General editor: Graham Handl

Brodie's Notes on John Webster's

The Duchess of Malfi

Peter Washington MA M.Litt.

Senior Tutor and Deputy Head, The Graduate Diploma, Middlesex Polytechnic

150th YEAR
M
MACMILLAN

First published 1986 by Pan Books Ltd

This revised edition published 1993 by
THE MACMILLAN PRESS LTD
Houndmills, Basingstoke, Hampshire RG21 2XS
and London
Companies and representatives
throughout the world

ISBN 0-333-58215-2

Typeset by Footnote Graphics, Warminster, Wiltshire
Printed in Great Britain by
Cox & Wyman Ltd, Reading

Contents

The author and his work 7
Webster's life 7
Webster and Revenge Tragedy 8
Sources and treatment 11
Date 15

Plot summary 16

**Scene summaries, critical commentary, textual notes
and revision questions 17**

The characters 63
Antonio 63
The Duchess 66
Ferdinand 72
The Cardinal 77
Bosola 80
Julia 87

Structure and style 90
Setting 90
Themes 90
Structure 96
Style 99
Literary terms 121

General questions and sample answer in note form 122

Further reading 124

Preface

The intention throughout this study aid is to stimulate and guide, to encourage your involvement in the book, and to develop informed responses and a sure understanding of the main details.

Brodie's Notes provide a clear outline of the play or novel's plot, followed by act, scene, or chapter summaries and/or commentaries. These are designed to emphasize the most important literary and factual details. Poems, stories or non-fiction texts combine brief summary with critical commentary on individual aspects or common features of the genre being examined. Textual notes define what is difficult or obscure and emphasize literary qualities. Revision questions are set at appropriate points to test your ability to appreciate the prescribed book and to write accurately and relevantly about it.

In addition, each of these Notes includes a critical appreciation of the author's art. This covers such major elements as characterization, style, structure, setting and themes. Poems are examined technically – rhyme, rhythm, for instance. In fact, any important aspect of the prescribed work will be evaluated. The aim is to send you back to the text you are studying.

Each study aid concludes with a series of general questions which require a detailed knowledge of the book: some of these questions may invite comparison with other books, some will be suitable for coursework exercises, and some could be adapted to work you are doing on another book or books. Each study aid has been adapted to meet the needs of the current examination requirements. They provide a basic, individual and imaginative response to the work being studied, and it is hoped that they will stimulate you to acquire disciplined reading habits and critical fluency.

Graham Handley 1990

Page references in these notes are to the Penguin edition of *John Webster: Three Plays*, but as reference is also made to the individual Acts and Scenes, the Notes may be used with any edition of the play.

The author and his work

Webster's life

Little is known about Webster's life. Even the dates of his birth and death are uncertain. Scholars believe he was born between 1570 and 1580, and he died in about 1630, which would make him a generation younger than Shakespeare, but contemporary with Ben Jonson. However, his enduring works – *The White Devil* and *The Duchess of Malfi* – were probably composed at the same time as Shakespeare's latest plays i.e., between 1610 and 1613, and have affinities with them. Both writers show the influence of the fashionable masque and pageant forms; and both use well-worn conventions, such as the revenge tragedy, to new effect.

There are also comparisons to be made with aspects of Jonson's stage-works. More important are Webster's relations with other fellow dramatists. The early 17th century theatre, though highly competitive, was also remarkable for the frequency with which writers co-operated. It is possible that Shakespeare himself had collaborators in *Henry VIII*, *Pericles* and *Two Noble Kinsmen* (a play not usually ascribed to him). It is certain that Dekker, Tourneur, Webster, Middleton, Rowley, Massinger, Beaumont and Fletcher, all worked with one another in various combinations. What concerns us here, however, is the fact that *The White Devil* and *The Duchess of Malfi* were, so far as we know, by Webster alone. He was not only a playwright: like his fellow professional writers, he turned his hand to whatever came up, including a lengthy elegy on the death of James I's eldest son (*A Monumental Column*, 1612). But the theatre seems to have been his main interest – perhaps natural in a period when it so dominated the literary scene. He has two other known plays to his credit – *The Devil's Law Case* (1619–20) and *Appius and Virginia* (c.1630) – but these are rarely performed or read. *The White Devil* and *The Duchess of Malfi* alone have held the stage.

One interesting and important fact which is known about Webster is that he worked from common-place books – notebooks in which he recorded quotations from his wide reading. For example, like Shakespeare, he often alludes to Florio's translation of Montaigne's *Essays* (1603) – an important source for *The Tempest*, which is nearly contemporary with *The Duchess of Malfi*.

The Elizabethans did not put our premium on originality: perhaps they understood that everything has already been said. They prized scholarship, witty allusion and acute quotation, and they saw no reason not to take from one another telling lines and phrases. If someone had a good idea it seemed natural to them to want to imitate it. Almost all their plots, for example, are borrowed from elsewhere, and translations of Latin tragedies provided many of the set-piece scenes which recur again and again in the drama of the period. Webster himself borrowed the Echo scene in *The Duchess of Malfi*; and he took the incident with the poisoned skull from *The Revenger's Tragedy* by his contemporary Tourneur. However, there is obviously a limit to the amount one can borrow without becoming a mere plagiarist, and Webster has often been thought of as a magpie. This is unfair, for at his best he has Shakespeare's capacity to transform his borrowings into something new, giving them a peculiar appropriateness to the context or an extra ironic twist, and his genius for dialogue, for the rapid establishment of character and situation, enables him to put borrowed material to good use. One side-effect is the rich verbal texture of his plays, which mingle the *sententiae* (moral truisms) so popular in the period with a dense, taut, and carefully thought-out patterning of imagery. As the common-place books suggest, Webster is a highly self-conscious artist, and it pays to bear this in mind when studying his work.

Webster and Revenge Tragedy

Between 1585 and 1625 England produced a body of drama comparable with the greatest years of the Greek theatre. But if the quality of the best work is extraordinary, equally extraordinary is the rapidity of the theatre's rise and decline. We are inclined to think of our own age as one of rapid change, but those years were just as volatile, socially, politically and

culturally. The drama reached its high point in the first decade of the 17th century in the tragedies of Shakespeare and the
comedies of Jonson. By the time Webster's plays appeared in
the first half of the second decade, the decline had already set
in. The last years of James I's reign (1601–1625) produced
some magnificent plays, including Webster's own, but they
are plays which are not only preoccupied – not to say obsessed
– with a corrupt society: they are also plays in which conventions are near the point of exhaustion, and technique has
become a matter of interest in its own right – always a sign
that something is near its end. We can see both these features
in Webster's work.

Revenge is the dominating tragic motif in the period; and
Revenge Tragedy is a particular form of a larger genre known
as the 'tragedy of blood'. This larger genre is usually defined
in terms of a quotation from *Hamlet*, itself a magnificent
example of Revenge Tragedy. At the end of the play (Act V,
Scene 2) Horatio addresses the remaining actors and the
audience:

. . . So shall you hear
Of carnal, bloody, and unnatural acts,
Of accidental judgments, casual slaughters,
Of deaths put on by cunning and forc'd cause . . .

and as Gamini Salgado points out in his excellent preface to
Three Jacobean Tragedies (Penguin 1965), these lines suggest a
strong connection between the tragedy of blood and modern
crime thrillers, in which mystery and violence are central to
the drama. Horatio goes on to speak of:

. . . purposes mistook
Fall'n on th' inventors' heads.

words which add to the seemingly chaotic brutality he has
described, some idea of justice. This notion forms the basis of
Revenge Tragedy, which brought to the horrors and slaughter
of the tragedy of blood the figure of the individual avenger,
who is the instrument of a justice ordinary laws cannot en-
compass. As we can see from the character of Bosola, this
avenger is by no means necessarily a virtuous man: more often

than not, he is deeply enmeshed in the train of savage actions which precipitate the tragedy. Nor is he necessarily the 'hero' of the play: again the role of Bosola poses problems about what we would mean if we spoke of him as the hero. Characteristically, the avenger's role is morally ambivalent: he punishes killing with more killing, and the vicious circle of murder can be cut only by his own necessary death. Revenge Tragedy thus highlights the problems of justice in an unjust world. It also pinpoints the problematic relationship between the human and the divine. The 17th century was a nominally Christian age – Christian to such an extent that wars were fought and men and women executed over small points of doctrine. In the end, justice was seen to be God's business.

Vengeance is mine, I will repay, saith the Lord.

is the crucial Biblical text. But though God may mete out rewards and punishments in the next world, how can He be seen to be working in this one, where there is so much evident *in*justice? And yet how dare men usurp his judicial function? When they do, like Bosola and Hamlet, they pay with their lives. On the other hand, they are irresistibly driven to vengeance by the circumstances, by their conscience, by honour. Caught between these two necessities – God's prerogative and human justice – men become tragic.

Webster's plays, however, although they exhibit the paraphernalia of Christianity, are hardly Christian. In *The Duchess of Malfi* many of the characters comment at the moment of death on their uncertainty about the future; and whatever the doctrinal basis of the play, its atmosphere overwhelmingly suggests that there is no world after this one, that we experience Hell and Heaven here. The absence of God, far from weakening the tragedy, sharpens it, putting all the more stress on the fragile nature of human justice, isolated between the animal chaos of this world, and the nothingness which comes after it; and much of Webster's tragic pathos arises from just this circumstance. This is both a refinement of conventional Revenge Tragedy and a reversion to its origins in the plays of Seneca, a Roman playwright and philosopher who adapted Greek plays for the Roman stage. The context of Seneca's plays is pagan: the gods mete out justice in this world, and the spectacle of the resultant human suffering forms the basis of Senecan tragedy. By witnessing the spectacle audiences are meant to reflect on their own frailty, and the mutability of all things human.

In Seneca's drama characters are not individualized beyond the necessary minimum, and the language prefers force to subtlety – traits found in the first important example of the form, Kyd's *Spanish Tragedy* of 1589. Kyd and Webster both inherited the heavy moralizing of Senecan tragedy, but Webster, setting the moral commentary in a superior dramatic context, and refraining from offering a consistent moral view (or being unable to), reaches a far higher level of intensity. The theme of mutability, expressed in the Duchess's fate, is framed, as it were, by Bosola's drama: we have two plays for the price of one – a domestic tragedy and a revenge drama. For the central predicament – the world's injustice – is Bosola's, and in his actions and deliberations it is most fully explored. Here Webster adds to his play yet another element of Jacobean tragedy. His avenger is also a satisist. We are accustomed to think of tragedy as wholly serious. Even in Shakespeare's tragedies, the comedy is kept apart from the tragic dénouement. The Jacobeans, however, were fond of tragicomedy, and although the effect is often unfortunate, at its best the form has a strange power of its own. In particular, the combination of tragedy and satire produced a whole genre of plays, among which *The Duchess of Malfi* is one of the best. While Bosola's scenes with the Old Lady are gratuitously nasty, and a miscalculation, aimed at a specific Jacobean taste for railing, Bosola's ironic detachment throughout most of the play only heightens the intensity of his resolve to punish the Duke and the Cardinal. And at the very end of the play, when his sardonic refusal of sentiment confronts death, the effect is both moving and disturbing. Morality is both the final justice and injustice, which come to all alike, the end of the comedy which leaves us, for all the feting of the new Duke of Malfi, with a question about human destiny unanswered.

Sources and treatment

Webster took the story of his play from the second volume of William Painter's *Palace of Pleasure*, a compilation of stories from various sources. Painter's tales were not original. The story of the Duchess of Malfi was translated from the French *Histoires Tragiques* of Belleforest, which appeared two years before Painter's book, in 1565. Belleforest in turn probably took his version from the original Italian source by Matteo Bandello, who wrote a series of novellas, of which this was number 26. It is possible that Bandello, who calls himself Delio in a series of sonnets he wrote, may have been involved in the action to the extent of being a friend of Antonio; for while they are substantially altered in the various retellings, the events of the Duchess's story are true in outline. The Antonio of the story was assassinated in Milan in October 1513; Bandello's novella, or long story, appeared not long after. The historical duchess was Giovanna d'Aragona, who married the Duke of Amalfi in 1493, at the age of twelve, bore him a son in 1494, and was widowed in 1498. In 1510 she left Amalfi for Loreto and then Ancona; where she married Antonio Bologna, her Master of the Horse. They were both murdered within a few years, together with two of their children.

The action of the play is clear in this account, but not its significance. There is nothing in the historical records, for example, to connect Giovanna's death with her two brothers, Cardinal Ludovico d'Aragona and Carlo, Marquis of Gerace. It was Bandello who added this detail. Nor is there any sign of Bosola in the various versions before Webster, who must take the credit for inventing this character, partly by amalgamating several agents and spies in the other accounts of the story. Webster naturally went to Painter's English version for his material. Painter translates Belleforest fairly closely, emphasizing some things, playing down others; but Belleforest does far more than translate Bandello, his retelling of the story being four times longer than the Italian original. He complicates and develops the characters, heavily moralizing the story and providing a good deal of detail. Painter largely follows him in this. What, then, are Webster's distinctive contributions to the narrative?

The first point to be made is that Webster, like most of his literary contemporaries, was a magpie: he took material for his play not only from the obvious sources but also from elsewhere, notably from Philip Sidney's *Arcadia*. This work is a long, rambling pastoral, enormously popular in the England of the early 17th century. It contains, for example, an echo scene, and episodes in which princesses are subjected to mental torture. There are also hints in *The Duchess of Malfi* of Cinthio's *Hecatommithi*, a collection of stories from which Shakespeare drew the plot of *Othello*. The details of such borrowings do not concern us here: what matters is the diversity of sources, the writer's readiness to adapt them, and the frequency of certain themes, such as the wronged and tormented woman. Above all, we look for the writer's ability to synthesize his borrowings and turn them to his purpose.

Webster simplifies his material by reducing the number of intermediaries between the Duchess and her brothers to one: Bosola. This entails developing a major character not present in the sources. He also brings the brothers into far greater prominence, introducing them at the beginning of the story, even before the Duchess herself. Again this involves developing character in greater depth: Ferdinand, in particular, is shown to have motives more complex than mere affronted honour. The distinction between this group of major actors – the Duchess and her brothers, Antonio and Bosola – and the minor characters, is sharpened: while at the same time a number of minor figures – Silvio, Grisolan, Roderigo, Pescara, the doctor – are added to enlarge the perspective of the various courts. Julia, too, is wholly an invention of Webster's: she plays an important role in the action and as a comparison for the Duchess. The playwright knits the characters more carefully together through the plot: Bosola is his means of doing this, impinging on the lives of all the characters and causing the deaths of the Duchess and her husband, her brothers and Julia, indirectly or directly. He also develops the character of Delio as Antonio's confidant, thereby giving greater interest to both characters, and allowing the Duchess's husband a less shadowy role. And by introducing the echo scene, Bosola's vision of the Duchess (V,2,345) and her son and heir, Webster gives the Duchess a kind of life after death, in which she can continue to influence the action up to the end of the play.

Various consequences follow from Webster's modification

of his material, not least the natural confrontation of Bosola and Antonio, the one embodying naked power and force of will, the other a timorous submission to fate. By virtue of their conditions they are enemies from the beginning, Bosola the predator, Antonio the prey. This adds a whole layer of dramatic interest to the play. Webster's more detailed revelation of character in the sister and brothers intensifies the action by making us consider the relationship between them: Ferdinand and the Duchess are evident twins, sensuous and passionate, while the Cardinal's nature is carefully distinguished from theirs as cold and calculating. His indifference to Julia contrasts sharply with Antonio's passion for the Duchess – and even with Ferdinand's – for Ferdinand shows a kind of fiercely possessive love which is only revealed when he looks on his sister's corpse after her death. Julia provides a foil to the Duchess: a loose, eager woman whose demise is as incidental as the Duchess's is prolonged, painful and dignified. Julia also highlights the theme of sexuality in the play which has a brooding erotic quality entirely lacking in the sources, whose prolix language cannot compete with Webster's for brilliance and intensity. Briefly sketched, Julia emerges as a rounded figure: the woman of pleasure, the epitome of the court lady for whom satisfied appetites are all that matter; yet who, like all the characters, has a glimmer of higher things too late. Julia also provides the only female interest in the play after the Duchess is murdered, a remote echo of her superior, like the voice from the tomb.

In the end however, it is the complex figure of Bosola who constitutes Webster's major contribution to the play and to drama. The contradictions in the characters of Antonio and the Duchess, for example, are hinted at in the sources: a good but weak and perhaps ambitious man seduced by a fine but foolish and lustful woman. These figures are developed, modified, subtilized. But the character of Bosola is a pure invention, belonging to a recognizable school of melancholy murderous heroes – Hamlet is one such – but quite unique. In him the peculiar genius of Webster's language and his mastery of dramatic structure are consummated.

Date

The Duchess of Malfi appears to have been performed for the
first time in 1614, two years after Webster's other great
tragedy, *The White Devil*. That puts it just after Shakespeare's
latest work, and roughly contemporary with Jonson's *Alchem-
ist* and *Bartholomew Fair*.

↳ Masculinity in Early 1600s
↳ Social mobility

Plot Summary

Unknown to her brothers and against their will, the widowed Duchess of Malfi plans to marry her steward, Antonio. The Duke and the Cardinal employ their henchman, Bosola, to find out the truth. Believing her to be pregnant, Bosola persuades the Duchess to eat unripe fruit, which induces labour. He then finds the child's horoscope, cast by Antonio, and informs Ferdinand. Not knowing who her husband is, Ferdinand surprises his sister in her room. His threats frighten her into exiling Antonio on false charges in order to get him out of Malfi. They plan to meet again in Ancona. Before leaving she tells Bosola her husband's identity.

The Cardinal, who exchanges his holy orders for a general's rank, persuades the council of Ancona to banish the Duchess and her husband; and although Antonio escapes to Milan with his eldest son, the Duchess is trapped by Bosola, with her other children and her maid. Ferdinand visits them in their confinement and initiates a series of tortures designed to break his sister's spirit. Bosola is ordered to preside over these and over her death. He does so, but immediately regrets it. When he then discovers that Ferdinand will not reward him, his eyes are opened to the enormity of his crime and he vows revenge. Ferdinand meanwhile goes mad at the sight of his sister's corpse.

Antonio now decides he must risk a direct confrontation with the Cardinal, unaware that his wife is dead. Bosola suborns Julia, the Cardinal's mistress, to extract from him the confession that he helped in the Duchess's murder. The Cardinal confesses, and kills Julia, but Bosola has overheard their exchanges. He pretends to agree to the Cardinal's request that he kill Antonio, while privately vowing to save him.

The Cardinal, feigning concern for Ferdinand, orders everyone to stay in their rooms, even if they hear cries for help: his purpose is to clear the way for Bosola's removal of Julia's body. Bosola, having overheard the Cardinal determine his death, kills Antonio, mistaking him for an assassin. He then kills the Cardinal and his brother, and is mortally wounded by Ferdinand. The Duchess's son is proclaimed her heir.

Scene summaries, critical commentary, textual notes and revision questions

Act I Scene 1

Antonio has just returned to the court from France. In prais-
ing the French king to his friend, Delio, he implicitly criticizes
Ferdinand and his rule. Bosola and the Cardinal enter in conversation, and when the Cardinal leaves, Bosola characterizes
him and his brother, Ferdinand, as corrupt men. Bosola is in
turn characterized when he leaves as brave but melancholy.

Webster gives us plenty of information in this scene –
establishing character and providing a vivid and detailed
picture of Bosola – but his main purpose is to establish
ambience and themes. Ferdinand's court is a rotten place, and
the scene's imagery is full of decay, disease and vermin. In its
81 lines an atmosphere both sinister and voluptuous is established, especially at 49–52. Only the image of the French
court as a pure fountain of good remains to suggest a different
world – but even this evocation of living water seems to be
nullified by the dead pool of Bosola's imagining (50). Within
this claustrophobic atmosphere a range of negative attitudes is
established, from Antonio's witty irony to Bosola's bitter resentment and the Cardinal's lofty disdain. All the themes
cluster round the idea developed in Antonio's first speech. A
good court requires a wise and virtuous ruler: in such a place
all men can be content, for they will get justice. It is such a
state as Ferdinand's which can produce a Bosola, suborned to
evil by his evil masters, unbalanced by 'melancholy', able but
frustrated. Notions of order and disorder, justice and injustice,
expressed in the natural metaphors of the fountain and the
stream, disease and health, breeding and rotting, suffuse the
scene.

A very formal In the very form of.
habit Dress.
at home With himself. In this speech, strategically placed at the
play's opening, Antonio expounds the idea that a healthy state
depends upon a just and honourable ruler. This reflects

ironically not only on the wicked Ferdinand and his brother, but also on the Duchess herself, whose behaviour is not without fault.

sweetly Antonio speaks ironically. The King of France means that his court, which should be an image of Heaven, is very far from that.

His Master's master-piece God's greatest achievement. Again ironic. Webster here sets up the first term in one of the play's main dualisms: Heaven/Hell.

duly Rightly.

in general Everywhere.

near the head At the source. The notion of things or persons poisoned in their very nature recurs in the play.

Death ... spread An example of the sententia or moral sentence: the play is filled with them.

Inform him Tell him about.

do ... foresee Antonio here distinguishes between instructing the ruler and advising him. He fails to follow his own sage advice; he counsels the Duchess badly.

gall This has the meaning of 'sore' and also of 'bile.' At his first entrance Bosola is therefore characterized as both tormenting and self-tormented.

railing Bitter scoffing.

haunt The hint that Bosola follows the Cardinal like a ghost or spirit becomes retrospectively ironic when Bosola later kills him.

I fell ... galleys Service as an oarsman in the galleys was a common punishment in Mediterranean countries at this time.

I ... mantle A typical example of Bosola's sardonic humour, comparing his misery with a Roman senator's dignity.

Slighted thus? Am I to be neglected like this? Despite their apparent rapprochement later, there is already a hint here of the fate Bosola has in store for his former patron.

blackbirds ... weather The first of the play's many vivid comparisons of the animal world and the human.

dog-days The hottest and unhealthiest days of summer, when the Dog-star is most clearly visible.

honest The Cardinal's wish is – to say the least – ironic, as Bosola's response acknowledges.

the devil Antonio associated the King of France with Heaven; here the Cardinal is linked with Hell.

suit Request

standing Stagnant. This extraordinary image brings together the various qualities, mainly negative, of the two brothers: corruption, decadence, attractiveness to parasites. It also implies

that their evil is like a natural growth: stunted but inevitable.
Notice also the contrast with I,1,12–15.

pies Magpies. The beginning of the play's many carrion images.

panders Procurers.

dependences Inherited appointments.

Tantalus Proverbially punished in Hades: he could never reach
the grapes over his head nor the water round his feet to quench
a burning thirst. The type of the frustrated man.

fearfully A pun: (a) full of fears and (b) dreadfully.

a kind of geometry Probably a bitter reference to the crutches
an old soldier might hobble on. See the following lines.

swing Slang – equivalent to our 'fling'.

hospital Courts have been compared to heaven and hell – now
to hospitals.

Gaston ... Naples Webster's invention. The French general
Foix was not concerned when a Franco-Spanish army conquered
Naples in 1501.

melancholy One of the four humours, in the 16th century,
melancholy was thought to affect great men in particular: many
people therefore affected it. The sense, stronger than ours,
includes the ideas of depression, disaffection, and near-madness.

malcontents Disappointed or frustrated – and therefore
dangerous – men. Antonio equates physical ills (excessive sleep)
with mental ones.

and their ... wearing The strange syntax here means: idle men
are spoilt by idleness like unworn clothes by moths.

Act I Scene 2

This long scene opens in a way familiar from many Jacobean
plays, with a passage of courtly banter, witty and occasionally
obscene exchanges between major and minor characters. This
provides a background to further discussion between Antonio
and Delio, this time about the characters of the Cardinal, the
Duke and the Duchess. The Duchess then enters and Ferdinand arranges that she shall take Bosola into her Household.
Ferdinand then takes Bosola into his confidence, and asks him
to spy on the Duchess: Bosola agrees and leaves.

The Cardinal brings the Duchess back, and he and Ferdinand bully her, insisting that she must not remarry. She
refrains from committing herself; but as soon as her brothers
leave, she places her maid behind the tapestry so that Cariola

may overhear her conversation with Antonio. He enters and the Duchess proposes marriage to him after a witty flirtation. Cariola then emerges, and the Duchess announces that she, the Duchess, is now married to Antonio – marriage requiring only the presence of a witness. The scene ends with Cariola's ominous prophecy of misfortune.

Webster's craftsmanship is clearly evident in this scene, as he prepares the way for the Duchess, letting her enter at line 67, but not speak until line 137, *after* her character has been described in rapturous terms by Antonio, sharply contrasted with her brothers'. As the play progresses the spectator is able to make his own assessment of Antonio's judgements: once again, as in the first scene, only one element lightens the darkness – this time the Duchess's character. Typically, Webster introduces the Duchess not with a great speech but a brief question – 'To me, sir?' – and in the light of Antonio's somewhat idealized portrait we soon see that she is a woman of many aspects: dignified, playful, passionate, wary, witty and wilful, commanding and voluptuous. Her proposal to Antonio makes his claim at line 126, that 'Her days are practis'd in such noble virtue ...' look both inaccurate and ironic: clearly the suspicions of her brothers are justified up to a point; she does want to marry.

Most of the scene falls into a sequence of significant duets and trios: Delio and Antonio discussing their rulers, Ferdinand suborning Bosola in a dialogue filled with Bosola's contempt for both of them and for all men, the Duke and Cardinal bullying the Duchess, the Duchess making passionate love to Antonio. While the various parts share similar imagery, each has its own tone and character. This is typical of the way in which the whole scene is carefully structured, building up from the cynical banter and double entendres of the beginning, through the different intimacies of Antonio and his friend, the Duke and Bosola, the brothers and their sister, to the deep if dangerous love of Antonio and his wife-to-be.

presence Audience chamber.
make ... of Inform me about. Thus Webster introduces a
  necessary piece of exposition.
took the ring Jousted.

gravity Ferdinand's aside indicates that he's going to make fun of Castruchio's seriousness.

do it i.e. flight.

jest she broke Joke she made.

tents A pun on the usual meaning, and the sense of dressings for wounds.

put up Sheathe their swords – but there is also the double entendre of 'make love'.

jennet A fast, light horse – hardly suitable for Castruchio.

Pliny A Roman naturalist who claimed – among other things – that mares sometimes conceived from the wind and thus gave birth to especially swift foals.

ballass'd Ballasted. Instead of slowing, quicksilver speeds.

reels ... tilt A pun: (a) shies from the course (b) regains his balance easily.

fool Ferdinand refers to the professional clowns noblemen kept in their houses.

my lady Another reference (see above I,2,24–35) to Julia, who is later to play an important part.

wrinkle A pun: (a) the usual meaning (b) moral defect. Julia's meaning is that merry company tempts her to vice.

out of compass Excessively.

I shall Notice the abruptness with which Ferdinand changes the subject, as he often does. This indicates not only dominance but also a disturbing, nervous quality.

first ... action Antonio's preoccupation with action is characteristic of the period, which believed that virtuous action was the true end of the noble life.

come about Come in to port.

temper Temperament.

play Gamble. The Cardinal is not our idea of a priest. For 16th century princes of the Church, the stress was on princeliness: they were expected to take part in public affairs and even war.

flashes Showy displays.

form Outward show.

inward character The contrast between inner and outer, appearance and reality, is positively obsessive in this play.

spring ... toads A curious expression which seems to mean: the spring-like expression on his face gives birth to toads i.e. dark thoughts and deeds.

Hercules A hero in Greek mythology who had twelve great labours imposed on him.

intelligencers Spies.

political Scheming.

primitive Fundamental.

it The papacy.

Some good ... Antonio speaks ironically here.

given Said.

Twins? As it happens, the Duchess and Ferdinand are born twins: Ferdinand and the Cardinal are twins in wickedness and deceit.

speaks ... ears Antonio puns here: the Duke uses spies, and pretends to be what he is not.

o' th' bench Here the play's justice theme is foreshadowed.

information False testimony.

they ... turns It means doing someone down.

oracles Profound truths.

Duchess Antonio naturally praises her to the skies – as Delio remarks (I,2,131) – but the main function of this portrait is to contrast her with the two brothers.

For her discourse ... As for her conversation.

She ... penance She thought it less vain to talk much, and less of a penance for those who listened.

galliard An energetic dance.

dead palsy Paralysis.

continence Chastity.

practis'd Occupied.

shrifts Confessions.

dress ... her Imitate her.

play the wire-drawer Overdo it.

case Cover.

only thus much To conclude.

grows Adds up to.

stains Overshadows. This hyperbolic couplet completes Antonio's eulogy and marks a change in the action.

suit Request.

provisorship ... horse Management of your stables. In a household such as the Duchess's this was an important post.

prefers Appoints.

leaguer Military camp.

bring ... haven Both 'accompany' and 'take' you down to the harbour.

entertain Engage.

intelligence Information. Intelligencers were spies.

I ... in't I don't want to be seen to be involved.

fitter More suitable.

you are deceiv'd Notice the irony that Ferdinand is blind to honesty – he is so corrupt. But the link is made between Bosola

and Antonio as comparable characters: men who serve the
great.

in my debt Bosola is consistently sardonic and blunt.

physiognomy The art of judging character from appearance.
This conversation takes up the theme of appearance and reality.

cozens Fools. Bosola's advice is to avoid appearances in favour
of realities. Yet he himself takes on disguises to torment the
Duchess.

For that As for that.

take their times Be watchful.

the oft shaking ... Ferdinand quotes a proverbial saying: when
a man is often tricked he becomes more watchful.

unworthily Without cause – but this also seems to imply
'basely'. As so often Bosola has a sharper wit than his
interlocutor, and caps his wisdom.

Whose throat ... Bosola delights in embarrassing Ferdinand.

rides post Rushes on.

Do not ... would not The mystery Ferdinand makes of this
should alert us to the complexity of his motives – which, we
later see, he does not understand himself.

familiars Bosola puns on the two meanings of 'close
acquaintance' and 'demon'. In 17th-century parlance a familiar
usually signified one who served another's interests, often basely.

thriving Ferdinand implies that Bosola will be doing himself a
favour by serving the Duke. Bosola's next speech shows that he
knows better.

Candies ... o'er Sweetens. Bosola returns to the appearance/
reality motif.

complemental Refined.

Be yourself Ferdinand's injunction is doubly ironic: he wants
Bosola to conceal his true role by maintaining his reputation for
bitterness, but in the end Bosola discovers a different 'self' to be
true to – a self which is revenged on the Duke and his brother.

politic Astute.

Feed ... dish Dine at a lord's table.

in a dream As though in a dream. The sleep/dream motif
recurs, most crucially at V,5,94, pointing up the gap between
conscious motive and unconsciously-driven action.

what's my place? Bosola cuts short his reverie.

Sometimes ... Bosola's sardonic humour covers his distaste.

addition Name.

luxurious Lecherous.

livers ... The liver was said to be the seat of the passions.

spotted Unclean.

Laban's sheep See Genesis, 30, 32. Laban was the father-in-law of Jacob, who took all his speckled sheep in payment.

Diamonds ... hands Like the other characters, the Duchess can quote proverbs to her own advantage. Here she is teasing her brothers. In contrast to their grimness she maintains a light tone through this exchange.

motion Intention.

rank Luxuriant i.e. tempting.

honey-dew Ferdinand changes his metaphor to the sticky substance found on leaves, which traps unwary insects. The over-rich texture of the Duke's speeches, and their complicated syntax, give them a disturbing quality.

Vulcan's engine The fine net in which Vulcan caught Mars and Venus committing adultery.

Your darkest actions ... This becomes ironic on several levels. Not only does it correctly forecast his sister's fate, but – more terribly – his own.

executed Threateningly plays on the meanings 'done' and 'put to death'.

some prison A double entendre. The prison is the womb, but also – for the Duchess – her actual fate.

joys Ferdinand continues the double entendre, echoing the play's persistent linking of sexual pleasure with danger, misery and death.

at the end By thinking about death. This is a common maxim in the period. It also ironically anticipates the later reflections of the Duchess and her husband on death.

poniard Dagger. Mention of her father is supposed to remind the Duchess that Ferdinand is now the guardian of her honour.

chargeable Expensive. Note how Ferdinand *assumes* she is misbehaving.

whispering-rooms Intimate quarters. Note the double entendre and those that follow.

lamprey A sort of eel.

neat Well-made.

Shall this ... Note the Duchess's abrupt change of tone after her brother's departure – showing that she does indeed deceive him about her feelings.

foot-steps Stepping-stones. The Duchess shows both determination and recklessness. She already has the marriage in mind, justifying her brothers' suspicions. Antonio, by contrast, is cautious.

secrecy Discretion.

poison A recurring image. See I,1,14. Here its use implies that the secret is dangerous for others.

ingenious Wise.

arras Hanging. She wishes to be overheard by her maid; later she is overheard by Ferdinand against her will. The arras points up both her forethought and her carelessness.

wilderness The Duchess speaks more truly than she knows.

What did I say? It is not clear whether she affects forgetfulness or experiences it.

husbands Stewards.

for your sake The Duchess is direct in her advances.

tane Taken.

upright A pun: (a) honest (b) erect.

Where?/In heaven The Duchess's playful manner is reminiscent of courtship scenes in Shakespeare e.g. *As You Like It*.

In perfect memory In sound mind.

procur'd Produced.

If ... But She continues the pun on husband/steward. Antonio is to progress from being the 'overseer' of her property to possession of her person.

quit Disposed of.

a good husband Antonio enters into the game.

In a winding sheet? Ready to accompany my dead husband? Winding sheets were wrapped round corpses.

couple A pun (a) pair of sheets (b) marriage (c) intercourse.

St Winifred A Welsh saint martyred for chastity.

as ... purgatory Like Protestants.

affect Like.

banishment Exclusion i.e., from marriage.

bare Mere.

wanton Child. Antonio playfully deprecates the pleasure of marriage in a way which (a) deflects attention from its sexual aspect and (b) becomes tragic when fate eventually overtakes his own children.

sovereign Effective.

eyesight As in *King Lear* eyesight is here equated with sexual desire. Antonio responds that he is blinded with love.

circle A pun: (a) ring (b) the magic circle created by her magical attraction. That the devil is 'saucy and ambitious' hardly bodes well.

conjuration Conjuring.

is it fit? Antonio kneeling to the Duchess makes a curious echo of Bosola submitting to Ferdinand's will (see I,2,211).

This goodly roof The Duchess refers to Antonio's head: kneeling, he is below her. But there are further layers of meaning: she wishes to raise him to her level socially, being equal in marriage. Besides, the constant undercurrent of double entendre hints at a sexual pun, following on from 'upright' at I,2,294.

Ambition Antonio takes up the theme of I,2,333. We must always bear in mind that he is aspiring above his station. All the characters are acutely conscious of this. Antonio's references to madness anticipate the Duchess's torments in Act IV.

a great man's madness i.e. only great men can afford it.

aim Understand.

You ... yourself You would not be good at 'selling' yourself.

dark'ning Obscuring.

that That method.

false lights In apposition to 'dark'ning'.

Are ... off Are designed to sell bad goods.

complete Various senses: handsome, worthy, virile.

progress Journey.

it Wages.

In riddles ... it is not Here the Duchess expounds her own version of the appearance/reality theme. The great are forced to act because of their greatness. Her tone implies the dangers of this approach.

multiply i.e. that the two hearts will mate.

tremble Whether from fear or love is not specified: the equivocation again links sexual attraction and danger.

This is flesh ... tomb A pre-echo of the scene (IV,1) in which the Duchess is shown waxworks of Antonio and her children.

half a blush i.e. because a widow is more experienced with men than an unmarried girl.

sanctuary A pun: (a) home (b) guardian (c) guarantor.

Quietus est Discharge. The formula was used both at the conclusion of financial business and as a phrase to intimate death.

But for But what about?

without this circumference Outside this circle.

easily This is the opposite of what happens.

mine Antonio means that he should be reassuring her, not vice versa.

of my counsel In my confidence.

Per verba de presenti 'Verbally in front of a witness.' Such a marriage was considered legally binding but not religiously valid.

Gordian A knot tied by king Gordius which only Alexander the Great could cut. The Gordian knot was proverbially intractable.

like the spheres The crystal spheres of the universe, in whose walls the planets were fixed, went one inside the other like Chinese boxes. They reverberated in harmony, setting up a cosmic music – unless the universal order was disturbed by a catastrophe.

the loving palms Palms were believed to flourish and fruit only if planted in pairs.

That Fortune ... Dramatic irony. This is what does happen.

faster More securely.

blind i.e., like Fortune. Presumably the Duchess refers to *good* fortune.

conceit Notion.

fortune Here the idea is extended to mean: good fortune, financial fortune, erotic fortune.

humorous Temperamental, difficult, tiresome.

Alexander and Lodowick Two men of similar appearance. One married a princess in the other's name, but slept separated from her by a sword, so as not to betray his friend.

treasury The Duchess takes up the chain of puns about stewards and treasurers.

of greatness, or of woman ... Cariola acts as a chorus here, making a vital link between the Duchess's femininity and her fate. Insofar as this is the Duchess's play it is very much the tragedy of a woman – a point all the characters allude to in different ways.

Revision questions on Act I

1 What do we learn about the main characters in Act I and how do we learn it?

2 Comment on the way in which Webster introduces us to (a) Bosola and (b) the Duchess.

3 What different aspects of royalty are presented in Act I?

4 Examine Webster's presentation of the relationship between the Duchess and Antonio.

5 What exactly is Ferdinand's objection to his sister's marriage?

Act II Scene 1

Bosola makes fun of the elderly courtier Castruchio, Ferdinand's butt in the previous scene. When an old lady enters, he turns to railing at women, dwelling especially on two of the play's preoccupations: the body's mortality and the deceitfulness of appearances. These reflections lead him back to the Duchess, who is now clearly pregnant. Bosola plots to reveal this, by inducing her to eat unripe fruit, safe for anyone else, but certain to make a pregnant woman sick.

Antonio then enters. After revealing to his companion, Delio, that the Duchess is married, he engages in a verbal duel with Bosola. When the Duchess comes in with her ladies, Bosola offers her the unripe fruit, which induces labour, and she is borne off. To conceal her plight Delio suggests that Antonio claim she has been poisoned by Bosola. He agrees.

At the beginning of the scene the action seems to pause as Bosola indulges himself in fantastic railing, but the purpose of this emerges at line 67 when he turns to speaking of the Duchess. Before this the language is obsessively concerned with decay, vermin and simple nastiness: Bosola revels in his disgust. His language has a dense, horrific vigour lacking in the other characters, as though he is determined to confront the world's vile reality; yet his exchanges with Antonio and the Duchess show him well versed in courtly wit too. In this scene we become aware that Bosola and Antonio are matched against one another – and the match is clearly unequal: Bosola dominates with ease. Bosola, like the Duchess, acts while Antonio reacts.

nightcap The white cap worn by lawyers.
expresses Proclaims i.e., that Castruchio has large ears and is therefore an ass. He is only the first of Bosola's victims in this scene.
band Neck-band with white tabs. Bosola sardonically envisages Castruchio as a pompous lawyer tugging at his tie as he speaks.
to ... memory Bosola catalogues affectations.
president Presiding magistrate.
stomach A pun on appetite.
roaring boys Rowdies.
nightcaps Lawyers. Bosola takes up the age-old satire of the legal profession.
painting Using make-up.
physic Medicine i.e., paint to cover her diseased skin.
inclines Comes.
sloughs Bogs.
the last progress The last time you appeared.

hedgehog Note the increasing savagery of Bosola's language.
The satire is conventional: women, like doctors and lawyers, are
traditional butts. This passage fits in with the appearance/
reality theme of the play.

careening Repairing or cleaning (applied especially to ships).

morphew'd Scurfy.

disembogue Take to sea.

There's ... plastic There's a crude way of describing your
artistry.

closet i.e. bed-chamber.

One would ... yields This extraordinary outpouring of 36 lines
is like an aria in opera, first developing variations on a theme
(up to line 66) then apparently changing mood and subject
abruptly. In fact both parts of the speech return obsessively to
the appearance/reality theme: the old woman appears as one
type of female deception, the Duchess as another.

fat ... ordure A typical receipt for witches' brew.

sin of your youth Desire to appear young.

is the very patrimony Makes the fortune.

footcloth A rich embroidery to protect horse-riders from the
mire: a sign of wealth.

Observe Here Bosola changes from prose to verse, and from
brisk raillery to a more formal style.

ulcerous wolf Ulcer – so named because of its ravenous
appetite.

swinish measle A skin disease in pigs, identified with human
measles.

Your wife i.e. Castruchio's wife, Julia.

Lucca A famous spa.

fins Rims.

wanes Grows thin.

married? Antonio has revealed his secret to Delio.

in your contemplation? What are you thinking about?

opinion Affectation.

tetter Skin disease. Bosola takes up the imagery of his insults.

simplicity Straightforwardness – as opposed to the subtlety of
wisdom. Once again Bosola is sardonic – playing the role of the
simple man.

inside Inner meaning.

honest The word comes to Bosola's lips much as it comes to
Iago's in *Othello* – most savoured when it is least appropriate.

lord of the ascendant Dominating influence. A reference to
astrology.

cousin-german remov'd First cousin, once removed.

heads Compare I,1,14. Bosola makes a rather different point to
  Antonio: that princes are like other men.

Come hither The Duchess reacts nervously to Bosola's
  insinuation, attempting to divert attention.

when? How long will you be?

sound Swoon.

mother Hysteria. But there is an evident pun.

Put your hat on The Duchess wishes Antonio to show his
  equality with her. It was common for princes to wear their hats
  while courtiers went bareheaded.

to-year This year.

Good ... Bosola's plan is to feed the Duchess unripe fruit which,
  in her condition, will produce sickness and even premature
  labour.

This grafting Double entendre applying to both the fruit and
  the Duchess.

farthingales Wide hooped petticoats.

springal Stripling.

undone Betrayed.

politic Prudent.

forc'd occasion Unavoidable situation.

For As for.

repoison Poison was so common at the Italian courts that
  Delio's story is a credible one.

Act II Scene 2

Once again Bosola meets the Old Lady and continues his
sportive exchanges with her, this time more mildly. Antonio
gives orders for the court gates to be shut and invents a story
about stolen treasure, as an excuse to confine the servants to
their rooms while the Duchess gives birth; but alone with
Delio, he gives expression to his fears, and his friend tries to
reassure him. When Antonio is left alone, Cariola enters with
his new-born son.

  Bosola's conversation with the Old Lady and the jokes
made by the servants are part of a background music which
runs through most of the play. Such moments are common
enough in Jacobean tragedy: they suggest the everyday world
outside the immediate drama, and give the variety and comedy audiences were inclined to expect. But Webster has far

more to offer than this: he integrates these episodes into the play, making them into commentaries on the main action. In *The Duchess of Malfi* they revolve obsessively around the themes of sexuality, death and false appearances, contributing to the intensity, thematic unity and sense of claustrophobia we often experience in the play. To the servants, jokes about the Duchess and her sex-life are incidental: to her and Antonio they will mean death. The scene once again highlights Antonio's timorousness in terms of a recurring motif: astrology is used in the play to suggest the world of incomprehensible forces which govern our destiny. Delio sensibly tells Antonio not to be superstitious: yet, ironically, it is Antonio's fears which prove to be well-grounded in the end. Superstition is seen to represent a truth of its own – namely, that our destiny is not within our control. All the main characters have to learn this.

glass-house Glass-factory.
Jupiter King of the Roman Gods.
Danaes Danae was pursued by Jupiter in the form of a golden shower.
laps Both thighs and genitals.
many ... centre Double entendre: many men make love to one woman.
hand ... girdle Sexually give pleasure to a woman.
posterns Back gates.
Switzer Swiss mercenary soldier. This is all speculation on the part of the excited servants.
pistol A pun on 'pizzle' (penis). This whole exchange plays upon the fact that cod-pieces – protective clothing for male genitalia – were often elaborate and enlarged.
approv'd Favourably judged.
Gentlemen o' th' woodyard Bosola sneers at the servants.
th'black-guard Scullions.
How ... danger Antonio's fears are being realized. His vulnerability is apparent.
post Hasten.
presents me/Somewhat Gives me visions of something.
mind Take notice of.
daunt whole man in us Make us effeminate.
best Notice the rhyming couplet which accompanies this salty saying.
figure Horoscope.

Act II Scene 3

Bosola encounters Antonio in the dark. They have another verbal sparring match in which Antonio feels threatened – so much so that he interprets a nose bleed as a bad omen. When he goes out, Bosola picks up a paper he has dropped: it is the horoscope he decided to cast for his son at the end of the last scene, which tells Bosola half what he wants to know, i.e., that the Duchess is indeed a mother. He plans to send the news to her brothers in Rome.

The most distinctive things about this scene are the battle of wills and the horoscope. Bosola is much stronger than Antonio: he contemptuously dismisses the charge of poisoning the Duchess and turns the tables on his adversary by questioning and accusing him. The contrast between Bosola's virile strength and Antonio's superstitious uncertainty is marked. Bosola laughs where Antonio trembles. Webster, who delights in using different styles in the play, makes a careful simulacrum of a horoscope. The scene is typical in its rapid movement from conversational exchanges of the tensest kind, to Antonio's fearful reverie on his nose-bleed, to Bosola's harsh humour. Bosola calls Antonio a 'precise fellow' and one can imagine his sardonic tone when reading the horoscope.

dark lantern Like a torch, a dark lantern only gave a beam of light when required.
list Hark.
several words Various rooms.
intelligence ... else My scent will go cold – I'll lose the track.
setting a figure Casting a horoscope.
'Tis rather ... Antonio asserts himself against Bosola. Each of their dialogues is a trial of strength.
my prayers Bosola's insolence shows he isn't afraid of Antonio. 'Hard luck if I offend you,' is the burden of his remarks.
a Spanish fig A term of dismissal – usually accompanied by a rude gesture.
scarce warm Just emerged from hibernation. Antonio refers to Bosola's recent freedom from prison, and his promotion.
it i.e. the libel.
My nose bleeds We may find this comically anti-climactic, but it serves its purpose as a further omen of doom – and an easy way to produce blood for the audience's excitement.

wrought Embroidered.

Mere accident Antonio is reassuring himself.

take order Give orders.

safe Held secure. But in the other sense – neutralized – Bosola is anything but safe.

quit Proved your innocence.

The Lord ... death ... A horoscope in characteristic style.

Caetera non scrutantur The rest will not bear examination.

bawd Procurer. Bosola is very near to, and very far from, the mark.

I ... wish I have the information I wanted.

cas'd up Confined.

galls Biles.

This Presumably Bosola refers to finding the horoscope.

Act II Scene 4

The Cardinal is seen talking to his mistress, Julia. Their theme is the inconstancy of women. The Cardinal leaves and Delio enters. He has come to Rome from Malfi and, in a semi-comic dialogue, asks Julia to be his mistress. A servant enters to announce the arrival of a letter for the Cardinal from Ferdinand.

Delio suspects that this contains news of Antonio's marriage.

The scene is divided into two dialogues which comment ironically on each other. No sooner has Julia indignantly rejected the Cardinal's charge of inconstancy than she is tempted by Delio's offer. Even Delio, Antonio's close friend, is shown to have loose morals; the Cardinal, theoretically celibate, is a man of pleasure. No-one in the play – certainly not the Duchess – is above their passions; and the link between desire and ambition is made quite explicit by Delio at line 81.

anchorite A religious recluse.

I mean to him This becomes retrospectively ironic when Julia and the Cardinal betray one another.

strongest thoughts Firmest resolution i.e. to be chaste.

fantastic glass i.e., the telescope. The Cardinal's words are a milder form of Bosola's at II,2,18–20.

jealously Passionately.

cuckold i.e. because they are not married.

perch Julia is compared to a falcon.

elephant A curious switch from the previous lines – typical of Webster's rapid pace.

When thou ... tune it The Cardinal implies that he is a passionate lover, as Castruchio is not.

in physic Being treated. Liver and heart were the seats of passion in Renaissance physiology.

commendations Praises. Delio's cheeky words are the prelude to his apparently surprising request. Julia's witty answer, however, suggests that she's known as a woman of loose morals and many lovers – in contrast to the Duchess.

breach Thighs. Castruchio remains a largely comic character.

Your ... pity What you joke about is my misfortune.

Lady ... This dialogue echoes the wooing of the Duchess and Antonio: witty but far less subtle.

cassia Cinnamon.

civet Perfume.

physical Medicinal.

fond Foolish

seethe't in cullises Braise it in broths.

Your husband's come The interruption of their courtly duet gives the scene a characteristic edge, and brings Delio smartly to business.

honesty Chastity.

Act II Scene 5

Ferdinand and the Cardinal have received Bosola's letter with news of their sister's marriage. They discuss it and plan revenge.

Whereas the Cardinal is angry but dignified, Ferdinand is almost out of his mind with rage. We see the first signs of his madness, expressed through his obsession with the grosser side of sexuality. His language is extreme, filled with images of hell and demons, and his passions out of control. We may note that Ferdinand and the Duchess are twins: two natures equally passionate but, in different ways, both determined to have their will, and both more than a little self-destructive.

mandrake A poisonous plant whose forked root makes it look like a human body. It was said to utter a maddening shriek if pulled up. But Ferdinand digs it up.

prodigy Amazing event.

loose i'th'hilts Lecherous – a double entendre of 'loose'.

conveyences Means.

service Punning on 'sexual' service.

Rhubarb This exclamation, which now strikes us comically, refers to the need for purging the liver – the seat of the darker passions Ferdinand is experiencing.

Here's This is. Ferdinand is indeed mad with a rage which foreshadows his full madness. The Cardinal remains calm.

balsamum Ointment.

cupping-glass A surgical instrument for drawing out blood.

mean Way.

Unequal Unjust.

left Animal hearts were thought to be in the body-middle. Man's left-sidedness indicated his fallen nature. The Cardinal implies that women are even more left-sided than men.

bark Craft.

Thus ... it The Cardinal refers to his sister: though she has honour she does not know how to maintain it. Typically the cool Cardinal attributes her behaviour to ignorance, the passionate Ferdinand to lust.

my imagination The high colour of Ferdinand's imagining becomes more and more apparent as the play progresses, as his next speech shows.

carries ... lodgings Double entendre, making fire and passion equivalent.

wild-fire Here the fire/passion analogy is to Ferdinand himself – neatly making the point that his passions are at least as torrid as his sister's.

palsy Paralysis.

beastly Beast-like. The Cardinal's comment is prophetic.

In tune See I,2,398. The body, like the universe, was held to have a harmony of its own. Intemperate passions created discord.

I will ... not Ferdinand here adopts the policy he recommended to Bosola (I,2,202).

in us The close relationship between Ferdinand and his sister is significant.

coal-pit Charcoal pit.

sulphur Ferdinand is persistently associated with images of hell, fire, and torment. They reflect his moral and emotional state.

cullis Broth.

renew i.e., restore him to the strength he required to conceive the child.

sin of his back Sexual intercourse.
leaps Sexually possesses.
general Total.

Revision questions on Act II

1 What is the dramatic purpose of the first 66 lines of Act
II?
2 Discuss the role of Julia in Act II.
3 Compare and contrast the characters of Ferdinand and
the Cardinal.
4 How important is astrology in this part of the play?
5 Compare and contrast the roles of Bosola and Antonia.

Act III Scene 1

Once again we find Delio and Antonio in conversation. Antonio is fearful, but certain his own secret is secure. Accompanied by Bosola, Ferdinand and the Duchess enter. Ferdinand
tries to pressurize his sister into marriage. She responds by
claiming that she is being slandered. The Duchess, Antonio
and Delio leave, and Ferdinand confers with Bosola

Deception is the theme of this scene. Antonio describes his
own success in keeping his marriage a secret, the Duchess
protests her innocence, Ferdinand pretends to believe her,
giving her false confidence. Ironically, the scene ends with
Ferdinand's praise of Bosola's frankness.

Feeder of pedigrees Producer of descendants. The irony is that
  Antonio's children by her would hardly be regarded as noble or
  legitimate by her brothers.
half hour Webster's joke: in terms of the play's action it *is*
  within half an hour.
reversion Inheritance. Antonio gives a conventional list of things
  which make time seem to pass slowly.
politic Shrewd.
censure Judge.
purchase Wealth.
left-hand A play on the word 'sinister'.
odious/Unto Unpopular with.
I am to bespeak ... Another abrupt transition from the
  Duke.

I will marry ... Just what she has not done. The Duchess is morally compromised by the need to lie.

How is't? What do you think? Ferdinand knows Antonio is involved with his sister – but not to what extent.

Pasquil A Roman of legendary sharp tongue who gave his name to a form of lampoon or scandal-sheet: the pasquinade.

A pestilent air See I,1,14. Ferdinand reverses Antonio's image again, to suggest the disease comes from without.

deadly air The Duchess takes up Ferdinand's image. We know that her safety is an illusion.

cultures Plough-shares.

some ... Antonio, for one.

desertless Undeserving – in the sense of unsuitable.

gulleries Trickeries. Ferdinand dismisses love-potions and magic in favour of better explanation: his sister's behaviour is the result of her disposition. Ironically, by taking this view, Ferdinand condemns his own behaviour.

lenative Soothing. The poisons were pleasant to take, but made the takers mad.

witch i.e. the supplier of the poison.

by equivocation By lying.

rank blood The blood was supposed to distil spirits which produced the passions – a process taking place in the heart and the liver. Because the word 'blood' is used both in this sense, and in another meaning of 'genetic inheritance' its usage becomes ironic: Ferdinand and the Cardinal – her brothers – inherited the same blood as the Duchess.

compass Fathom.

drifts Intentions

Are ... chronicle Blow your own trumpet.

Flatter Note Bosola's abrupt honesty and Ferdinand's acceptance of it.

entertained Accepted/employed/listened to.

rails ... belief Teases him into admitting.

Act III Scene 2

The scene opens with a passage of banter between the Duchess, Cariola and Antonio. Then the Duchess is left alone: she talks on, thinking her maid and husband are still in the room, but meanwhile Ferdinand has let himself in with the false key Bosola procured for him (see the previous scene). He threatens her with a dagger and she confesses that she is married. After abusing her he departs saying he will never see her again. Cariola and Antonia, who have been hiding behind the arras, come back into the room and Antonio accuses Cariola of betraying them. She denies it.

Someone knocks at the door. Antonio leaves, and Bosola enters, explaining that Ferdinand has ridden off in a passion proclaiming betrayal. The Duchess explains that she is indeed betrayed: Antonio has cheated her of money for which her brother stood guarantor. She sends Bosola off to rouse her servants and quickly makes a plan with Antonio: he must pretend to be guilty and accept banishment. When he has gone Bosola pretends to be disgusted with the way the others have turned against him, and tricks the Duchess into admitting that Antonio is her husband and the father of her three children. She is then persuaded by Bosola to make a fake pilgrimage to Loreto, which is only a few miles from Ancona, Antonio's refuge. Cariola is doubtful, but the Duchess is convinced. When Bosola is left alone he reflects sardonically on his own perfidiousness which will surely bring him a reward.

In this crucial scene the Duchess is first surprised by Ferdinand, then tricked by Bosola – the one direct and violently abusive, the other flattering and skilful. Webster's taste for dramatic effects is exploited to the full, as the play's web of deceptions tangles more and more. The warm, witty intimacy of Antonio, the Duchess and her maid is sharply contrasted with Ferdinand's dark threats, as is their easy style with his fierce rhetoric. Ferdinand's surreptitious entry, like Bosola's deceitful confidence, marks him out as an embodiment of the Duchess's inescapable fate. Every precaution she takes is rendered ironically null by the apparent omniscience of these two: thinking herself fraught but free, in fact she has all her actions from now on determined by her brother and his creature. This highlights one of the play's themes: the notion that we act as though free, but cannot control even the most limited consequences of our actions. Nor can we know why we perform those actions, issuing as they do from desires, not from reason. Bosola sums up this view in the play's last lines when he says Antonio came by his death. In a mist: I know not how . . .

lord of mis-rule A pun. Mis-rule was a feast or revel, headed by a junior member of the household.

in the night i.e. as the Duchess's husband.

rise Double entendre – continued in Antonio's reply.

ended i.e. at the moment of orgasm. This saucy banter is quite conventional for the time.

Daphne Turned into a bay-tree to protect her from rape by a god. To avoid the same fate Syrinx was turned into a reed; and Anaxarete was changed into marble for being indifferent to the fate of a man who hanged himself for love of her.

peevish Perverse.

transhap'd Transformed. Antonio returns to the theme of fruitful love.

Paris Priam's son, Paris, was made to judge between three goddesses – Hera, Aphrodite and Athene – which was the most beautiful. He chose Aphrodite (Venus), goddess of love, who promised him Helen as a bride.

motion Display.

benight the apprehension Confuse the understanding. The allusion is ironic: 'benighted' by the Duchess' beauty, Antonio, like Paris, has chosen a dangerous course. Paris's choice led to the Trojan War, Antonio's to his and the Duchess' downfall.

hard-favour'd Ugly. Another passage about the appearance of women and its importance.

chaf'd Become irritable. This is a theatrical moment for which the use of hangings in 17th-century theatres made every opportunity.

arras Orris powder. The theme of female vanity is opportunely placed just before Ferdinand's entrance.

I ent'red ... keys A reminder that the Duchess initiated the wooing, thus compounding her guilt in her brother's hearing.

Love ... sweetest An important clue to the play's erotic nature. See also I,2,369.

gossips Godfathers.

like a prince The Duchess is brave and self-possessed even when surprised – a stance she maintains throughout.

essential Real.

O most ... prevent A curiously solemn conclusion from Ferdinand which serves two purposes; (a) it articulates a general principle, moralizing the moment; (b) it points up Ferdinand's hypocrisy and ignorance when he fails to anticipate the results of his sister's murder.

there's ... shame The only benefit shameful deeds bring is a deadened sense of shame. In the speaker's case the opposite proves to be true – but here he refers specifically to sexual dishonour.

Happily As it may happen.

basilisk A fabulous creature; its look or breath was fatal.

wolf Prefigures Ferdinand's lycanthropy.

screech-owl He adapts the Duchess' bird-image to his own taste.

beget Produce. Ferdinand here seems to withdraw from his earlier extreme position.

use Ability. Ferdinand constantly harps on the idea of names in these exchanges. Honour depends on having a pure name – even if deeds are bad, apparently.

bewray Reveal.

bullet ... wild-fire A typically grotesque image: wild-fire was both fire and a disease. A bullet was a cannon-ball

shook hands with Said good-bye to.

standing on my guard Ready to fight. But Antonio hardly emerges from the episode with credit: at no point did he step forward to protect the Duchess.

warrantable Justifiable.

Tane up Borrowed from.

lets ... forfeit Has allowed Ferdinand to become liable.

cunning Bosola is filled with admiration for the Duchess' resourcefulness. Once again she thinks for her husband.

weak safety Precarious state.

enginous wheels The wheels of a machine i.e., things are rushing out of our control.

short ... periods Brief words must take the place of sentences.

Tasso In the *Gerusalemme Liberata* (II,22) of the Italian poet Tasso, Soprina tells a lie for a noble purpose.

Quietus See I,2,383.

I am all yours Antonio follows the Duchess in his double entendre.

extortion Extortioners.

officer Policeman.

hermaphrodite One with organs of both sexes. A sly reference to Antonio's marriage. Notice how the courtiers follow their mistress's lead.

chippings of the butt'ry Crumbs from the kitchen.

gold chain i.e. Antonio's chain of office.

these i.e. the courtiers

in a ring Led by a ring – through the nose.

intelligencers Spies.

flatterers Bosola takes up one of the play's themes, and suggests that flattery produces its own justice when the flatterers are deceived.

poor gentleman By taking Antonio's side Bosola lulls the Duchess into a sense of security.

Pluto Properly Plutus, confused with the god of the underworld.

by scuttles Scuttling.

He was ... Compare this with Antonio's encomium of the Duchess (I,2,112–29). Where Antonio is hyperbolic, Bosola offers a portrait of the noble well-balanced man, concentrating on the distinction between being and appearance.

basely descended The Duchess tries the ground.

herald Registrar of genealogies.

politicians' Plotters'.

it cannot ... virtue i.e. it is no real evil to fall from grace if you are virtuous.

O ... music This is music to my ears.

shadows ... painted The obsessive appearance/reality motif.

unbenefic'd Without a church post.

curious engine Beautiful instrument. Bosola is practising the flattery he so cogently condemns.

cabinets Private rooms.

coats i.e. coats of arms. The absurdly flowery final couplet might alert the Duchess – but she is too delighted with Bosola's apparent friendship – an ironic vindication of the play's warnings about flattering princes.

th'inside Ironic: Bosola almost immediately reveals the truth to Ferdinand.

your direction Bosola is masterly where Antonio was passive.

base Bosola's self-consciousness is acute: he is always aware of – even delights in – the baseness of his deeds.

Prefers Promotes.

Act III Scene 3

The Cardinal is persuaded by the Emperor's envoys to give up his holy orders and become a soldier again – as he was before. The courtiers discuss Count Malateste behind his back, until Bosola arrives with news of the Duchess's pilgrimage. Now Ferdinand knows the full truth about his sister. He and the Cardinal agree to get them banished from Ancona.

The action of the scene takes place against a background of courtly chatter, in which the minor characters again discuss the vices of the great: Ferdinand, Bosola, the Cardinal. There is a cruel irony in the way her brothers condemn the

Duchess's pilgrimage: after all, it is their agent, Bosola, who suggested it. In hypocrisy the Duchess hardly approaches her brothers.

Pescara Historically, Ferdinand's brother-in-law. But Webster is only using the name.

Lannoy The Viceroy of Naples – the largest town near Amalfi.

Malateste A foolish nobleman.

muster book Register of military forces.

leaguer Military camp. Malateste and Pescara are opposite types: the foolish old man, and the honourable soldier.

scarf Malateste affects to be a knight taking his mistress' scarf as a sign of his service to her and her favour.

pot-gun A child's toy weapon.

touch-hole The opening where the gunpowder was lit.

guarded sumpter-cloth Ornamented cloth to cover a horse.

remove Movement. Silvio means that Malateste is purely ornamental, a piece of baggage.

What ... business? What is the matter?

Foxes ... for't An allusion to Samson's destruction of the Philistine corn (Judges 15). He tied pairs of foxes together by the tails, attached fire-brands to them, and sent them into the fields. They are divided because they don't know which way to run, having two heads.

fantastical Absurd.

knots ... toothache Typical of the foolish problems troubling academics, indicating Bosola's excessive subtlety.

salamander An animal supposed to live in fire – with which Ferdinand is persistently associated.

bad faces i.e. the miserable looks of his victims.

up's nose Up his nose – a play on 'haughty' and 'watchful'.

like ... storm A proverbial saying.

honesty i.e. dishonesty – also unchastity.

A slave Ferdinand's obsession seems to be more with caste than with sex.

counters Disc used in accounting.

audit-time The regular examination of accounts. Ferdinand means that only on such special occasions could Antonio even look like a gentleman.

Act III Scene 4

Two pilgrims discuss the Cardinal's decision to give up his hat, and the Duchess's pilgrimage. In dumb-show we then see the Cardinal's investiture as a soldier and the banishment of Antonio, the Duchess and her children from Ancona. A song is sung to glorify the Cardinal's military prowess. The two pilgrims then explain the action. The Pope has seized the dukedom of Malfi and made the Duchess a kind of outlaw.

This extraordinary scene is the first of several tableaux which Webster uses to vary the drama and to sum it up. The commentary of the pilgrims serves to put the action in context, but what counts is the visual show. The artificiality of the whole business reminds us that the play is fundamentally a kind of passion or progress: a symbolic enactment of suffering, in which the Duchess is reduced by stages to mortification before she is killed. In this scene the ritualistic side of the drama is emphasized. The juxtaposition of the Cardinal's new military role and his sister's banishment make the point economically: there is war between them, and it is a war very much of this world. The play is suffused with images of heaven and hell – but only when they suffer acutely do the characters turn their minds to the possibility of another world which is not merely one of animal satisfaction.

Act III Scene 5

The Duchess and Antonio discuss their situation, the Duchess describing an ominous dream in which her diamonds turned to pearls. Then Bosola comes in with a letter from Ferdinand demanding Antonio's presence. The Duchess advises Antonio to flee to Milan with their eldest child. This he does. Almost immediately Bosola enters in armour with a troop of soldiers. They have been instructed to take the Duchess prisoner.

The Duchess's separation from her husband is to be final, and she suspects as much: yet still she shows presence of mind and concern for Antonio's safety. Both of them acknowledge the power of misfortune, and the tone is one of noble resignation as they recognize the inexorable working of Providence. Bosola is the embodiment of that Providence, changing his role from friend to gaoler, rehearsing the arguments of the brothers about Antonio's low birth and weakness. But the Duchess replies with a magnificent parable about the Salmon and the Dog-fish. Like the tableau of the previous scene this parable highlights the ritual quality of the play, when the Duchess speaks not only for herself but for suffering humanity. She speaks appropriately, for she rises to heroic stature in proportion to her wretchedness.

Lightens Rests.

take Share.

fledg'd Grown up, i.e. now they are provided with what the Duchess (their 'parent') can give them.

politic Shrewd.

I stand engaged Ferdinand has cynically adapted the Duchess's story (III,2,166–70) to his own use. Note how the impression of the play's action as a great and horrible game is reinforced by the way all the characters play with their words.

breeding Bosola is both wrong and right: wrong because Antonio's caution is justified, but right because compared to his wife the steward is timid.

adamant Magnet.

bottom Boat.

For all . . . sorrow The Duchess here enunciates one of the tragic functions, as the characters do throughout the play. The tragedy is a highly self-conscious one, played out in foreknowledge.

O Heaven The Duchess begs a critical question about the play i.e., the degree to which this is a divinely ordained sequence of events.

scourge-stick Whip.

laurel The evergreen laurel was proverbially supposed to shrivel at the monarch's death.

vizarded Masked. This is the first of Bosola's physical 'disguises' – not his first moral one.

Fortune's wheel This allusion links the play with the Senecan tragedy of the 16th century: another aspect of its self-consciousness.

adventure Quarry.

Charon's boat Charon was the ferryman of Hades who took the dead across the River Styx.

virtue The very same argument Bosola himself put forward at II,1,91–112.

A Salmon . . . As with most parables, it is possible to interpret this in a number of ways. The Duchess gives her own version at line 140.

Revision questions on Act III

1 What is the effect of Ferdinand's entrance to the Duchess's room in Scene 2?
2 Why does Webster use dumb-show in Scene 4?
3 How many people tell lies in this Act and what is their significance?
4 What is the significance of the Duchess's last speech in Scene 5?
5 Comment on the Duchess's reference to 'Fortune's wheel'.

Act IV Scene 1

Bosola reports to Ferdinand on the Duchess's behaviour in adversity. Ferdinand leaves and Bosola draws a curtain revealing the Duchess and Cariola. It is dark when the servants take out the lights. Ferdinand enters and gives the Duchess a dead man's hand to kiss, pretending to make peace with her. The lights are then brought back and the dead hand revealed, after which another curtain is drawn, revealing wax figures of Antonio and his children, which the Duchess takes for their dead bodies. Bosola then talks with the Duchess, half-tormenting, half-comforting her. She leaves and Ferdinand returns, explaining that he wishes to make his sister despair, and that he has not finished yet. Bosola insists he will only see the Duchess in disguise, and the Duke implies that he will soon be sent to Milan to deal with Antonio.

Having introduced the notion of the tableau in III,4 Webster here develops it in startling ways. We see one tableau within another when the wax figures are exposed. Among other things, this confuses our sense of reality. Until Ferdinand tells us that these presentations are but framed in wax we may believe, like the Duchess, that they are indeed bodies. But they must also make us wonder about the extent the Duke is prepared to go to in his cruelty, and this compels the audience to pay as much attention to him as to his sister. Despite the play's name, it does not focus on one character with the intensity of a Shakespeare tragedy: it is a communal, not an individual drama. The play's purpose is not to explore the predicament of a unique character, but to stimulate the response of the audience through examination of a representative tragedy. This is the function of sensational devices such as the dead hand, popular in Jacobean drama, which probes extremes of sympathy and hatred. In this scene the rapid comings and goings, changes of perspective, abrupt alternations of light and dark, the vivid language and the bitter images all contribute to the creation of high tension, maintained until the Duchess's death at the end of Act IV.

Nobly Nobility is the key to our idea of the Duchess as a tragic heroine. It is this which raises her above the level of the other characters, despite her weaknesses.

I'll describe her Compare these lines with I,2,112–29. Both paint pictures, present the Duchess as an emblem, first of virtuous beauty, then of suffering beauty. Both comment on her reticence.

apprehend Recall.

traverse This rapid change is both dramatic and artificial, making Bosola appear the manipulator of the drama, the master of ceremonies.

a sacrament o'th' Church i.e. marriage. The children are not bastards, and Ferdinand should not speak of them so.

i'th'light But it is Ferdinand who becomes decisively associated with darkness by the play's end. Here he says the opposite of Antonio and Bosola – See IV,1,2 above.

a dead man's hand On one level this is sophistry: Ferdinand can break his promise because it isn't sealed with his hand. More importantly, it is the first of Act IV's horrors. While exciting, these are not merely gratuitous: they highlight the Duchess's calvary, her progress through suffering, and make visible the mental and emotional torture she undergoes. They also confirm our sense of Ferdinand's sheer nastiness.

a traverse ... Another tableau, this time exactly so. This revelation of scenes within scenes disturbs our sense of theatrical 'reality' – and Webster plays more and more with the stage illusion as the play progresses.

piece Body.

wastes The word is used literally, as the following lines show: the Duchess imagines a wax doll of herself in the 17th century equivalent of voodoo.

in hell See I,1,10. This is a stage on the way to her conclusion that death is a release.

Portia Who killed herself after the death of her husband, Brutus, by eating burning coals.

The bee ... The bee, only having one sting, is safe once it is discharged

pity One of the two tragic emotions (pity and terror) according to Aristotle. Bosola becomes instrumental in focusing both for the audience.

daggers Pains.

vipers Russell Brown comments that this may be a misprint for vapours – which would certainly make more sense. But as the following lines show, the Duchess is distracted and the mixing of metaphors ('blow' and 'vipers') may be deliberate.

pray ... curse The Duchess is torn by her sufferings – torn between acceptance and rebellion.

O fearful! Bosola's tone is difficult to judge, but his exchanges with Ferdinand after the Duchess's exit, suggest that he is now experiencing remorse and genuine pity. Although he still proceeds with the murder he does it 'Never in mine own shape' (IV,1,132) – which suggests a kind of controlled schizophrenia only transcended at the play's end. Like the Duchess, Bosola experiences his own progress through suffering. Unlike her, he changes during the play.

three smiling seasons i.e. spring, summer, autumn.

the world It is characteristic of the tragedies in this period to invoke cosmic imagery in association with the central character's downfall, widening and dignifying the drama.

the stars shine still Ambiguous. Bosola may be comforting the Duchess – or he may be deepening the pathos by citing the immutable cosmic order, indifferent to her sufferings.

them i.e. her brothers.

plagu'd in art Distressed by the illusion (of her dead family).

my blood ... soul Ferdinand's obsession – and his pride – are fully revealed here.

she'll needs be mad She must be made mad. The irony is that, as the Cardinal has already hinted (II,5,67) Ferdinand's hysteria verges on the madness into which it finally falls.

practise Meaning both: 'go about their business' and also 'copulate'.

gambols Frolics – again with a sexual undertone.

full o'th'moon Madness was supposed to be at its height at the full moon.

intelligence Bosola is beginning to feel twinges of guilt.

last cruel lie i.e. the waxworks.

Thy ... thee Ferdinand suggests that Bosola's pity is not his true nature. He is both right and wrong.

Act IV Scene 2

The Duchess and her maid, Cariola, can hear the madmen Ferdinand has stationed outside their rooms to distress them. As they discuss their predicament, a servant enters to announce the entry of the madmen. They come in prancing and jabbering. After they have danced, Bosola enters disguised as an old man who has come to make a tomb for the Duchess. He exhorts her to think on mortality. The executioners enter and Bosola changes his story: now he says he has been sent to prepare the Duchess for death. Cariola is dragged off, and the executioners strangle the Duchess. Bosola orders them to kill the children and fetch Cariola, who is then also strangled. Ferdinand enters and is shattered by the sight of his sister's dead body. He then tries to put the blame for her death on to Bosola and refuses to give him the promised reward. Bosola is angry but sees that Ferdinand is seriously disturbed. The Duke leaves and Bosola expresses his regret. When the Duchess briefly revives, he tells her that Antonio is living. Her death makes Bosola reflect on his deed and promise that he will at least see to her decent burial.

The theatricality of the previous scene is continued in this one. Webster revels in the grotesque and shocking, contrasting the play's blackest moments with violent comedy. Like death and sex, madness was an obsession of the Jacobean tragic writers: in this work we find all three. The madmen provide yet another sensational element in the play; more significantly, they also point up the idea of awful futility, their pointless babbling and capering both suggesting the inevitable end of all human vanity, yet also contrasting with the calm purposefulness of the Duchess. Like them, she may be engaged in an ultimately futile exercise, but she remains dignified and loving: her humanity is not destroyed by suffering, as theirs has been. Her dignity is also emphasized by the contrast with Cariola, who struggles against death to the end. In this scene the Duchess, for all her weaknesses, takes on truly tragic stature. Her brother, on the other hand, reveals a panic which is to destroy him, trying to evade the consequences of his action, which catch up with him in the form of madness when his perversion of justice appears in its full horror and, as Bosola says 'murder shrieks out ...'

But perhaps the most interesting development is that of Bosola himself, who finally gives free rein to his doubts and his conscience. Until this scene he has believed it possible to separate his actions from what he knows to be dishonourable, by maintaining a thoroughly cynical attitude. Now his cynicism is no longer strong enough to repress his sense of injustice and emotional revulsion. Yet it is not the murder itself which finally tips the scales, but Ferdinand's attempt to unload responsibility for it.

consort Company. There is also an ironic pun: referring to a group of musicians, consort often meant harmony – the last thing the madmen have.

Th'heaven ... mad Life has now become hell for the Duchess: she lives in her brother's element, fire.

her eyesight Traditionally, Fortune was blind.

sport Ambiguous: the Duchess will be made sport, as well as seeing some.

imposthume Abscess.

secular priest i.e. not a monk.

failing of't When it failed to happen.

usher Porter.

knave in grain A pun: (a) in the grain trade, (b) a rogue.

hind'red transportation Refused permission to export.

broker A salesman, whether of things or people i.e. a procurer. The list of madmen is probably full of topical allusions, now lost.

O let us howl ... An appropriately dreadful song for the madmen, in which Webster burlesques the very Gothic horrors which are an integral part of his drama.

perspective Telescope.

glass Magnifying-glass.

tithe Turn.

woodcock's head The woodcock was thought to be simple, hence this means proverbially brainless.

Greek is turn'd Turk Greeks and Turks were proverbial enemies.

Helvetian Swiss. The Genevan translation of the Bible, was Puritan in bias, emphasizing salvation by Grace, not by Works.

lay Expound.

rope-maker i.e. the hangman's suppliers.

placket Skirt. The linking of lechery and death here is obviously relevant.

possets Hot milk mixed with ale or wine.

throw ... me Copy me.

made ... costive Difficult: soap-makers were subject to diarrhoea. This comic moment gives a clue to the mad scene's nature – somewhat like the comedy in Shakespearian tragedy, sharpening the pathos, pointing up the central character's noble isolation by contrast.

insensible Invisible i.e. spiritual.

worm seed A medicinal dried flower.

salvatory Ointment box.

mummy Medicine prepared from corpses.

puff-paste Light pastry. This extraordinary sequence of images suggests decay, worms, flimsiness.

riot Debauchery – to which the great are especially prone, according to Bosola. But see I,2,360.

That makes ... light The illusion of greatness is disturbing – but it is only an illusion.

resolve me Explain to me.

they are not ... world Bosola here takes on the role of moralizer, railing against the time.

charnel Burial-place.

obedience, in my blood A contradiction of Ferdinand's obsessive point.

bellman One who made speeches on the morning of, and the night before, an execution.

'Twas ... mortification Bosola here defines his role. Mortification is both the coma preceding death and the soul's release from bodily concerns.

whistler Any bird: a singer, not a screecher.

such vain keeping Such a pointless fuss about keeping.

Sin ... weeping They are conceived in sin and born in tears.

reversion Inheritance.

catarrh Cerebral haemorrhage.

whispering A characteristic Websterism: shot.

fault i.e. talking. The Duchess is so calm that she is able to make a joke.

feed A disturbing line, suggesting the sensuality of the brothers, and the way in which they 'feed' off their sister's death emotionally.

strangle the children Bosola's brusque orders reveal that, for all the pity he expressed earlier, he can still kill in cold blood.

come to my answer Be answered.

discover Reveal. Cariola does anything to prolong her life.

When! Really! – Bosola's sardonic humour.

credit Reputation.

She is ... her Bosola puts the responsibility firmly on Ferdinand's shoulders.

Cover her face ... His broken remarks reveal that Ferdinand is shaken by the results of his orders. Bosola − the actual killer − remains calm. But then, the *appearance* of the Duchess has always stirred men's emotions.

infelicity Unhappiness.

twins This is crucial, not a mere circumstance: it explains much about the closeness of Ferdinand's identification with his sister, and about his rapid collapse after her death.

It seems ... Bosola drily corrects Ferdinand's point. It is several minutes since the Duchess died. This is of a piece with his insistence on facing reality.

approv'd Proved.

distracted Ferdinand's reproaches show his weakness. They also ironically show he has no inkling of the madness to come.

the main cause An implausible explanation, quite at odds with his earlier passion. As we have seen, Ferdinand's instinct is to conceal his deepest feelings − which he's just revealed to Bosola. Ironically, he lights on the pettiest possible lie, before turning to blame the only available person − the assassin.

Let me quicken ... Bosola is not willing to let his patron get away with this. 'Quicken' means 'jog'.

challenge Claim.

pardon Ferdinand is determined to unload responsibility for the murder onto Bosola.

study Bring myself.

Mine? Ferdinand has now mastered his emotions − it seems − and retreated into equivocation.

wolf Wolves were superstitiously believed to locate murdered corpses and dig them up.

fear of him i.e. God. Ferdinand's hypocrisy is complete.

worthy Ironic: they are worthy of something terrible.

take ... blood Gets a grip on members of one family. In view of Ferdinand's hysterical comments on his sister's 'blood' this is ironic.

tane Had.

lov'd A strange distinction. Bosola claims he has put loyalty to the Duke above honesty.

I'll go ... darkness With this characteristically abrupt change of tone and exit, Ferdinand seems to crack. When we next see him he is mad. In fact we can see these last lines as the culmination of mounting hysteria from line 263. The Duke's evasions are a part of this.

owl-light Twilight.
painted False. Quite what Bosola means by his honour it is hard
to say: presumably the marks of distinction accorded him as a
servant of Ferdinand. But see I,2,202.
sensible Perceptible.
cordial Restorative.
So pity . . . pity i.e. if he calls Ferdinand will hear.
he is living Apart from dramatic suspense, the main point of the
Duchess's revival seems to be this news, which allows her to die
in peace.
turtles Turtle doves – a symbol of both innocence and ease.
good . . . bad i.e. because it registers the painful difference
between the two.
suffer'd Allowed. Bosola, too, seems to be excusing himself.
estate Condition.
dispose Attention.
dejection Humiliation.

Revision questions on Act IV

1 What is the purpose of Bosola's various disguises?
2 Does the Duchess change or develop in this Act?
3 In what ways does Webster use spectacle in Act IV?
4 Comment on the imagery in Scene 2.
5 What happens to the relationship between Bosola and
Ferdinand in Scene 2, and why?

Act V Scene 1

Delio explains that Antonio's lands have been seized by Pescara. When the Marquis enters and Delio begs the estates for
himself, Pescara refuses, then grants the same lands to Julia,
the Cardinal's mistress, explaining that he will only give
something unjustly confiscated to someone unworthy. Antonio has decided that he will now risk everything on confront-
ing the Cardinal, and stirring his conscience.

As Antonio himself remarks, Pescara is one of the few
virtuous men in the play. Though his role is small he reminds
us that this is not a world entirely without virtue and honour.
Delio's pledge of friendship is in the same vein. On the other
hand, it is clear that Antonio's enterprise is futile: troubled as

he later is by visions, the Cardinal never gives up the game until he is mortally wounded. The introduction of Julia, who has played a very minor role up to now, prepares the way for her crucial intervention in the following scene. If Pescara embodies honour, she embodies self-interest, soon to be hoist with its own petard.

brethren i.e. the Duke and Cardinal.

in cheat A legal term. Were Antonio without heirs or a convicted criminal, the lands would revert to Pescara – who has indeed repossessed them under pressure.

To be invested in To be the recipients of.

an heretic ... shape myself A dispeller of any belief I can cultivate in my safety.

suit Request.

demesnes Lands.

engag'd Indebted.

main Great.

ruddier Kindlier – i.e. bringing a blush of pleasure into their cheeks. Pescara shows what a just man he is by this action.

his lust i.e. the Cardinal's.

To ... malice On the hope that even the Cardinal may not be completely wicked.

fraught with Foiled by. Antonio hopes that the Cardinal, expecting attack, will be surprised by loyalty.

keeps rank with Keeps in step with.

Act V Scene 2

Pescara and the doctor discuss Ferdinand, who now believes he is a wolf. The Cardinal enters with his brother, Malateste and Bosola. Ferdinand is clearly mad. The doctor tries to treat him but is assaulted by the Duke, who runs out. The Cardinal, when questioned, invents a ghost-story to explain his brother's madness, and then pretends to Bosola that he knows nothing about his sister's death.

Julia enters briefly and notes Bosola's attractiveness. The Cardinal commissions Bosola to find and kill Antonio. When he goes out Julia returns and makes love to Bosola, who decides to use her infatuation to find out the truth from the Cardinal. Bosola withdraws. The Cardinal returns and Julia presses him to tell her his secret. He does so, but only after making her swear discretion by kissing a poisoned book. Bosola, who has been hiding nearby, rushes in, but Julia dies. The Cardinal first threatens him, then promises great rewards for killing Antonio. Bosola agrees to do this and to remove Julia's body, but privately decides to warn Antonio and let him escape.

The contrast between the two brothers is made explicit in this scene: while the Cardinal remains icy-calm, Ferdinand cracks under the weight of his guilt. But the Cardinal is outdone in calmness by Bosola who, though appalled by what happens, is able to keep his head until he has done what he must. He is now acutely aware of the dangers on all sides. The Cardinal's ruthlessness is demonstrated by his treatment of Julia and his readiness to do any temporary deal with Bosola which will serve his turn. Like his brother, however, he is keen to avoid responsibility for what has happened. Both of them fatally trust in Bosola. Ironically, Ferdinand has now become like the madmen with whom he persecuted his sister.

lycanthropia Imagining oneself a wolf. The disease is an appropriate punishment for one who constantly invoked vermin and animals of prey as human comparisons. Sufferers were remorseful and guilty and the disease was associated with witchcraft. The doctor offers some details below.

melancholy Ferdinand is transformed from his usual choler to the opposite humour, melancholy.

nearer More direct.

Paracelsus A doctor, sage and magician (1493–1541).

Eagles ... together Compare this bird-imagery with the Duchess's. Ferdinand thinks naturally of birds of prey and scavengers.

your shadow A man and his shadow are inseparable. So are twins.

six snails ... Ferdinand is, as usual, extreme.

sheep-biter Sheep-worrying dog.

civil Becoming.

mad tricks The mixture of comedy – and medical satire – with the pathos of Ferdinand's madness, is typical of such scenes in the period.

salamander's skin Supposed to be fire-proof.

cocatrice Another name for the basilisk. See note p. 40.

Physicians ... contradiction An ironic reflection on Ferdinand's own former manner.

fetch a frisk Cut a caper.

cullis Broth.

anatomies Dead bodies.

beasts ... belly In sacrifices the tongue and the entrails were left for the gods.

I must feign ... Compare III,2,166–72. The Cardinal offers a curious parody of Ferdinand's excuse to Bosola (IV,2,281–84).

worse and worse But see V,2,21. Do the Cardinal's words indicate his intentions for Ferdinand?

Any thing i.e. anything but what he is and has been – the murderer of the Duchess.

For ... begin Thinking too much about the result stops them beginning. Had Bosola considered his murder he would not have done it.

kill him The Cardinal talks one kind of ruthlessness in order to evade the guilt of another. It is not clear why the Cardinal minds about Bosola's knowledge of his complicity.

style me ... advancement Call me your patron.

not freeze Not be slow off the mark.

I would see ... /be happy Bosola and the Cardinal have different meanings. Bosola really wants to see Antonio; the Cardinal thinks this is merely the desire to kill him.

He's ... murder He thinks of nothing but murder – but Webster's far more vivid words suggest that the Cardinal is murder incarnate.

trace Proceed.

fox Ferdinand is a wolf, the Cardinal a fox.

your pistol There is an equivalence between the sexual and the physical threat.

kissing-comfits Sweets to scent the breath.

a pretty way Sardonic.

arm Embrace.

Compare ... eyes ... Julia has been gazing longingly at Bosola.

nice Delicate.

familiar Familiar spirit – one who comes when called.

compliment Finesse.

a heart A desire.

I have it This almost comical aside puts Bosola's compliments – and Julia's infatuation – in perspective.

use to cut off Are used to ending.

excuse Reason i.e. the object of desire. Julia's account of how great ladies 'of pleasure' behave throws light on the Duchess's more delicate wooing.

express I love you To express my love for you. Julia's offer is opportune. The speed of this courtship accentuates its comical aspect.

cabinet Private room – bedroom

Yond's There is. Julia's entrance in the midst of his decision to dispose of her is ironic indeed – the more so since she is on a mission which will help Bosola dispose of the Cardinal.

What ails you? Again ironic: the Cardinal has just described his disease.

and not me But don't tell me this.

true unto yourself Julia means that they are so close, telling her will be like telling himself.

rack Torment.

hoop'd with adamant Bound with steel.

poison The recurrent image of courtly life.

How settles this? We might say now 'unsettles' – 'You find this disturbing?' – spoken in ironic satisfaction.

equal Equitable.

I know not whither This disturbing comment characterizes the last part of the play. Compare V,5,89–90 and V,5,105.

Wherefore For what.

a great man Bosola's irony.

as she intended Which she intended to satisfy by this.

your fellow Like Ferdinand, the Cardinal brazens things out, but by cooler means.

fair ... /purposes i.e. as though painting rotten wood like marble, pretending better to me than you intend.

honours Equivocal: the Cardinal may mean a reward – or he may mean funeral honours.

that body i.e. Julia.

a very happy turn Bosola is ironic. The Cardinal takes no notice.

estate Condition.

frost-nail'd i.e. have studs on their boots.

Bears up in blood This may either mean 'persists in killing' or 'keeps up his courage' or 'continues to show his family traits'. Webster may be playing on all three.

Security Confidence.

dead Unbroken. Bosola suggests that the Cardinal's assurance is separated from hell by a thin divide.

biters Animals of prey.

thy blood i.e. his children.

It may be Bosola is still uncertain of his course. Note also how he lays responsibility for the children's death at other feet, hardly acknowledging his own part.

my melancholy See above V,2,304–5.

O ... up A characteristic sententia to end with. One might trace the play's development in terms of such sayings.

Act V Scene 3

Unknown to them, Antonio and Delio are near the Duchess's grave. Their words are echoed by the vault, and a vision appears to Antonio, which seems to warn him of his fate. Though unnerved, he regains his courage and resolves to stake everything on a surprise visit to the Cardinal.

The irony of Antonio's resolution is underlined by his ignorance of the Duchess's death. We know this – as much as we know that his gesture is a futile one. The uncertainty of what he sees – whether or not it is his wife's face – hardly matters: the strangeness and vagueness are of a piece with the play, and with Bosola's later sentiment that everything in it has happened as though in a mist. The echo – an aspect of the play Webster took from the masque – intensifies the pathos of Antonio's predicament, besides gratifying Jacobean taste for the sensational.

I do ... we have This whole speech is sententious. Like his wife, Antonio, being put in a suitable frame of mind for death. 'Memento mori' – 'think upon death' – was a favourite 17th-century motto.

Churches and cities This puts Antonio's own tragedy in the larger context.

Like death ... have The echo picks out a series of pertinent phrases.

Wisdom ... for't Wisdom has no more effect on exhausting grief than time does – so take your time.

a face Antonio sees the face of the Duchess.

ague Fever i.e. of uncertainty.

Spread Presented.

Fortune Here Antonio explains that Fortune may bring misery, but it depends on the individual how he or she reacts to it. The noble mind rises above pain: at last Antonio rises above his fears.

Act V Scene 4

The Cardinal ensures that his brother will be left alone that night so that he, the Cardinal, may safely smuggle out Julia's body while the others are in their rooms, bidding them not to come even if he should call. Bosola enters, overhearing the Cardinal decide on his death, and Ferdinand comes in and goes out muttering about murder. Antonio and a servant enter; and Bosola, mistaking Antonio, kills him. Before Antonio dies Bosola tells him his wife and children are dead. Stricken with remorse Bosola decides to take immediate revenge on the Cardinal.

The irony of mistaken identities compounds Bosola's immersion in crime. Earlier in the play he would have indifferently killed Antonio; now he does it by accident, preparing the way for his conclusion at the play's end that it is

Such a mistake as I have often seen
In a play . . .

Antonio dies concluding, like his wife, that life is worth little and death, therefore, not so terrible a thing. This is in line with the memento mori theme of the play: the moral lesson which teaches us to remind ourselves how insignificant are the desires and pleasures of this world, and how subject to chance. While the play as a whole shows moral design in the shape of punishment for the wicked, it offers little hope of happiness for the good in this world, and little sign of the effectiveness of human will. The events of the last few scenes occur almost casually, and this is how the characters take them on the whole.

enjoin'd Urged.
sensibly With feeling.
osier Reed.
his own child This small remark gives a clear indication of how Ferdinand is regarded.
The reason . . . Rather awkwardly, the Cardinal gives the reason for his strange behaviour – which is, of course, necessary for the final stage of the action.
He dies Note the abrupt transitions in this speech – which show the Cardinal's family resemblance to Ferdinand: one moment he longs to pray, the next he decides on Bosola's death.

one's footing Someone's footsteps. As the end draws near the action quickens, with entrances and exits rapidly following. Death is the obsessive topic.

We value ... /death A sententia: the Cardinal's fear will make him utterly ruthless.

suit Quest. Refers back to 'pray' in the previous line.

banded Bandied.

in sadness In earnest.

balm'd Treated with ointment.

preparative Preparation.

process Causes.

I ... that Bosola does not want to know about such things when he is intent on killing the Cardinal – and when he has just killed Antonio in error.

tender Value.

direful misprision Terrible mistake.

represent Bosola addresses himself. 'Represent' contrasts with 'imitate'. Like Antonio (V,4,48) in the final test Bosola will abandon disguise and deceit and be himself 'for silence' – i.e. he will not speak, but act.

Act V Scene 5

The Cardinal is puzzled and disturbed by visions and by thoughts about the nature of hell. Bosola enters, announcing his intention to kill the Cardinal, who shouts for help to no effect: he has already warned people not to respond in the previous scene. Pescara, however, decides to investigate. Bosola wounds the Cardinal as Ferdinand enters. They fight and Ferdinand wounds his brother and Bosola, who kills him. The Cardinal dies and Bosola's wound also proves to be mortal. Delio enters with Antonio's son, whom he proclaims his mother's successor.

In this brief final scene events move very fast, as the protagonists are despatched by an apt justice killing one another. For the first time we see a chink in the Cardinal's armour: like his brother he is now troubled by guilt. When attacked he is terrified for his life; but once he knows he is dying, an extraordinary resignation grips him. The same is true of Ferdinand: in death the two brothers proclaim their own symbolic roles as evil-doers justly punished. Bosola, too, hints at his symbolism, referring to the drama in his last speech. He dies perplexed, and the note of hope at the end is conventional, quite overshadowed by the darkness into which all three descend. The scene marks the consummation of revenge tragedy: the vengeance is symmetrical as the two brothers are killed by their instrument of murder, and he by them. The theatrical self-consciousness, present throughout the play in dozens of allusions to actors and the theatre, is made explicit in Bosola's admission of the roles he has played. The end of the play, referring to 'Integrity of life' and 'lords of truth', ironically hints at the futility and illusoriness of what we have witnessed — yet it is the impression of pity and terror which remains.

in By.

He i.e. the author of the book.

one material i.e. the same throughout. The Cardinal has begun to worry about judgment.

a thing A disturbing vision of vengeance, sharpened by the precision of the setting and the curious substitution of a rake where one might expect a sword or a scythe.

ghastly Full of horror.

it lightens i.e. the expression on his face. He's stirred both by action in general, and by the particular action he proposes.

You would not bawl ... The combination of horror and humour is both effective and characteristic of this writer.

engines Implements.

aloof Some way after.

***kills the* SERVANT** Bosola is cold and calculating even in his revenge.

equal Impartial.

of thyself By your own momentum.

leveret Young hare. A striking image of vulnerability for the apparently powerful Cardinal.

vaunt-guard Vanguard.

honour of arms Honour of soldiers i.e. I salute you. Ferdinand is quite mad.

your brother./The devil? This juxtaposition makes the point effectively.

adverse Opposite.

There ... ransom Bosola cannot be held for ransom if he is dead.

Caesar ... Pompey Both these Roman rulers were murdered, Caesar at the height of his power, Pompey in exile.

revenge Bosola's words remind us that this is, among other things, a revenge drama.

broken winded ... dog-kennel Ferdinand madly mixes his metaphors.

vault credit Outleap expectation.

come to himself Compare V,5,48 and V,5,81. The notion that extreme suffering forces self-knowledge pervades the end of the play.

our own dust Ferdinand may mean that a man is his own worst enemy – or that he had been brought low by his own kind – i.e. his sister.

payment Death wound.

in my teeth i.e. about to depart through the mouth.

Revenge ... /Neglected Bosola neatly sums up the situation.

actor The double meaning – doer/performer – reflects back on the play's chain of theatrical motifs.

'gainst mine own good nature So Bosola turns out to have been a 'goody' in disguise all along. It is questionable how much we can believe in this self-assessment. Alternatively, we can take 'good' as meaning 'better'.

let ... /thought of The Cardinal's conversion to humility is not so sudden as appears: it has been growing at least since the beginning of the scene.

In a mist Retrospectively this characterizes most of the play's action: the characters are rarely in possession of their motives. The following reference to the drama – which confirms the strand of similar allusions throughout – is linked thereby to the mist imagery, the two being aspects of the more general questions about the relationship of appearance and reality which pervade the play.

womanish An ironic usage in view of the Duchess's brave behaviour.

heir The appearance of the next generation, as so often in Jacobean tragedy, hints at continuity.

this great ruin i.e. the mound of bodies!

things Bodies. No longer persons, corpses are things – but the word here suggests the dehumanization of death after an all too human drama.

Fall ... snow A wonderful image of transience – which links with mist (See above line 94).

lords of truth In the context of recent events this seems to refer especially to self-knowledge.

Integrity of life One can hardly say this of anyone in the play.

Revision questions on Act V

1 What does Ferdinand's madness contribute to the play?
2 What is the point of Scene 3? Can it be related to anything else in the play?
3 Discuss Delio's role throughout the play.
4 Do Bosola's last words throw any light on the play?
5 What is the purpose of the various rhyming couplets scattered through the last scene?

The characters

Antonio

A most wretched thing
That only have thy benefit in death,
To appear myself.

Like the Cardinal, Antonio is more important for the roles he plays than as a developed character. For most of the play he acts as a foil to his wife, to Ferdinand, or to Bosola: only towards the end is he given any kind of 'independent' life – after the Duchess's death.

This should not obscure the fact that Antonio at times plays a crucial part – never more so than in the first act, when he doubles as participant in the action and commentator on it. The play's opening sequence depends upon a conversation between Antonio and Delio. The Duchess's steward has recently returned from France – a visit which gives rise to his reflections on corrupt and virtuous courts (I,1,4–22). Antonio's first speech lends the play a vital keynote: in it he expounds the doctrine that a good court – and therefore a happy country – depends upon a wise ruler supported by 'a most provident Council'. We are about to witness the acts of headstrong and self-interested princes who rule autocratically, with the help of liars, spies and flatterers. Ironically, even the Duchess's household, to which Antonio belongs, is not immune from this poison: the Duchess is a good but wilful woman, and her servant, Antonio, fails to give her shrewd advice, despite his suspicions that her marriage can only bring trouble. In retrospect his speech thus becomes ironic.

His discussion with Delio is interrupted by Bosola's entrance. this is significant on a number of levels. It gives Webster the chance to offer Antonio's characterization of Bosola, before and after his talk with the Cardinal – who is in turn summed up by Bosola. It provides an immediate and vivid illustration of Antonio's point that bad princes make bad men. And it establishes a comparison between Antonio and Bosola – servants of the brother and the sister. At this stage

Bosola is the outsider and Antonio the safe insider. These roles are soon to be reversed, and the fates of the two men are entwined through the play – until Bosola finally kills Antonio by mistake, and is himself killed avenging him.

The pairing of Bosola and Antonio is not accidental in a play which features twins. The two servants reflect and comment on their masters, who bring them both to disaster. The work is full of echoes, both literal and metaphorical. The mirror into which the Duchess looks in III,2; the painting Cariola compares her with (IV,2,31); the echo (V,3); Ferdinand's rage with his own shadow (V,2,38) – are all examples of Webster's preoccupation with doubles, self-images, reflections and twins. Bosola is Antonio's doppelgänger or shadow: in IV,1, when he begins to pity the Duchess, he paints a picture of her which resembles Antonio's first image of the woman both lovely yet chaste. More tellingly still, both of them refer to her quietness. It is the sight of the Duchess stirring in her death throes, able to utter only two words which calls forth Bosola's tears and makes him resolve on revenge – just as a silent vision makes Antonio determined to act in V,3. Throughout the play the actions of the two men mirror one another, even in death. As he lies dying, Antonio ruefully reflects that he should:

. . . only have thy benefit in death,
To appear myself. (V,4,47–8)

A few lines later Bosola resolves that:

I will not imitate things glorious,
No more than base: I'll be my own example. (V,4,80–81)

Both men discover themselves in action.

For most of the play, however, Antonio is passive to fate, whether in the shape of the Duchess, her brothers, or Bosola. His role as commentator is continued in I,2 when he provides character sketches of Ferdinand, the Cardinal and their sister. At one level these sketches are meant to be objective – and so they are: subsequent behaviour largely bears them out. But the portrait of the Duchess is clearly designed to show that Antonio regards her with more than respect. As Delio comments: 'You play the wire-drawer with her commendations' (I,2,131). It is up to the audience to work out how accurate Antonio's picture is. In a play filled with shifting perspectives, this is not always easy. In the second part of I,2 Antonio himself appears in a rather different light: no longer the wise servant, he becomes witty and amorous, ready to respond to the Duchess's invitations, though he trembles (369). Even the Duchess's deception – hiding Cariola behind the screen – does not flummox him. Socially he may be his wife's inferior: in love and wit he equals her.

It is the question of Antonio's inferiority, however, which preoccupies the Aragonian brothers and their agent. Again and again they declare his baseness. When arresting the Duchess Bosola tells her to: 'Forget this base, low fellow' (III,5,116) calling him 'One of no birth'. This contrasts sharply with the beginning of the next scene in which Bosola calls the Duchess 'noble' twice within a few lines. The Duchess's response to attacks on her husband's birth is to say, as she does to Bosola:

Man is most happy when's own actions
Be arguments and examples of his virtue. (III,5,119–20)

and it is precisely this conclusion which Bosola himself reaches at the end of the play when he vows to be his 'own example'. The oppressed Antonio thus becomes the model for virtuous action. This is not to say that social distinctions are not maintained. Far from it: Antonio recognizes his own baseness and speaks to the Duchess of his 'unworthiness'. But he understands, as the Duchess does, that in moral matters:

The great are like the base; nay, they are the same,
When they seek shameful ways to avoid shame. (II,3,51–2)

And Antonio is by no means a moral paragon himself. For one thing, he is frightened and inclined to duplicity. He hides from Ferdinand (III,2) and allows the Duchess to send him away just before her own arrest (III,5). He is highly superstitious. Having cast a horoscope for his newly-born son, he drops it when encountering Bosola, who scares him; and he takes the

bleeding of his nose as an ominous sign. In the previous scene
Delio has warned him against superstition, using this very
example. When things go badly, Antonio is inclined to think
the worst. He interprets a dream of the Duchess as a sign that
'you'll weep shortly' (III,6,16), and tells Delio that it is impossible 'To fly your fate' (V,3,34). On the other hand, this
pessimism puts him in tune with a reality which the other
characters ignore until too late. As he puts it to the Duchess:

> Do not weep:
> Heaven fashion'd us of nothing; and we strive
> To bring ourselves to nothing. (III,5,78–80)

Once again Antonio acts in the role of commentator or chorus:
he enunciates a truth which is enacted in the play. This is
hardly a help to the development of a substantial dramatic
character, and the trouble with Webster's presentation of
Antonio is that he can all too easily strike one as wooden, flat
and lifeless. Only after the Duchess's death, when he becomes
the Aragonian brothers' main quarry, does he take on a life of
his own, deciding to visit the Cardinal and confront him in the
hope of reconciliation. The very unlikeliness of this shows how
hopeless Antonio's case is, and how justified his pessimism;
and his new role is short-lived. In death his role is once again
to enunciate a gloomy truth: 'Pleasure of life, what is't? Only
the good hours/Of an ague: merely preparative to rest'
(V,4,66–7).

The Duchess

She stains the time past, lights the time to come.

Given the play's name audiences have often wondered about
this character's status: apart from her three or four great
scenes she appears relatively little, and not at all in the last
quarter of the play. To what extent can she be called the
heroine, or even the main character? Are these two necessarily
the same? And what is her importance relative to the other
major figures – Bosola, Ferdinand, the Cardinal and Antonio?
These are questions which can be answered partly in theatrical

terms. The play shows signs of Webster's awareness that the Duchess stands apart from the other characters, not only morally and in stature, but because she is a woman in a play otherwise _dominated by men_. Thus instead of giving her a formal entry or a great soliloquy to begin with, he introduces her almost casually in the second scene of Act I, keeping her on stage for nearly seventy lines before she makes a few inconsequential remarks. While she dominates the second half of I,2, this is really a separate scene. Our first 'meeting' is with her face, figure and bearing, not with her words.

In performance it is impossible to keep our eyes from wandering to her, even though she is silent. Even if it were, Antonio's vivid comparison of the brothers and their sister would direct our attention to her, inviting us to compare our visual impression of the Duchess with what we are being told. Antonio's description is idealized, even romantic, suggesting more than loyalty to an employer. Compared to other women, the Duchess is chaste, noble and silent, beyond reproach yet attractive enough to stir any man. Antonio's portrait treads a thin line between describing his mistress as sexually provocative but at the same time pure (I,2,120–25). Delio rightly suggests that his friend is overdoing things, but Antonio responds with even greater hyperbole:

All her particular worth grows to this sum:
She stains the time past: lights the time to come (132–3)

a curious couplet echoed many pages later by the miserable Ferdinand as he looks on his sister's corpse (IV,2,263) and again when Antonio sees a vision of her after death. The Duchess is associated with light as her brothers are with darkness, though not so completely, for she is not presented as virtuous in the way they are shown to be evil i.e. completely. Central to the character are her faults: it is not as a paragon that she is shown to suffer, but as someone who learns patience in suffering.

The complexity of the portrait begins to appear in I,2. In the second half of the scene Antonio's glowing portrait of the chaste woman is counterpointed by wilfulness and coquetry. The minute Ferdinand leaves the room a very different person is revealed. Without any of his cruelty, the Duchess's speech shares the energy and vivid metaphors of her brother Ferdinand's and shows an even greater energy – highlighted in the force necessary to spit out 'If all my royal kindred' and 'low foot-steps', and borne out by the vigorous way she gets down to business: 'Is Antonio come?' (I,2,278). During the rest of the scene she is flirtatious, decisive, witty, tender and shrewd by turns. Here is no submissive female but a human being at once passionate and level-headed, who understands very well the dangers of her chosen course. Having said this, she matches Ferdinand in persiflage and use of the double entendre and takes the lead throughout in her courtship of Antonio, bidding him be brave when he trembles. In particular, she reassures him about her brothers: 'Do not think of them'. It is this miscalculation which proves to be her downfall. And she is not only over-confident, but also deceitful. Having explained to Antonio that:

> we
> Are forc'd to express our violent passions
> In riddles, and in dreams, and leave the path
> Of simple virtue, which was never made
> To seem the thing it is not. (I,2,363–7)

she then reveals how she has tricked him by concealing Cariola and thus effecting the marriage between them. So she not only deceives her brothers but also him.

These small deceptions may seem, like her overconfidence, small faults in the context of her evil surroundings, yet they are decisive – not only in the consequences but in their moral import. For the Duchess, in however muted and acceptable a form, suffers from the classic tragic flaw of pride. She believes that she can overcome all adverse circumstances and work her will, in the face of the evidence. Her manipulation of Antonio shows that even where her lover is concerned she will still assume control to get what she wants. At this stage in the play the good things of this world count for everything with her. Though she is a good woman, she shows no more sign than her brothers of caring for the spiritual life, or liking the classic Christian conclusion she is brought to by her sufferings: that all flesh is grass. Whatever religious or metaphysical views we may wish to attribute to Webster, this stark moral lesson forms the play's heart, and it is the Duchess who learns it most painfully – which is why she gives *her* name to the play.

By the end of Act I we have the image of a complex woman: sensuous and proud, spirited, practical and quick-witted, wilful and tender. It is left to her maid Cariola to put these qualities in perspective:

Whether the spirit of greatness or of woman
Reign most in her, I know not, but it shows
A fearful madness: I owe her much of pity. (I,2,420–22)

Cariola, like Antonio, largely lacks her mistress's nobility, but she is altogether more realistic, and her mention of madness makes a curious symmetry with Ferdinand's fate at the play's end – reminding us again that the two are twins. Ferdinand is debarred from tragic status by his fundamentally evil character; but Cariola's words, echoing Aristotle's requirement that tragic action should stir the emotions of fear and pity in the audience, make it clear that his sister is being presented as a tragic heroine. On the other hand, doubt about her motives – the spirit of 'woman' or of 'greatness' – show that this status is by no means uncomplicated. Like Shakespeare's tragic protagonists, Webster's have faults in proportion to their qualities. It is the large scale on which their destinies are acted out, and the magnificence with which they meet them, that count. We can see this clearly enough if we compare the Duchess's behaviour in the execution scene (IV,2) with Cariola's. Where her mistress accepts the end with dignity and even gratitude, Cariola howls for just one more minute of life. Ferdinand and the Cardinal die likewise, in a muddle and without repose. Only Bosola's last words, black, theatrical and sententious though they are, can compare with his victim's in dignity.

Before her last noble hours the Duchess undergoes many dangerous moments which test her resolution: black comedy often results. When she parries Ferdinand's insistence in III,1 that she take a spouse, she complains of rumours which sully her honour, saying that: 'when I choose/A husband I will marry for your honour' (43–4). It is difficult to tell how ironic she is being here. But *we* know that Ferdinand knows the truth – that she is married – and he is unmistakeably ironic. The

Duchess leaves, claiming that 'This deadly air is purged' and the Duke immediately snarls at Bosola that: 'Her guilt treads on/Hot burning cultures' (56–7). The Duchess is forced to become an actress – to do what she complained of at I,2,364–6 i.e. pretend to be that which she is not. In a play filled with theatrical metaphors these moments take on a special significance. Both Bosola and his victim find themselves constrained to uncongenial roles. The irony is that these roles are cruel parodies of what they really are. Both of them become 'criminals' under pressure of circumstance – Bosola a murderer, and the Duchess – in the eyes of her brothers – a whore.

Theatrical metaphors are common in the literature of a great dramatic age. *Hamlet*, to cite one famous contemporary example, is full of them. There, and in comparable plays, they naturally connect with the question of identity. If I play roles of one sort or another it is likely that I will speculate on the nature of the 'real' me – especially when the roles played bring that very reality into doubt. At the beginning of *The Duchess of Malfi* there is clearly a gap between the way in which the heroine perceives herself and the ways in which others see her. To Antonio she is a chaste saint, to her brothers a potential whore, to herself simply a woman who wishes to fulfil her natural desires. In order to deceive her brothers she is forced to play a role, and it is the gradual exposure of this role for the sham it is which forms the core of the tragedy. This begins in III,2 when the Duchess lies about her husband, to find an excuse for banishing him from Malfi. Not only is she quick-thinking: she and Antonio then act out a curious exchange in front of Bosola which is meant to appear dismissive to him but reassuring to them (III,2,182–208). It is ironic, then, that the Duchess is shortly fooled by the play's other great actor, Bosola, into revealing the truth. Here she fatally forgets her part, throwing away her one advantage in the duel with Bosola: secrecy. This opens the way to her expulsion from Ancona (III,4) and subsequent arrest (III,5). It is these catastrophes which set in motion the Duchess's Passion – her realization that disaster is in sight and her acceptance of it. In Act III Scene 5 both she and her husband reiterate the point that – as Antonio puts it:

Heaven fashioned us of nothing; and we strive
To bring ourselves to nothing. (79–90)

When he leaves and Bosola arrives to arrest her she puts it
another way:

When Fortune's wheel is over-charg'd with princes,
The weight makes it move swift. I would have my ruin
Be sudden. (93–5)

Her long parable at the scene's end emphasizes the almost
impersonal nature of her fate; she suffers representatively.

In IV,1 and 2 the drama is played out through a number of
fantastic theatrical tricks – the dead hand, the waxworks, the
madmen, Bosola's disguises – which emphasize the ritual,
theatrical nature of the Duchess's torment and death; and
Webster indicates her passive acceptance by constantly plac-
ing her within a frame, as it were. Thus, at IV,1,17 a curtain is
drawn to reveal her; then Ferdinand visits her in the dark;
then a further curtain is drawn exposing the wax figures of her
husband and children. In each case she is like an animal in a
cage, on show to Bosola, Ferdinand and the audience. Just as
she has exercised her ducal role in public, so she now perishes
in full view, each stage reducing her desire for life a little
further – so that when the executioners arrive she can turn
Ferdinand's obsession with the honour of his blood back on
him. But it is not a character we watch suffering – as we watch
a character in a Shakespeare tragedy: it is a role, a stripping
away of attributes gathered together under the Duchess's
name. When she says, a little earlier:

Who am I? (IV,2,123)

and then

Am I not thy Duchess? (133)

and finally

I am Duchess of Malfi still. (141)

the growth in confidence is not only apparent; it sounds ironically in the context of Bosola's macabre funeral games. The
statements are invitations to Bosola to prate about mortality.
They also serve to remind us that her grand title is of no
account before the reality of death – a sententious conclusion
characteristic of Jacobean tragedy's obsession with the theme
of memento mori. She affirms her identity in the process of
losing it.

Ferdinand

Like diamonds we are cut with our own dust.

The Duchess's twin is a fierce, passionate, unstable man who
reflects his sister's wilfulness, pride and sensuality as though
in a dark, distorting mirror. His obsessive imagining of her
desire, and the 'punishment' he wishes to mete out to it,
indicate a preoccupation with his sister well beyond honour's
demands or the greed for her gold. To Ferdinand, the Duchess
is not simply a sister: she is the focus for all the ungovernable
passions which, in the end, destroy him, and which are shown
to be self-destructive. When he kills her physically he effectively kills himself mentally. In this play Webster shows a
subtle insight into the close psychology of twins and their
tendency to identify with one another.

As one of the play's four major characters, Ferdinand is
carefully put in context for us by Antonio. The first lines of
I,1, contrasting the noble French king with less worthy
princes, are an implicit criticism of the two brothers. As if on
cue, Bosola enters: the lines (19–22) ironically foreshadow his
complete submission to Ferdinand's will, even as he seems to
be telling the Duke the truth about himself. When the Duke
declares later that

I never gave pension but to flatterers,
Till I entertained thee ... (III,1,90–91)

he means himself to flatter Bosola; but once again the lines are
ironic, for Ferdinand speaks the truth in spite of himself.
While seeming to speak frankly, Bosola only faces the whole

truth about Ferdinand too late – too late, that is, for the Duchess and for himself. He flatters his royal master in the subtlest way by speaking rudely to his face, but nevertheless doing his bidding. They flatter most effectively who tell a part of the truth: the limited insolence of their servants is a luxury to men bored with absolute power. Ferdinand is such a man: the theme of flattery, a particular manifestation of the discrepancy between reality and appearance, is consistently associated with the Duke through the play. Even in madness the doctor flatters him. And though Ferdinand sees through the tricks and beats the doctor, he remains mad. Surrounded by informers and spies, claiming to know everything, the Duke no longer even knows himself.

This is a long way from his first appearance as a courtly monarch, the paradigm of an Italian Renaissance ruler: polite, urbane, cultured and witty, engaged in the sort of verbal banter with his courtiers we find so often in Shakespearian comedy. In his first appearance he even makes a joke of flattery itself, suggesting that he well understands life at court (I,2,43–4). Such light-hearted irony contrasts sharply with the characterization of the Duke offered by Bosola in the previous scene. He and his brothers are:

... like plum trees, that grow crooked over
standing pools, they are rich and o'er-laden
with fruit, but none but crows, pies, and
caterpillars feed on them ... (I,1,49–51).

At this point, in view of Antonio's earlier dismissal of Bosola as a talented moaner, we might write off this description of Ferdinand, though the vivid images are haunting – were it not that the Duke's witty first scene is rapidly followed by Antonio's assessment of him in terms which establish his deceitfulness (I,2,94–107). Yet when the Duchess briefly comes on stage for the first time the Duke sustains his urbane manner until his conversation with Bosola (I,2,156–215), when the mask slips again. The use of shifting perspectives and the contrast between what is said and what is shown – apparent here – are both techniques favoured by Webster, serving to disturb any settled judgements of character and motive the audience may reach, and to emphasize the sense of unease.

While the Duke and the Duchess are twins by blood, the Duke and his brother are twins 'In quality' as Antonio puts it (I,2,97). They are not merely bad, but evil. Ferdinand soon gives evidence of this in his dry reproof to Bosola: 'Your inclination to shed blood rides post/Before my occasion to use you' (I,2,174–5). The lines are typical of his chilling wit. But it is only at the Duchess's second appearance in the play (I,2,216) that his obsession with her is revealed in a series of disturbing images. Ferdinand's words generate a sense of claustrophobia and unnaturalness not dispelled by the Duchess's impatient dismissal of them when he leaves. When he next appears, in II,5, his obsession has turned – as he says himself – almost to madness, and his ravings culminate in lines which fuse the claustrophobic and the unnatural with the hellish (II,5,67–9). The sinister warning of his earlier images is here translated into brutal savagery. This change also serves to highlight the contrasting temperaments of the brothers: for 80 lines Ferdinand rages and the Cardinal coldly attempts to calm him. The Duke speaks of his vivid imagination (II,5,40) while the Cardinal points out – rightly – that his rage is merely blinding him to his own weakness.

But Ferdinand is overwhelmed by his obsession with the Duchess's sexuality. This is contrasted with the Cardinal's apparent preoccupation with honour. While Ferdinand, like the Cardinal, has made this the motive of his suspicion to his sister, the sheer violence of his response suggests other causes. Not only is his family honour betrayed, but also a deeper bond: both are expressed in the notion of 'blood' in its several senses associated with Ferdinand in the play. Descent, kinship, affinity, temperament and passion are all comprised in the word. Honour is the public expression of personal pride, valid only when it takes due notice of other personal and social obligations: charity and love among them. In Ferdinand's case these are lacking: his 'honour' therefore becomes the mere assertion of personal vanity – *my* honour – and a cover for an incestuous possessiveness.

When the Cardinal points out the futility of his brother's rage he links it with an image of witchcraft. The imagery of hell and devils is associated with both the brothers. Here it hints at the Duke's inhumanity – a point immediately made explicit in another sense by the Cardinal, who compares his brother to a beast: 'there is not in nature/A thing that makes man so deform'd, so beastly . . .' (II,5,57–8). These lines are profoundly ironic: the innumerable animal images point to a world in which bestiality is always just below the human surface. In Ferdinand's case the surface is broken when he literally becomes a beast – a wolf, transformed by the 'witch-craft' of his own excessive passions which destroy his reason. His words to the Cardinal:

> So, I will only study to seem
> The thing I am not. (II,5,63–4)

confirm the irony: irresistibly Ferdinand changes until the urbane surface is cast off and he becomes what he really 'is' – a beast.

In III,1 Ferdinand's rage is reported by Antonio: evidently he has not succeeded in seeming the thing he is not, for he 'Doth bear himself right dangerously . . .' (III,1,19). To make the point Antonio compares Ferdinand with a dormouse. If the dormouse image suggests, among other things, subtlety, it is not the subtlety of self-knowledge, which is a thing the Duke fatally lacks, until the very last moments of his life. In III,1 he dismisses Bosola's idea that the Duchess may be enchanted, insisting that 'The witchcraft lies in her rank blood . . .' (III,1,78). Once again 'blood' points towards relationship: the excessive passion he finds in the Duchess is what we, the audience, find in him: yet this is the point he cannot see. For Ferdinand, her blood is 'rank' because poisoned and therefore changed from the true stream which flows in his veins. But the imagery of witchcraft recalls the Cardinal's words at II,5,51, confirming the blood relationship: both the Duke and the Duchess are possessed by a kind of witchcraft because both are ruled by their passions. Expressed in terms of the four elements or humours – earth, air, fire and water – they are both fiery. And they are both proud of their passion. Only at the play's end does he acknowledge that: 'Like diamonds we are cut with our own dust' (V,5,73) his last words before death.

The ironies generated by Ferdinand's lack of self-knowledge

are developed in III,2, when he creeps into his sister's room and surprises her. He speaks sententiously of the 'most imperfect light of human reason' (III,2,78) which, presuming he has ever had more than a parody of it himself, he is soon to lose; and bids the Duchess '. . . be past all bounds and sense of shame . . .' (82). If we are not to regard Ferdinand's hypocrisy as merely ludicrous at this stage — who is he to prate of honour? — we need to grasp the multiple moral standards of the time. Not only was there one code of conduct for women and another for men: public and private morality were also distinguished. Great men were allowed a latitude forbidden to others: princes, charged with the responsibility of controlling men, were seen by some to have the right to commit acts such as treachery and murder, forbidden to private citizens, so long as they were in the interests of the state as a whole. Ferdinand holds a perverted form of this doctrine, in which he identifies the interests of the state with his own whims and desires. Thus his homily on Reputation is not *only* hypocrisy — though it is that too — but the exposition of one familiar view i.e. that woman's chastity is a different thing to man's, that she has obligations he does not have, and that her lack of discretion will be disastrous. Ironically he is proved right.

Having apparently decided in this scene not to kill his sister, only to frighten her, the subsequent news that her lover is the base-born Antonio rekindles Ferdinand's passion. Once again we are faced with an unfamiliar moral problem: the absolute ban on marriage between persons of widely differing social rank. And once again we need to note how seriously this was taken at the time if we are to put Ferdinand's behaviour in its proper perspective. This said, his course of action remains indisputably evil. Through the agency of Bosola he embarks on the torture of his sister. The playfulness shown in I,2 is horribly transformed and we now understand the meaning — and the exactness — of Antonio's claim that the Duke has: '. . . a most *perverse* and turbulent nature . . . (I,2,94).

In one sense Ferdinand is merely the instrument of his sister's mortification in the middle of the play. When asked why he tortures her he replies: 'To bring her to despair' (IV,1,115). In the process the depths of his savagery are revealed. He is mad with vanity and rage:

that body of hers,
While that my blood ran pure in't, was more worth
Than that which thou wouldst comfort, called a soul. (IV,1,119–21)

Ferdinand's pride here reaches its peak: not only does he arrogate to himself all the family honour – *my* blood – but he puts it above even the soul in importance. It is appropriate, then, that at his next appearance Ferdinand's sanity finally collapses under the weight of his own pride and the shock of seeing in his sister's corpse the consequences of his actions. Ironically, in castigating Bosola, he anticipates his own fate. When we next see him he is suffering from lycanthropy. Ferdinand is now frightened by his own shadow – an ironic comment on his relationships with his sister and with Bosola, both of whom he has treated as mere extensions of himself. His one remaining function in the play is to complete the ironical symmetries in the final scene, when he and Bosola kill one another.

The Cardinal

He is a melancholy churchman.

The Cardinal's character remains undeveloped when compared with Ferdinand's, but his role is of crucial importance in the play. He is a man of fewer but more effective words than the Duke, and clearly the controlling spirit. If Ferdinand directs Bosola, so the Cardinal directs Ferdinand. This is hinted in his very first appearance in I,1, when his previous association with Bosola is established; and Delio, speaking of an earlier murder, opines that:

. . . 'twas thought
The Cardinal suborn'd it . . . (I,1,70–71)

confirming Bosola's claim that he has suffered in the prelate's service – and also confirming – '*twas thought*' – the Cardinal's skill in avoiding direct responsibility.

The elaborate character sketches in I,2 show the points at which the brothers compare. They are both described in terms of misleading appearance and true reality; both are devious, ruthless, amoral; both use spies and informers to achieve their ends; both are brilliant and treacherous. As Delio points out, despite his priestly robes, the Cardinal is every inch a courtier (I,2,76–9). Later in the play he finds the transition from Cardinal to General easy. Even for an age which relaxed the distinctions between temporal and spiritual power, he can be seen as a thoroughly worldly man. Only once (V,5,1–6) does he show any sign of his holy orders – and then of the most perfunctory sort. But as Antonio tells his friend, even the Cardinal's worldly brilliance is a show: 'Some such flashes superficially hang on him ... ' (I,2,80). Underneath this display lies 'a melancholy churchman'. At first this phrase appears to be contradicting the image of the showy courtier with the notion that the Cardinal is fundamentally serious. Antonio's next words soon dispel this impression: by 'melancholy' he means bad or poor. But there is a further sense to 'melancholy' which complicates the meaning here. Antonio refers to:

... the spring in his face (which is) nothing
but the engend'ring of toads ... (82–3)

Toads were symbolic of the dark, heavy, lugubrious and poisonous qualities associated with the notion of melancholy as it is used about Bosola (see I,1,75). Thus beneath his superficial liveliness the Cardinal conceals a character which is the exact opposite of Ferdinand's fiery passion: his evil issues not from mania but from a completely cold nature.

This contrast of humours shows up in exchanges between the two brothers. In I,2 the Cardinal shows his decisive superiority to his brother in a few curt words about Antonio: 'You are deceiv'd in him ...' (153) and when his brother rants in luxurious imagery at their sister, the Cardinal speaks plainly. Even at life's end his words have a simplicity which becomes almost touching for a moment:

    ... let me
Be laid by, and never thought of. (V,5,89–90)

This is in marked contrast with Ferdinand's self-consciously tragic formula (V,5,73). It is clear the Cardinal would never try Ferdinand's melodramatic tricks – the dead hand, the madmen. Only at the beginning of the play's last scene does his business-like manner briefly desert him.

Yet the Cardinal is not presented without human weakness, as his relations with Julia show. We first see them exchanging banter in II,4. Here the Cardinal's cold dominance is made plain. Julia is his creature – a hawk or a tame elephant – a woman to whom he gives the sexual fulfilment her husband cannot provide. He is openly cynical about the nature of women. His wooing, as Julia tells him, has been purely conventional: 'You told me of a piteous wound i'th'heart . . .' (37). This is the language of courtly love, reflecting the Cardinal's worldly side. In this spirit, his mistress is easily won, and just as easily disposed of when she becomes a nuisance. The contrast with Ferdinand's frantic sexual obsession and the Duchess's warm passion could not be clearer. The Cardinal's real weakness in this respect is not his desire for Julia but his entire lack of warmth. His passions are stirred only when he is angry – as when he responds to Bosola in a brief moment of panic with: 'I'll have thee hew'd in pieces' (V,2,289). Here the spirit of Ferdinand shows through his brother's habitual calm. The Cardinal at once regains his self-possession, refusing to respond even to Bosola's blunt speaking (V,2,294–8). But the murder of Julia marks the turning-point in his fortunes, forcing him into a fatal involvement with Bosola.

It is fitting that a man famous for employing spies and intrigue should be undone by them. The Cardinal's plan to get Julia's body out of the house turns against him and he dies of wounds at the hands of Bosola and Ferdinand. In this final incident the play's irony is compounded. Calling for help from Ferdinand the Cardinal pleads: 'Help me, I am your brother' (V,5,51) and Ferdinand, wandering in his wits and confused further by the darkness, replies: 'The devil?' thus confirming the identification established by Bosola at the play's outset. And this is rendered even more ironic by opening the play's final scene with the Cardinal's perplexity about the nature of hell:

I am puzzl'd in a question about hell:
He says, in hell there's one material fire,
And yet it shall not burn all men alike. (V,5,1–3)

This reference to the notion of different degrees of punishment for different degrees of sin is aptly voiced by the Cardinal; for he, his brother and Bosola all participate in the guilt for his sister's murder, but while Bosola, who did the deed, is the least guilty, as a mere instrument, the Cardinal must bear the heaviest responsibility for instigating the crime which now haunts him. These reflections, which open up a new perspective on the Cardinal, are cut short by Bosola's entrance with the body of Antonio.

Bosola

This foul melancholy will poison all his goodness.

Bosola's power and presence are evident from the way he dominates the play's first scene: Antonio, Delio and the Cardinal form a background to his bitter reflections. As Bosola enters he is immediately characterized for us by Antonio as 'The only court-gall . . .' (I,1,23) a phrase which unites the notions of bitterness, soreness and courtliness. Antonio, who has just compared the virtuous court of France with – implicitly – the corrupt courts of Ferdinand and the Cardinal, explaining that virtue or corruption issue from the head downwards, sees Bosola as both a product and a source of the court's vicious atmosphere, perverted by his masters, but disposed to be so. The 'railing' Antonio refers to is a common feature in the period's dramatic literature: a kind of sour, indiscriminate condemnation of things, issuing from a deformed or poisoned nature. This can be mild and comic – as we find it in Shakespeare's fools – or savage, as it is in Bosola, who suffers from the general disease of his milieu: an indifference to moral standards and a belief in the primacy of self-interest. Where there is no justice from above, every man must look to himself. Bosola has decided to devote his great energies to doing just this, and it has twisted his whole view of life. As a result he reverses all the higher moral virtues. Taxing the Cardinal with neglect, he berates the

Miserable age, where only the reward of doing
well, is the doing of it! (I,1,32–3)

thus overturning the idea that virtue is its own reward. It is indeed reward which Bosola pursues throughout the play until he is ironically gripped by the opposite passion, determined to see that bloody justice is done on the Cardinal, whatever the cost to himself – though even then he has no certainty of any worth in his actions, driven, as he is, not by the rational self-interest he claims to cultivate at the play's beginning, but by obscure and incalculable emotions.

But even at the beginning Bosola is confused. On the one hand he asserts that:

Could I be one of their flattering panders,
I would hang on their ears like a horse-leech ... (I,1,52–3)

but on the other he dismisses all such hopes: 'Who would rely upon these miserable dependences ...' (I,1,25). His bitterness about lack of rewards for service is combined with contempt for the potential rewarders – a contempt which grows throughout the play. It stems in part from experience and in part from his natural melancholy i.e. his disposition to see everything in dark colours. Antonio describes this condition with some care (I,1,75–81). The 'goodness' Antonio speaks of is not so much moral virtue as excellence, and he makes the point that when great gifts go neglected or unused, they turn against themselves. Energy and talent need an outlet: without one they become destructive. It is Bosola's talents, not his vices, which make him dangerous. This doctrine fits well with the 17th century notion of hierarchies and order: that everything has a proper place, suitable to its qualities. Disturbance of this order inevitably results in trouble. Bosola's neglect represents such a disturbance: both he and Antonio are aware that he has not been given his proper reward or place.

But there is another important aspect of melancholy we must take into account when thinking about Bosola – namely that it entails a temperamental disposition to inwardness and reflection. Bosola is essentially a man of action, like the characteristic renaissance hero. But he is also a man of sensibility and intelligence – fully displayed in the brilliant and subtle imagery Webster gives him. These are unstable qualities, for they prevent the resignation to circumstance which might

make frustration bearable. Thus it is that even when he *is*
commissioned to act by Ferdinand, with promise of reward,
this murderer is unable to refrain from reflecting on his deeds:
his relatively conventional outbursts of spleen concerning
women and the world's mutability are transmuted into a
specific horror at his part in the Duchess's murder. These
aspects of Bosola's character are by no means unusual in 17th-
century drama. Perhaps the most famous parallel is Hamlet,
another gifted man disappointed of his true place – as King of
Denmark – and compelled to a melancholy and inaction
which bring him to the brink of self-destruction and madness.
Bosola lacks Hamlet's powers of self-examination: he is not,
like Hamlet, a playwright manqué, nor does he achieve a
degree of enlightenment at the play's end. Nevertheless, the
essential formula is the same in both characters: the gifted
man of action, frustrated and turned in on himself, forced to
examine the morality of his predicament.

In one respect Bosola is a more puzzling character than
Shakespeare's, for while Hamlet is self-evidently the hero of
his play, Bosola's dramatic status is constantly in doubt.
Though he is not nominally the central figure, he dominates
the drama from beginning to end as the most developed
character and the one with – in the end – the most power.
One can hardly fail to notice that he kills all his main fellow-
characters. On the other hand, we might view him as being
somewhat apart from the play's main action, in that he is only
an agent of it. The plot would seem to be concerned with the
Aragonian family: the Duchess, her husband and brothers. In
this sense, Bosola merely supplies the connections between
them, acting as a puppet for the brothers, and embodying
doom for Antonio and his wife. Yet we do not need to learn
from a study of the sources that Bosola was Webster's main
invention and addition to the play to realize quickly how vital
he is to it.

This combination of apartness and centrality marks Bosola
out from the start. In the very first scene Webster uses his
favourite framing device to show Bosola in conversation
with the Cardinal, observed by Antonio and Delio. Bosola's
immediate repudiation of the Cardinal after his exit and
Antonio's lines closing the scene contribute to our sense of

Bosola's importance and isolation. In Scene 2 he does not so much converse with Ferdinand as engage in a parallel soliloquy with him. While it is Bosola's role to serve the Duke, he shows no sign of subservience, but speaks bluntly, in a way which Ferdinand relishes. Indeed he speaks as cynically as the Duke himself (I,2,197–201). He deceives himself into thinking he *must* oblige Ferdinand, while showing his self-contempt. The idea that evil turns even good things into bad ones suggests Bosola's wilful passiveness: only after the Duchess's murder does he discover his own will to good – and even then it is embodied in revenge, not in mercy. Most important of all, his words show very clearly what a product of his environment he is, so imbued with the need for 'advancement' that he takes it on any terms. Antonio's very first speech in the play states the familiar doctrine that the vice or virtue of the ruler determines the condition of his state: Bosola, for all his strength, is the walking proof of that doctrine. In this sense we can interpret his apartness as spiritual alienation and his centrality as moral complicity. The play shows that Bosola is too deeply corrupted to be saved, but sufficiently virtuous to be an instrument of salvation.

Both the corruption and the virtue are evident in the two episodes of Act II which show Bosola enacting his role of the melancholy railer at life i.e. II,1,1–66 and II,2,1–27. In both women are the main target of attack. We can guess from Julia's sudden infatuation that Bosola is attractive to women (V,2,121), but he takes the role of their tormentor – in the persons of the Duchess, Cariola, and the Old Lady. His satire on female artifice and lechery is conventional, if perhaps more brilliant and disgusting than usual – and is only saved from redundance by its reinforcement of a central theme: the sexuality of women. In the context of the whole play, however, this increases Bosola's prominence and exhibits him in a dominant role. His savage wit easily exceeds Ferdinand's in power, and this makes him a suitable match for the Duchess: the torturer and his victim are well balanced. These 'virtuoso' passages are the equivalent of the Duchess's long speech at III,5,122 –not opportunities for developing character traits so much as dramatic set pieces in which the audience's attention is concentrated on the role. Bosola's fantastic imagery and his bullying manner show him well aware of human weakness but only capable of a vicious pleasure in it. The violence of his language is an index of his frustration.

Bosola's dominance in the play – and the manner of it – raise another question, about whether he is not the hero but the villain of the piece. There are many moments when he behaves like the rogue of melodrama. He seems to revel in appearing before the Duchess in disguise, overhears the Cardinal plotting his death, and self-consciously proclaims both his crimes and his penitence in ways familiar from the lurid sensational drama of any age. Webster uses the full battery of theatrical devices in the play to heighten the tension, many of them associated with Bosola – who does not have Ferdinand's excuse of madness for his excesses. He thus appears as both hero and villain, changing from evil to good during the course of the play. Alternatively, we might say that he is neither hero nor villain – and it is just here that the 'apartness' commented on earlier becomes important, for the character's presentation derives its peculiar strength from refusing to fall clearly into one category or another. Just as Webster uses changing perspectives to make us think more deeply about the Duchess and Ferdinand, so he refuses to allow us to come too easily to a conclusion about Bosola. It is this which saves the play from being a mere morality or sensational blood-and-thunder drama. The character of Bosola is therefore essential to the moral range and subtlety of the play.

We can see this most clearly in his changing responses to the Duchess. At first she is merely part of his task – a challenge to which he must respond to get advancement. He is aggressive and reckless. His distaste for the approach Ferdinand enforces is impersonal. He is contemptuous of Antonio but begins to be susceptible to the Duchess, describing her to Ferdinand in terms not dissimilar to Antonio's own in I,2:

You may discern the shape of loveliness
More perfect in her tears, than in her smiles ... (IV,1,7–8)

Yet he is still ready to follow the Duke's order and torture her, revealing more and more clearly his pathological condition. For Bosola is attempting to accommodate opposite demands:

personal ambition and pity, justice and advancement, obedience and self-knowledge. In consequence the intensification of the Duchess's torments results not in her breakdown but in the collapse of Ferdinand and Bosola's resolution, under intolerable strain, that he will go no further. Yet this is only awakened when the Duke tries to push the blame for his sister's death entirely onto Bosola. Up to that moment the killer expects his reward – even though he, like his master, has refrained from doing the actual deed. Only then does he conclude that:

What would I do, were this to do again?
I would not change my peace of conscience
For all the wealth of Europe. (IV,2,337–8)

Once again it is *ingratitude* which stirs Bosola's deepest feelings and awakens them to the enormity of his crimes. Psychologically this is right: he has been so preoccupied with himself that only a deep wound to that self can arouse him. For though Bosola has a strong sense of evil and fine phrases to describe it, he can only respond to good when he sees it. He is insensitive to the notion of a moral order. At the end of the play he makes this explicit.

O this gloomy world,
In what a shadow or deep pit of darkness
Doth, womanish and fearful, mankind live? (V,5,100–102)

The world is merely a deep pit of darkness in which a few lights fitfully shine. Our sense of his complexity is deepened by the fact that he knows about this lack: 'My estate is sunk/ Below the degree of fear ...' (IV,2,361–2) he says, weeping over the Duchess's body. Yet even now he only responds personally: he is moved by feeling, not by moral consciousness: 'somewhat I will speedily enact/Worth my dejection' (IV,2,372–3) is a conclusion which shows he has only moved a small way along the road. Lack of feeling has been replaced by feeling: this is at least the beginning of justice.

In the last Act Bosola is the agent of this justice – as ferocious as ever, though now in a different cause. He pretends that he wishes to serve the Cardinal, thus becoming an actor in a play filled with theatrical metaphors. But this is only the latest in a series of roles. In I,2 Ferdinand bids him 'Be yourself' in order to deceive others; and in Acts III and IV he self-consciously takes on a series of roles in his pursuit of the Duchess: policeman, gaoler, gravedigger, bellman, executioner. At a more fundamental level, Bosola can be said to be acting a part throughout the play: his cynicism leads him to the conclusion that advantage in life is only to be gained from acting: '*And men that paint weeds, to the life, are prais'd*' (III,2,329).

His very last speech takes up the theme, when describing Antonio's death:

In a mist: I know not how;
Such a mistake as I have often seen
In a play. (V,5,94–6)

The ironic force of 'mistake' here gains from the play's obsession with acting and the necessary confusions which ensue. Bosola pretends to be the Cardinal's servant, Julia's lover and Antonio's opponent in this last act: as a result he brings to light the truth and a kind of justice is done. Yet even in his last words he continues to oscillate violently between good and bad, faith and despair. On the one hand he says that:

We are only like dead walls, or vaulted graves
That, ruin'd, yields no echo. (97–8)

On the other hand he insists that:

... worthy minds ne'er stagger in distrust
To suffer death or shame for what is just ... (103–4)

With his dying breath Bosola juxtaposes the two deepest themes of the play – themes which seem irreconcilable: that life has no meaning, and that the fight for goodness and justice is essential. The implication is that men must act for the best in spite of the discovery that, as Bosola says:

We are merely the stars' tennis-balls, struck and banded
Which way please them ... (V,4,53–4)

Bosola has attempted to combine two mutually exclusive roles: the good man and the good servant. He has done this by pretending that they are separable, that duty to Ferdinand comes before honesty with himself, because Ferdinand represents the duly constituted authority which – as Antonio explains at the beginning – is essential to the right ordering of society. But when the ruler is corrupt he must be resisted. If his will does not reflect a higher will to good, it must be set aside, and the individual must abide by his own lights. 'I'll be my own example' as Bosola himself puts it (V,4,81) when he vows to take revenge on the Cardinal. Thus, at the play's end, Bosola still stands outside the social order, apart from the main action, yet at the very cause and heart of it, as he has throughout.

Julia

We that are great women of pleasure . . .

Like Bosola, the character is Webster's invention. And like Antonio and the Cardinal, her importance depends not on detail of character development but on the roles she plays in the action. We first hear of her in I,2 as Castruchio's witty and saucy wife. She then appears with the Duchess, but says nothing. In II,4 her role is suddenly developed. She is presented both as a 'typical' court lady – pleasure-loving, treacherous – and as the object of the Cardinal's cold superiority. He has:

. . . taken you off your melancholy perch,
Bore you upon my fist, and show'd you game . . . (II,4,28–9)

There is an implicit contrast with the Duchess in two respects: that Julia is loose where the Duchess is chaste, and that Julia is subordinate where the Duchess is dominant. The scene divides into two parts: after the Cardinal's exit, Delio enters, and there is an almost comic exchange between Delio and Julia about whether she will become his mistress – showing that Antonio's trusted friend has much the same attitude to women as the Cardinal. Julia's response to his offer: 'Sir, I'll go ask my husband if I shall' (II,4,75) shows that her reputation for bold wit is not unfounded. She is a strong-minded woman, like the Duchess – but she lacks her superior's inner strength. Her energy is based on desire.

Clear evidence that Julia was an expedient creation is given by her disappearance from the play until V.2 when she reappears in order to forward the plot. Attracted by Bosola, she approaches him in a parody of the Duchess's approach to Antonio, brandishing a pistol. But the domestic happiness of the Duchess's marriage is contrasted with Julia's quest for sexual pleasure. As she tells Bosola:

> . . . had you been i'th'street,
> Under my chamber window, even there
> I should have courted you. (V,2,193–5)

Julia is what Ferdinand believes his sister to be. She says it herself: 'We that are great women of pleasure' (V,2,190) need immediate satisfaction of desire. When Bosola offers her this, Julia pays the price with her life; yet at the end she demonstrates that she has the virtues of her vices. She is stoical, uncomplaining and quite prepared to take the responsibility for her actions. And her last words anticipate the last words of the Cardinal, Bosola and Ferdinand in their uncertainty: 'I go,/I know not whither' (V,2,285–6).

Structure and style

Setting

The setting recreates the claustrophobic atmosphere of 16th-century Italian courts, famous throughout Europe for intrigue and violence. Italy was divided into dozens of small states, most of them ruled by autocrats like Ferdinand. While Rome's importance was recognized as the centre of religious authority, each city or duchy was a little political world in itself – a point Antonio makes in his first speech. Webster does not distinguish the court of Malfi especially, and he is vague about why Ferdinand and the Cardinal – who presumably have estates of their own – should be there. Instead he concentrates on the representative quality: Malfi is any small court filled with plots and gossip. In the same way, Ancona has no significance except as a place from which the Duchess and her husband are exiled. While Italy was an exotic, exciting and frightening place for 17th-century English audiences, the aristocrats among them were no doubt able to make easy comparisons with less sensational events at their own court.

Themes

Webster calls *The Duchess of Malfi* a tragedy on his title page, and like all tragedies the play is concerned with the conflict between circumstances – or 'fate' – and human desires. At the centre of this conflict is the Duchess herself: her love for Antonio is in conflict with what her brothers see as her duty to the family honour. This basic discord generates others. Ferdinand is caught between his desire for revenge and his sense of wrong-doing. The Cardinal wants dominance, but finds himself outwitted by his own agent, Bosola. Antonio's love for the Duchess betrays him. Bosola himself is destroyed by his awakening conscience, which prompts him to exact vengeance. This last example is characteristic of the play in that the conflict is not only external but internal. Bosola, like the Duke, is at odds with himself, torn between incompatible demands for advancement and for justice. The Duchess is determined to have her way and marry Antonio; but once things start to go wrong she acknowledges that it is not only her brothers who are opposed to the match. One cannot fight destiny. Ferdinand makes the point in his dying words: 'Like diamonds we are cut with our own dust' (V,5,73). The Duke is actually referring to his sister as the cause of his downfall, but the words are applicable at a deeper level than he knows: it is Ferdinand's own passions which have brought him low.

The theme of fate is explored from different aspects. In one sense it is embodied in the inexorable march of circumstance beyond the control of any individual. All the main characters in the play – and several minor ones – are killed, almost by the way, as though, once the chain of events had been set in motion, there was no escaping it. The terrible commitment of actions is demonstrated: once married, the Duchess cannot change her mind; once promised, Bosola cannot withdraw from his work for Ferdinand. Accidents – such as overhearing secret words, meeting the wrong person in the dark, mistaking one meaning for another – play a large part in emphasizing the triviality of human will. Desires seem to have little to do with character or moral disposition. Individuals are surprised by passions and driven by them. Death finally makes a mockery of all their ambitions. In all these ways the powerlessness of human beings is made clear. In another sense fate signified the logical working out of a situation, once it is brought into being. Though the Duchess cannot see it, her venture is doomed to failure from the start. If Ferdinand only knew what the consequences of his action were to be, he might never embark on it. Bosola does not calculate that he will be turned from a savage, cynical automaton into a feeling man. Yet Webster presents the action in a tight casual chain, issuing inevitably from the natures and situations of the characters. God is hardly ever mentioned, though the Devil's name figures frequently; but both are only invoked as comparisons for the human protagonists, making the point that Hell is here on earth, that there is no external malign fate, but simply the consequences of human action.

And this leads us to another theme – the theme of knowledge. Each of the main characters begins in ignorance and, by experiencing the working of fate, comes to some kind of knowledge which – in each case – is summed up in their final words. Ferdinand's conclusion has already been quoted. The others all reach a comparable point, with one exception. Where Antonio, the Cardinal and Bosola all conclude that this life is without meaning, the Duchess dies content to go to another world. Yet doubt hangs about them all – doubt caused by uncertainty about the meaning of what is happening to them. Things occur, as Bosola puts it, 'In a mist' (V,5,94). That disaster descends alike on the innocent and the guilty – the Cardinal and the Duchess's children – suggest that there are no innocents or that whatever providence there may be is inscrutable.

Given that there is no providence, in the sense of an evident divine hand managing affairs; that the inscrutability refers not only to events but to persons; that the lack of knowledge pertains not only to a generalized fate but to the self; the insight the characters reach is thus a kind of self-knowledge, in each case different and in each case brought to a head by the imminence of death. Only extinction seems to relieve the pressure of immediate circumstance for a moment and clear the air so that the truth can be briefly perceived. And what is this knowledge of self to which the protagonists finally gain some limited access? In the first place it is an understanding of their limitation – in the starkest terms their limitation by circumstances and by death. Added to human frailty, disaster brings them acquaintance with the deepest theme of tragedy: mutability. All human fortunes change: the pride generated by prosperity will always be brought low. Once again this theme is most clearly represented in the Duchess's downfall, and it is a truth she and Antonio come to accept early on. As the Duchess herself puts it:

> For all our wit
> And reading brings us to a truer sense
> Of sorrow. (III,5,66–8)

In the earlier part of the play Antonio is constantly warned against 'ambition' which, in this sense, means not only the desire for advancement but the aspiring to a good fortune beyond our proper deserts.

The second kind of self-knowledge explored in the play is knowledge of identity – and this is developed through the many allusions to, and variations on, the idea of acting. The text is filled with theatrical metaphors, and all the central characters take on 'roles' in the sense that they pretend to be what they are not. Spies and intelligencers are frequently mentioned, deception is a subordinate theme, and everyone tells lies and plays tricks. Only when the end approaches are they forced to throw off their disguises and discover their 'true' selves – though as Bosola's last speech hints, the nature of such selves is by no means clear. Webster pursues the theme of identity through a number of spectacular dramatic devices. Bosola's various roles in his torment of the Duchess, Ferdinand's madness and his obsession with secrecy, the Cardinal's sinister refusal ever to acknowledge his part in events unless he is forced, Julia's horrific death while playing a role of her own, the Cardinal's dumb-show change of persona from cleric to general – they all contribute to the theme, which is also enriched in the linguistic patterning. Like Webster's other great tragedy, *The White Devil*, this play is seething with animals: wolves, dogs, tigers, mice and all kinds of vermin. The human beings are repeatedly compared to and even identified with these creatures. In one spectacular case – lycanthropy – Ferdinand 'becomes' the animal he resembles. The humanity of the Aragonian brothers is constantly brought into question, their identity challenged at the deepest level. As he is wounded the Cardinal cries out 'Shall I die like a leveret . . .' (V,5,45) and Ferdinand, just before his death, says

Give me some wet hay, I am broken-winded.
I do account this world but a dog-kennel . . . (V,5,66–7).

Paradoxically, to be human is to acknowledge that we are also animals – but that we are animals with reason which can conceive of abstract qualities such as goodness and justice. It is these qualities which even the Duchess forgets, for she herself is driven by her passions and animal desires, though it so happens that these lead her to gentleness, not cruelty. But Ferdinand is right, in the play's last scene, when he blames the catastrophe on his sister – though in another sense this is an example of him trying to shift the blame: it is her desire for Antonio which has set in train the events of the drama, as she herself acknowledges when she says to Cariola:

> ... nothing but noise, and folly
> Can keep me in my right wits, whereas reason
> And silence make me stark mad. (IV,2,5–7)

In the same scene she declares that 'Necessity makes me suffer constantly' – an admission that there is a kind of justice in her pain. Indeed, it is part of her moral grandeur that she is able to convert patent injustice into the acceptance of Necessity, for she has made the painful discovery that the expression of our deepest desires and the consequences they produce are parts of that very Necessity we must then endure. Like Ferdinand she is enunciating the doctrine that we are 'cut with our own dust'. Our knowledge of identity is sharpest at the very moment when it is self-destructing – the moment before death when we are faced with the pattern of our lives – or the lack of it.

Against the darkness of this view we can identify a third aspect of the self-knowledge theme. In IV,2 the Duchess's execution is preceded by a conversation between Bosola and his victim in which she first asks 'Who am I?' (123) and then affirms:

I am Duchess of Malfi still. (141)

This proclamation, which goes against all the obvious evidence that she is imprisoned and humiliated, rings out against Bosola's baroque elaboration of the theme that all flesh is grass. It is therefore both pathetic and magnificent, an affirmation in the face of imminent death. Not an affirmation of aristocratic pride, but an insistence that not until the actual bodily dissolution of death do we cease to be what we are – in sharp contrast to Ferdinand's collapse, which offers another kind of affirmation that Ferdinand remains what he has always been i.e. a wolf. Thus it is that Bosola can say – before *his* death – that he:

... was an actor in the main of all,
Much 'gainst my own good nature, yet i'th'end
Neglected. (V,5,85–7)

Here the themes of acting and knowledge are brought
together, as Bosola admits to his inner conflict, and the theme
of self-knowledge points to the notion of enduring identity
which is one secure thing to hold onto in an uncertain world –
if it can be located. The problem is to know it for what it is,
and Webster shows this happening, in each case, too late.
Only the 'base' Antonio suspects from the beginning that he is
not fitted for this savage aristocratic world, but the compara-
tively minor nature of his role may cause us to disregard this
insight until late in the play. Ironically, had the nervous
Antonio been true to his self, the drama would not occur –
and he points this out himself:

A most wretched thing
That only have thy benefit in death,
To appear myself. (V,4,47–9)

he says to Bosola's enquiry 'What are thou?'

Connected with the themes of fate, identity and knowledge
is the question of woman's sexuality, for it is by dramatizing
this that Webster presents these themes. *The Duchess of Malfi*
resembles other early 17th-century plays in its preoccupation
with this theme – which is, of course, as old as 'literature'
itself. The very first human drama of the Old Testament links
the desire for knowledge with the temptation of woman. Biblical authority for this link naturally made it a popular subject
in a Christian culture.

The Duchess wishes to marry: she can see no reason against
it. She loves Antonio and cares nothing for the opposition of
her brothers. At no point in the play is it implied that she is
wrong to marry again. Webster shows no sign of sharing the
brothers' obsession with honour – which is anyway a cloak for
darker motives in Ferdinand's case. Yet her marriage leads to
disaster because it involves her in subterfuge and in flouting
the will of her brothers. Her sexuality is thus problematic not
in itself but because, in the circumstances, it leads to conflict.

We are implicitly invited to compare her sensuous simplicity with Julia's forwardness; and we are told – though by the prejudiced Antonio – that no hint of vulgar lust mars her life. Though she takes the lead in courtship, this is necessary because of her social position in relation to her husband's. Once again, it is not her sexuality itself which causes trouble, but the rigid social distinctions of 16th-century Italian courts.

Yet having said all that, there is no doubt that female sexuality is a major motivating force in precipitating the tragedy. How can this be? The answer is that it obsesses not the woman, but two of the men – Bosola and Ferdinand; and entraps a third – Antonio. Perhaps 'obsession' is too strong a word for Bosola: in his castigation of the Old Lady he repeats the usual charges against women, and he is coldly prepared to use Julia's infatuation with him. He shows no signs of weakness, and is converted to Antonio's view of the Duchess when he sees her suffer. But Ferdinand is obsessed throughout: his imagery is often intensely, even horrifyingly, erotic, and he admits that he cannot get his sister's copulation out of his mind (II,5,39). Antonio's case is the saddest: out of true love and in response to the Duchess's desire, he marries her and pays the price. Nothing could make it clearer than this marriage does, that lust is not the direct cause of the catastrophe. The Duchess's passion is transmuted into domestic affection and loyalty – a point expressed most vividly through her devotion to the children. One of her last requests is that Cariola should:

> giv'st my little boy
> Some syrup for his cold, and let the girl
> Say her prayers ere she sleep. (IV,2,203–4)

At the play's heart is a struggle between what a woman wishes to be and what men expect of her. One might well then say that the theme is as much about power as sexuality. Ferdinand wishes to dominate his sister just as his brother, the Cardinal, claims to dominate Julia in II,4. In discussing the pleasure he gives her, the Cardinal arrogantly demands that Julia shall thank him for it. In his view, all women are instruments, not principals; beholden to men for their happiness and even their lives. The Cardinal's cold nature and Ferdinand's passionate one produce the same result: women must obey. The Duchess's marriage is, among other things, a show of independence, unacceptable to her brothers.

Finally, it may be remarked that 'independence' is itself a preoccupation of Webster's, both here and in *The White Devil*. Characters struggle to assert themselves and are defeated, not only by time and death, but more immediately by the enormous power of social constraints and by the competing desires of others. Again and again Webster shows the characters as each other's fate, inescapably reacting and interacting, while desiring a kind of freedom they cannot achieve – whether it is the freedom of love, prosperity, or power. This is a major source of the claustrophobic atmosphere generated in his plays. The animal imagery appropriately suggests creatures in a cage: it is only a matter of time before they tear one another to pieces.

Structure

The complications of the play's structure are connected with its curious proportions and hybrid nature. We expect from the title to spend most of our time with the Duchess. Certainly, her betrayal, torture and death constitute the play's core – but this core is finished two-thirds of the way through. When we consider that she makes only two extended appearances in the first two acts (I,2,137–420 and II,1,112–63) it becomes clear that the dramatic interest concentrates directly on the Duchess only in the middle of the play. I say 'directly' because, of course, the beginning and end of the play lead up to and away from this core and are deeply affected by it. Nevertheless Webster rations his heroine's appearances, and extracts the maximum effect from them. One example will demonstrate this. The Duchess first appears on stage at I,2,68, but it is almost seventy lines before she speaks. In the interval we have time to study her and listen to Antonio's encomium. The characters are exhibited and commented on as though in a tableau. When the Duchess does speak, her words are inconsequential – 'To me, sir?' It is up to the actress to make maximum effect with those few sounds.

This rationing means that the Duchess's appearances are, as it were, framed by the rest of the play. Framing, and the perspective it allows, were techniques which fascinated Webster: they are used throughout the play both incidentally and as structural devices. One of his tricks is the revelation of the stage within the stage: midway through a scene curtains are drawn showing a figure or figures within. Thus Antonio is introduced into the Duchess's presence at I,2,283; the Duchess is discovered by Bosola at IV,1,17; and the waxworks at IV,1,55. These are typical *coups de théâtre*. Ferdinand's unobserved entrance to the Duchess's bedroom at III,2,62 is another sudden change of perspective, as are Bosola's various disguises in Act IV and the different views we get of Ferdinand in Act I. In each case the audience experiences sudden changes of level, abrupt intensifications of the drama. This technique is put most thoroughly into practice during the Duchess's 'mortification' and death as we progress through a series of increasingly macabre scenes to the sudden calm of her death scene, which is itself framed by poor Cariola's hysterical struggles, sharpening our sense of the Duchess's dignified resignation.

In broad terms, then, the structure can be divided into three parts: the preparation (Acts I and II, plus Act III, Scenes 1–4); the Duchess's 'Passion' (Act III, Scene 5, and Act IV); and the conclusion (Act V). However, such a division only holds if we regard the Duchess as sole centre of attention in the play, and this is unconvincing. While she may be the *major* focus of attention, she by no means engrosses it: both Bosola and Ferdinand also have major roles which develop in different ways through the play – Bosola towards a degree of enlightenment, Ferdinand towards madness. They can be seen as parallel to the Duchess and also in contrast with her. If we think of the play as a tragedy, Ferdinand has many of the characteristics of a hero, Bosola of a villain. Yet neither fits these roles. Like everything else in this play, they refuse to accept the strait-jacket of conventional tragic form.

Instead, we can think of the play's structure in terms of two conventions common in the period: Progress and Revenge. The notion of the Progress is commonly found in medieval allegory, both literary and visual. It depends upon identifying a series of moments or typical stages in the rise or fall of a character. Thus, the soul might be pictured journeying to redemption through a series of trials and temptations. Biblical parallels were popular in the period, and the story of Job would serve as a good basis for this Progress. The most significant example of the genre was Christ's journey to Calvary, which medieval art breaks up into a series of scenes or "Stations". Christ's suffering and death was seen to have analogies with the idea of tragedy in which a protagonist undergoes and finally accepts suffering at the hands of an inescapable fate. Even when not specifically Christian, early 17th-century tragedies are full of Biblical allusions, and *The Duchess of Malfi* is no exception. The Duchess's tragedy can be seen in terms of Christ's Passion. Bosola's speeches over her body make this clear. She is not just, like the tragic hero, a figure who stirs pity and fear in the spectators. He begs her soul to lead his out of hell; he describes her as the innocent who brings him to a recognition of his guilty conscience, and thus of the pains of hell; she is characterized as a redeemer, whose briefly opening eyes open the gates of heaven. She acquires significance as the emblem of heavenly virtue in a dark world where the very existence of heaven is in doubt.

It is in the context of this doubt that we must consider the other convention on which the play depends. Revenge tragedy is common in the period: perhaps the most famous example is *Hamlet*. The form is based on the notion that revenge constitutes a kind of justice outside the ordinary laws of men. In an uncertain world the theme of justice is naturally a vital one, and revenge is often seen as the expression of the divine will. The other side of this coin, to which Webster's work inclines, is that revenge is a *substitute* for divine providence. Bosola, having been the instrument of injustice, becomes both judge and executioner in the cases of the Cardinal and his brother. This forms the substance of the last act. The play's many references to heaven and hell point to the heaven and hell of this world. As Bosola says in another context:

Their minds were wholly bent upon the world. (IV,2,160)

Thus the play's structure depends upon one crucial factor: Bosola's change of heart after the Duchess's death. We can therefore understand it better if we think of it not as the story of one person – the Duchess – but as the story of several – in particular the Duchess and Bosola. The two are complementary and parallel. Both pursue their desires without calculating the consequences; both experience the central drama of murder, as victim and executioner; both undergo a process of self-recognition. Most important of all, they determine each other's fate: Bosola presides over the Duchess's death, but the Duchess guides him to revenge.

Style

In general Webster's style is characterized by the extreme richness of the imagery and the careful patterning of the language. His range of reference is narrower than Shakespeare's but more luxuriant; yet he rarely suffers from the obscurity Shakespeare's fondness for complicated syntax leads to, and he is more self-consciously dramatic. Comparison of the two dramatists suggests that Webster always had his eye fixed on the stage: he thinks in terms of theatrical effectiveness, sometimes at the expense of subtlety. Shakespeare prefers to round off his arguments, to create well-finished speeches. Webster is a master of the conversational exchange and the finely placed image. He lacks Shakespeare's intellectual comprehensiveness and breadth of sympathy, but he sometimes cuts deeper and more intensely. Shakespeare illuminates a whole world, Webster throws the most searching light on a single continent.

T. S. Eliot took the view that there were passages in both Webster and Tourneur which exceeded in vividness anything to be found in Shakespeare. In *The Duchess of Malfi* Bosola has many lines which might make us agree with that view. The very first scene is brimming with them. He describes his own fate:

I fell into the galleys in your service, where,
for two years together, I wore two towels instead
of a shirt, with a knot on the shoulder, after the
fashion of a Roman mantle. Slighted thus? I will
thrive some way: blackbirds fatten best in hard
weather ... (I,1,35–9)

The passage is characteristic of Webster at his best: the forceful, witty style and tone appropriate to the speaker, and the two images of the mantle and the blackbird trenchantly making their point. The language is at once racy and poetic, the dry, angry irony exactly caught in the question – 'Slighted thus?' – which undercuts the speaker's wordly comedy. A few lines later the same speaker describes the Aragonian brothers:

He and his brother are like plum trees, that grow
crooked over standing pools, they are rich, and
o'erladen with fruit, but none but crows, pies and
caterpillars feed on them. (49–52)

The image is startling and resonant: the cumulative notions of 'crooked', 'standing', 'rich' and 'o'erladen' build up an oppressive sense of over-ripeness and corruption, in sharp contrast to the earlier lines about the blackbird. The language is dense and rich, constantly suggestive yet never over-elaborate. The metaphors are grounded in the persistent distortion of the 'natural' images we associate with the good and fruitful. Later in the same scene Antonio speaks of the foul melancholy which will poison all Bosola's goodness. In a comparable sense the images, too, are poisoned or tainted. This effect pervades the play. Only descriptions of the Duchess, and some of the language associated with her, are exempt.

Verse and prose

It will be noticed that the quotations from Bosala are in prose, not verse. In terms of richness of texture, Webster makes no distinction between them. His choice of one medium or another is dictated by suitability or expediency. In the first scene, for example, Antonio's elaborate comparison of the French court with inferior establishments is couched in verse, Bosola's racy commentary in prose. The more dignified parts of the play – especially those connected with the Duchess – are commonly in verse; the humorous exchanges in prose. Yet just as often, the two are mixed. When Ferdinand enters in the play's last scene he speaks first in verse, then in prose. When

Bosola berates the Old Lady (II,1) he changes from prose to verse in the course of his speech to indicate a change from raillery to a formal statement of man's condition.

Forms and techniques

More important than the distinction between verse and prose is the use of certain formal techniques: the parable, the sententia or aphorism, the rhyming couplet, the song, the homily. Both Ferdinand (III,2,120–36) and the Duchess (III,5,122–40) are given parables. Webster uses these like arias in an opera: the action stops while the character develops a theme. Ferdinand uses personification, while the Duchess employs the fable. Her story is the more vivid for it – but it is also more ambiguous. There is no mistaking the Duke's meaning, which is made clear in his narrative's last lines:

You have shook hands with Reputation,
And made him invisible. (III,2,135–6)

The Duchess, too, offers an interpretation of her fable about the Dog-fish and the Salmon: 'Men are often valued high, when they are most wretch'd' (III,5,140) but the audience may well conclude that the real meaning of what she says is concerned with salvation and damnation. If

Our value never can be truly known,
Till in the Fisher's basket we be shown ... (135–6)

this is because we are only 'truly known' when we come to the final judgment. The Duchess's own conclusion does not even fit with the beginning of her story, which springs from a quarrel with Bosola about Antonio's baseness. She is not, of course, talking about Antonio, but about herself. Ferdinand's parable, too, is more suited to his predicament than to hers. This is typical of a play in which what the characters say about others always reflects on themselves.

So it is with Bosola and his homilies on death in Act IV. In Scene 2 he recites a traditional litany of humbling analogies, showing that the body is less than nothing:

Thou are a box of worm seed, at best, but
a salvatory of green mummy: what's this flesh?
a little crudded milk, fantastical puff-paste:
our bodies are weaker than those paper prisons
boys use to keep flies in ... (IV,2,124–7)

This is very close in tone to the sermon – the kind traditionally delivered on the morning of an execution. The purpose of
such sermons was not only to prepare the victim for death, but
to remind the congregation that, however virtuous, they must
in the end share the same fate. Bosola's fantastic style here is
not unlike the real thing, though more sculpted and elaborate,
but it is easy enough to find comparable passages in the
sermons of another great poet of the period, Donne. The
reader at home, the audience in the theatre, the church congregation, the crowd at a public execution – these were the
same people in a tightly-knit community, used to the same
thing. They expected to find both sensational excitement and
moral improvement in the theatre, and this is what Webster
gives them. It is worth remembering that this was an intensely
dramatic age in every sphere of public life – and most significant life was inevitably public. Television, radio and news-
papers, the whole apparatus of domestic comfort and our
immense and complex technology have made it easy for us to
live privately in the 20th century: people may inhabit the
same street or block of flats all their lives and never meet. In
the 17th century this was inconceivable, even for the very rich.
Life was by nature public and communal: it was therefore
natural that the church and the theatre, the street market, the
court, public entertainments and executions and all kinds of
ceremonies should be the focal points of life. It is worth
remembering this if we are inclined to look at Webster's style
and call it excessive or melodramatic.

Baroque style

And there is another reason for tempering our judgment on
this score. The characteristic style of all 17th-century arts has
come to be known as the Baroque. Baroque is an intensely
theatrical phenomenon: it is concerned with reality and illu-

sion and the vague barriers between them, with dreams and visions, with vivid contrasts, heroic gestures, and magnificent monumental effects. It is exuberant, energetic, powerful and richly – even excessively – ornamented. Parts of the Vatican, especially the statues of Bernini, the paintings of Rubens, Louis XIV's palace at Versailles, Milton's poetry, Bach's music, are all Baroque: massive, proportioned and concerned to express the invisible in the visible, the metaphysical in the physical. It is perhaps natural that this style should characterize much 17th-century art, for there are two aspects of that era which together seem to point inevitably towards it. First, there is the public, theatrical manner of life I have already mentioned, and second, the atmosphere of religious crisis which pervades these years. For the Baroque is a style which heroically combines the worldly and the unworldly: it is both sensuous and yet spiritual. This is the case even when, as with Webster, we suspect an absence of belief in a spiritual realm. For although Webster constantly invokes heaven and hell, devils, demons and angels; and although the Duchess's torments are set in a strongly Christian context of resignation, everything in the play constantly points us back to this world and our life here. This is where we suffer or are happy, this is where our crucial experiences take place. Heaven and hell are merely extensions or developments of the pleasures and torments we know here. When Bosola says at the end: 'Mine is another voyage' (V,5,105) he says nothing about salvation or damnation, and indeed, his preceding words give the strong impression that there is none: 'We are only like dead walls, or vaulted graves/That, ruin'd, yields no echo' (97–8).

Bosola is a typically Baroque hero, like the prince in *Life is a Dream* by the Spanish writer Calderón (1600–81). Prince Segismondo is confused between dream and waking: the play presents his attempts to distinguish between transient insignificant experiences and lasting ones. Bosola, too, has been in a kind of dream: he killed Antonio: 'In a mist: I know not how . . .' (V,5,94). Ferdinand, plagued by fantasy, slips into madness. The Duchess fools herself into thinking her brothers will not mind her marriage. The Cardinal is plagued by visions of 'a thing, arm'd with a rake'. Both Antonio and his wife have dreams or visions of disaster. The basic contrast in the play is not between this world and the next but between different orders of reality within this world. This contrast pervades the action. The Duchess, for example, thinks she is speaking to Antonio, when it is in fact her brother who has crept into the room (III,2). Later, she thinks it is Antonio's hand she is holding when her brother gives her a dead man's (IV,1). Bosola kills Antonio by mistake and the Cardinal is hoist with his own petard in V,5. Julia thinks she has tempted Bosola, and then that she can inveigle her way into the Cardinal's secrets for her own ends (V,2): in both instances she is mistaken. Bosola thinks the Duchess is dead, but then she briefly comes to life; she has believed Antonio dead, but in her brief moments of revival, Bosola tells her Antonio is alive (IV,2). Later (V,4) this motif is reversed: the dying Antonio is perversely comforted by the news that his wife and children are murdered. All these surprises and changes point to the uncertain order of reality.

At a more minute level, too, the style is redolent of Baroque with its richness of imagery, fondness for grotesque metaphors, elaborate comparisons and metaphysical conceits. The abrupt changes of rhythm, mood and tone, the wide variety of linquistic usages, from the formal to the incoherent – all contribute to the fantastic, varied texture of the work. Bosola, in particular, is given telling, extraordinary lines. In IV,2 for example, he says of the Aragonian brothers:

You have a pair of hearts are hollow graves,
Rotten, and rotting others: and your vengeance,
Like two chain'd bullets, still goes arm in arm (317–19)

The oddity of the grave metaphor is compounded by the immediate succession of the bullet simile: not only are the images curious, they are quite unlike one another. Yet Webster's writing is not arbitrary, for the implied link between violence and rottenness is used in the play to characterize the brothers. In V,2 Bosola asks the Cardinal:

And wherefore should you lay fair marble colours
Upon your rotten purposes to me?
Unless you imitate some that do plot great treasons,
And when they have done, go hide themselves i'th'graves
Of those were actors in't. (294–8)

Both these passages distantly recall Bosola's initial characterization of the brothers as 'plum trees, that grow crooked over
standing pools . . .' (I,1,49). Standing pools rot and fester like
empty graves. Again the image is fantastic, linking two apparently disparate ideas: the rich fruit trees and the mouldy
water. These passages are examples of what Dr Johnson complained of in Webster's contemporaries, the Metaphysical
Poets:

The most heterogeneous ideas are yoked
by violence together; nature and art are
ransacked for illustrations, comparisons
and allusions; their learning instructs and
their subtlety surprises . . . (Johnson, *Life of Cowley*)

As may be guessed from the tone of these lines, Johnson
objected to the Metaphysicals (principally Donne, Cowley
and Crashaw) on these very grounds. Yet it is just such
qualities in Webster which intensify the dream and hold our
attention in spite of a plot which has dated.

Versification

Webster was not alone in his fondness for elaborate 'conceits'
– the 17th-century term for fanciful comparisons or startling
images. Most Elizabethan and Jacobean writing is characterized – and frequently ruined – by them. Webster's peculiar
gift was to combine this taste with an acute ear for the nuances
and rhythms of speech. It is this combination which saves his
work from mere cleverness or obscurity. In the lines quoted
above from IV,2 for example, Webster is using the, by then,
traditional line of iambic pentameter – the line which forms
the basis for all the work of Jonson, Shakespeare, Marlow, and
their contemporaries. This line has five beats (pentameter)
arranged in iambs (units consisting of an unstressed beat,
followed by a stressed one). If regularly maintained, this
pattern soon becomes monotonous: the poet's skill lies in
varying it; the dramatist's skill lies in adapting it to colloquial
speech patterns. In the three lines quoted above, the first is
perfectly regular, the stresses coming on every second syllable:

You hāve a pāir of heārts are hōllow grāves

But in the next line, Webster changes the stress pattern on the first word only, so that the stressed syllable comes first:

Rotten, and rotting others: and your vengeance

Furthermore, he inserts a brief pause after 'rotten', and breaks the line in the middle, after 'others'. These are all small changes, and there is no awkwardness of transition: we are not jolted by the change in rhythm. But together they make all the difference in the world: they reinforce the stress on the repeated syllable 'rott' which is, in itself, a vigorous sound, at the same time breaking the verse flow slightly. The emphasis is put where it belongs: on Bosola's contemptuous description of the brothers as essentially rotten and corrupting those around them. The tension is further heightened by the careful patterning of the sound: 'rotten' and 'rotting' take up the 'o' sound from 'hollow' in the previous line and carry it on to 'others'. This is again a small point: but the accumulation of such minor touches builds up the whole picture of the play, whether in imagery, language, rhythm or sound. Webster uses a wide range of techniques to vary his basic verse form. As already noted, he intersperses it with prose. He breaks up lines between two and even three characters, and stretches and shortens them, especially at moments of great intensity. When the Duchess is dead, Bosola confronts Ferdinand with her corpse:

Bosola: Fix your eye here.
Ferdinand: Constantly.
Bosola: Do you not weep?
      Other sins only speak; murder shrieks out:
      The element of water moistens the earth,
      But blood flies upwards, and bedews the heavens.
Ferdinand: Cover her face. Mine eyes dazzle: she di'd young.
  (IV,2,259–63)

Here the rhythm is stretched to breaking-point: it is almost impossible to find five regular beats in Ferdinand's last line, however one says it. 'The normal number of syllables in an

iambic pentameter line is ten: five stressed and five unstressed. Four out of the five lines here have eleven syllables.
The one with ten –

Other sins only shriek: murder shrieks out . . .

reverses the normal stress pattern on the first word and the
fifth. Once again, all these variations from the norm combine
to transform the verse into almost unbearable distortion: it is
very near collapsing into prose. Webster is fond of packing
extra syllables into his lines, increasing the sense of pressure.
Later in the same scene, Ferdinand is trying to wriggle out of
responsibility for his sister's death. He says to Bosola:

'And, for my sake, say though hast done much ill, well' (289)

The snaking syntax of the line reflects the twistings of Ferdinand's motives; but it is the last, ironic syllable which really
tells, awkwardly added on as it is. At other times Webster
shortens lines – most tellingly in Bosola's last speech, which is
worth quoting in full for the light it throws on Webster's
methods:

In a mist: I know not how;
Such a mistake as I have often seen
In a play. O, I am gone:
We are only like dead walls, or vaulted graves
That, ruin'd, yields no echo. Fare you well;
It may be pain: but no harm to me to die
In so good a quarrel. O this gloomy world,
In what a shadow, or deep pit of darkness
Doth, womanish, and fearful, mankind live?
Let worthy minds ne'er stagger in distrust
To suffer death or shame for what is just:
Mine is another voyage. (V,5,94–105)

The first short line follows Malateste's question 'How came
Antonio by his death?' which is also a stress short. Line 95
is then the usual length and rhythm and line 96 then echoes
the pattern of 94, even in its sounds: 'In a mist/In a play, I
know not how/O I am gone'. The play is linked with a mist,

Bosola's imminent death with his lack of knowledge. The echoes and the broken rhythms save the theatrical metaphor from banality – just as, at the end of the speech, the couplet 'distrust/is just' is lifted above staleness by that last haunting line – 'Mine is another voyage'. Bosola's valediction is rendered the more affecting by its contradiction: he praises those who strive for justice while conceding the futility of human life. It is uncertain whether the 'We' of line 97 refers to humanity or to the characters of the play. Either way, the image is ironic, for it resembles closely what Bosola said earlier about the Aragonian brothers – that they were 'hollow graves'. The idea has now been extended to cover everyone, and is taken up in the notion of the world's shadow or deep pit – an image which implicitly compares this world with hell. Bosola's voyage is therefore *out* of hell. Like Antonio, who also had a vision of the hollow tomb in V,3 he:

> . . . would not now
> Wish my wounds balm'd, nor heal'd: for I have no use
> To put my life to. (V,4,61–3)

Unlike Bosola's image, Antonio's tomb in V,3 does give forth an echo – an echo which warns him of impending disaster. By opposite means – with and without an echo – the grave beckons to both men. This is typical of the way in which Webster patterns his imagery. Bosola's speech is full of allusions. Not the least important is his description of humanity as womanish, when we recall that the Duchess has shown more calmness and resolution in the face of death than any other character. That we are meant to note this is made clear by the rhythm – the hesitation on 'Doth' before 'womanish' comes out, and is suspended between commas, with two stresses on the word: 'wōmanīsh'. The sententia with which the speech seems about to end:

> Let worthy minds ne'er stagger in distrust
> To suffer death or shame for what is just.

appears grotesquely out of place in this context – its level pulse emphasizing the contrast with the other broken lines; and in the context it becomes, if not ironic, at least interrogative. Bosola seems suddenly to have remembered what he *ought* to say at the end of a tragedy, but cannot quite believe it. Taken together with his earlier words about what he has 'often seen/In a Play,' these lines invite the audience to speculate about their status, and about the status of the whole drama. It is, after all, a play and not reality. What we have seen, however painful, is fiction. It is typical of Baroque art to emphasize its own fictionality, to flaunt its elaborate artifice, and to dwell on a central paradox of art: that a work may at the same time move us by its evocation of reality and entertain us by rendering that reality unreal. Bosola's last words do just this; and it will pay us to attend just as much to Webster's artifice as to his insight.

Artifice

This approach is nowhere more important than in the play's central section, the torture and execution of the Duchess. Here Webster pulls out all the stops, abandoning all semblance of conventional 'realism' and producing an effect which is at once exotic and moving. Effectively Act IV is a sequence of tableaux which correspond to the Stations of the Cross in Christian iconography. Medieval and Renaissance religious paintings often take for their subjects the stages on Christ's way along the road to Calvary, his place of crucifixion, and his experiences in the days immediately before his death. These are ritualized into a series of symbolic moments, or Stations, and given qualities which are both unique – relative to Christ's unique status as the Son of God – and general – relative to the sense in which his pain and death represents the pain and death of any man. In certain altar-pieces, these Stations are shown in sequence. Just as Christ is the innocent victim of human evil, so the Duchess can be seen as the victim of her brothers' wickedness, sacrificed in their interests. She does not, of course, 'save' them by her death – but her passion may have an effect on the audience, just as Christ's did on millions of people unconnected with the event. In that sense the audience become more than mere spectators: by virtue of their participation in human evil, they became accomplices in the Duchess's death, just as they are in Christ's. The analogy is not an exact one: the Duchess is not herself without faults, nor does Webster draw close attention to the comparison. But he has no need to: 17th-century audiences were too familiar with the idea of redemption through acceptance of suffering to need much prompting, nor would they expect an intimate identification of Christ and the Duchess – they would, indeed, have found such a thing shocking. The point of the analogy is the general moral, emotional and dramatic one: that this world is a world of pain, and that heroic virtue consists in resignation to inevitable suffering when there is no alternative. Christ had to die to save mankind; the Duchess dies to stir in the audience the tragic emotions of fear and pity.

Just as there is something static about paintings of the Stations of the Cross – moments of agony frozen in time – so the various scenes of Act IV have a quality of symbolic immobility. Scene 1 divides into a number of sections. First (I–17) Bosola gives Ferdinand an account of the Duchess. Her executioner has been converted to Antonio's view of the Duchess both passionate and noble, sensuous and majestic. He paints her portrait: this is the first picture in the sequence. Then he draws the traverse to reveal the Duchess, Cariola, and the servants. In this one gesture attempts at stage realism are abandoned: the next picture is quite literally revealed. This picture is then altered by the removal of lights, and the third section begins: Ferdinand's torment of his sister, to whom he gives a dead man's hand. The lights are then brought back and the next picture is produced by drawing another traverse to exhibit the waxworks of Antonio and his children. Once again, artificiality and sensationalism are the keynotes: the screw is turned further. Then the Duchess goes through a ritualized conversation with Bosola about despair and the desire for death – the ritual quality being emphasized by the entrance of a servant purely and solely to tell the Duchess that he wishes her long life, so that she can reply:

I would thou wert hang'd for the horrible curse
Though hast given me: I shall shortly grow one
Of the miracles of pity. (IV,1,92–4)

The Duchess thus announces her own status as a spectacle – 'one/Of the miracles of pity'. The scene then ends with exchanges between Bosola and the Duke in which Ferdinand, speaking of the waxworks, uses a phrase which exactly sums up the whole of Act IV. The Duchess, he says, is 'plagu'd in art' (IV,1,110). One curious effect of the waxworks is to make the actors seem more 'real' – and thus to add another dimension of mystery to the play's preoccupation with appearance and reality.

In IV,2 Webster surpasses himself in the manipulation of artifice. Our first picture shows the Duchess and Cariola in conversation. When the Duchess asks her maid 'Who do I look like now?' – a thoroughly, almost outrageously gratuitous question – Cariola replies:

Like to your picture in the gallery,
A deal of life in show, but none in practice:
Or rather like some reverend monument
Whose ruins are even pitied. (IV,2,31–4)

Once again the pictorial, emblematic nature of the Duchess's suffering is proclaimed: she is a picture and a monument. The ruined monument and the grave are images which recur through the play. As if to drive the message home the Duchess replies that:

. . . Fortune seems only to have her eyesight,
To behold my tragedy. (35–6)

The scene's second section presents a tableau proper: the dance and song of the madmen. The atmosphere of chaotic riot generated by the lunatics contrasts sharply with the sombre dialogue between Bosola and the Duchess which then follows, in which Bosola once again uses a visual image to describe the Duchess – this time in her grave:

. . . Princes images on their tombs
Do not lie as they were wont, seeming to pray
Up to Heaven: but with their hands under their cheeks,
As if they died of the tooth-ache; they are not carved
With their eyes fix'd upon the stars; but as
Their minds were wholly bent upon the world,
The self-same way they seem to turn their faces. (155–62)

These magnificent lines – the more magnificent for their hint of comedy – again point to the notion of the monumental, and again suggest hollowness, and contradiction. The body within the tomb rots, but the image survives. The image points to the world, not to Heaven: it is therefore the idea of worldliness which is eternal, not the notion of eternity itself. The irony is doubled because the lines are addressed to the Duchess who, worldly as she has been, is now growing into her shroud, accustoming herself to cast off the world. Typically, Webster makes Bosola say that the shell tells more truth than the core – a reversal of the usual appearance/reality hierarchy, in which the outer surface obscures the inner truth.

The executioners enter, Bosola sings his song and the action proceeds to what appears to be its consummation: the Duchess's death. But her murder and Cariola's prove to be only the doorway to the scene's climax, which is a conversation between Bosola and Ferdinand. Their exchanges are filled with theatrical allusions and metaphors of blindness and insight:

Bosola: Fix your eye here . . .
Ferdinand: . . . Mine eyes dazzle . . .
     . . . Let me see her face again . . .
     . . . See: like a bloody fool . . .
Bosola: . . . who shall dare
     Reveal this . . .
Ferdinand: . . . Never look upon me more . . .
     . . . That I may never see thee . . .
     Tis a deed of darkness. (IV,2,258–332)

Ferdinand's wandering reason may remind us of Vaughan's lines about 'A deep but dazzling darkness' written only a few years after Webster's play. The significance is clear: the consequences of the tableaux we have been witnessing are too much for Ferdinand, he cannot face them. He turns to the theatrical metaphor:

. . . as we observe in tragedies
That a good actor many times is curs'd
For playing a villain's part . . . (286–88)

in order to shield himself from the responsibility: Bosola has 'acted' his part too well, and deserves the opprobrium. But

Bosola answers him with the same idea of the good man playing a bad part:

And though I loath'd the evil, yet I lov'd
You that did counsel it: and rather sought
To appear a true servant than an honest man. (329–31)

We may doubt the nature of Bosola's 'love' for Ferdinand: standing in apposition to 'loath'd' it means loyalty rather than affection. The last line is clear enough: 'playing a villain's part' is all being 'a true servant' seems to come to, where Ferdinand is concerned. Bosola makes the unpleasant discovery that his cynicism, to which he has sacrificed all principles, doesn't even bring him profit. The contrast with the Duchess's behaviour earlier in the scene could hardly be stronger. She has offered herself up as a 'miracle of pity', while her killers argue over the remains. It is then that Webster produces his riskiest coup de théatre, for it transpires that Bosola's row with Ferdinand is not the end of the scene after all. The soliloquy we might expect to provide the closing lines turns out to be an introduction to the Duchess's revival. Like Desdemona, she comes briefly back to life: she turns from a lifeless monument, a pale picture to a breathing body and opens her eyes. But the climax turns out to be an anti-climax. Even as Bosola gives her the news that Antonio lives she expires, and Bosola is indeed left to conclude the scene vowing vengeance against the Aragonian brothers. The Duchess's revival, like Desdemona's, reaches the heights of improbability: it is the moment in the play when we are most immediately aware that this is indeed a play. Yet the surprise, the dramatic shock, if well produced, is enough to convince us that this is also the most moving moment in the play, if only because the Duchess utters no more than her husband's name and a plea for mercy. It is both sentimental and sensational, against all the rules of probability and good taste. It is also thrilling theatre, once again compelling the recognition that the moving is not necessarily the natural, especially in Baroque art. And yet the single most interesting stylistic stroke in this whole act, the one which shows Webster a great dramatist rather than merely a good one, is, in a sense, as close a rendering of 'natural' behaviour as it could be. When the Duchess briefly revives, Bosola, already disgusted with Ferdinand and his own part in the murder, is so moved that when she murmurs her husband's name he replies:

Yes, Madam, he is living.
The dead bodies you saw were but feigned statues;
He's reconcil'd to your brothers: the Pope hath wrought
The atonement. (IV,2,348–51)

The first two lines are true: out of pity for the dying woman Bosola adds the next two. The point here is that he lies, and that he lies out of kindness: under stress he throws off his cruelty. Is this, then, the real Bosola? The lie is brilliantly placed, for not only is it 'natural' – far more important, in line with the play's equivocal nature, it at once compounds our doubt about just who the 'real' Bosola is. So that once again the 'naturalness' is the effect of consummate art. The tears which follow it do nothing to mute Bosola's savagery in the last act: instead they proclaim him as the play's most elaborate and therefore most credible character creation. He is the best exemplar of the truth that Webster's style is no mere excess or adjunct but inseparable from what he wants to say.

Imagery and irony

Two further features remain for comment: imagery and irony. The two are closely related. The striking richness of Webster's style has already been remarked: paradoxically, this richness of texture does not preclude a narrowness of focus – on the contrary, it is the combination of richness and narrowness which gives the play its intensity. The imagery is varied but most of it can be identified within a network based on recurring motifs. It is also communal: different characters use images which are recognizably the same. On the one hand this no doubt reinforces the claustrophobic atmosphere of the play – our sense that the characters are inextricably bound up with one another, however much they struggle to be free. On the other it contributes to the sense that the play is self-consciously developing themes and exploring arguments in a way foreign to – say – Shakespeare. This impression is confirmed by the work of scholars which suggests that Webster was indeed a highly self-conscious and painstaking artist, who worked hard on his plays, drawing from many sources but striving to blend them into a unity. In consequence, whereas it is possible and profitable to examine Shakespeare's plays in terms of theme and structure, they do not offer the inducement to look for coherence as Webster's do. This has virtues and vices. Webster lacks his contemporary's scope and range, his abounding sense of a plural world existing on many different levels. On the other hand, he has a distinctive sharpness and sense of intellectual coherence, often lacking in Shakespeare. In this sense only he is closer to the French tragedy of Racine and Corneille, which is more concerned with the play's overall shape than with the vivid life of the details. This is a matter of emphasis. It is also a useful corrective to readers and play-goers who are disappointed because Webster doesn't give them what Shakespeare does – or vice versa. Comparative discussion of writers is useful, comparative assessment futile.

The most prominent groups of images derive from animals, especially vermin. This was hardly an original move on Webster's part: animal metaphors are as old as literature itself. They were also popular with his contemporaries. Shakespeare's *Coriolanus* and *King Lear*, to name two examples, are filled with them. The distinctive quality of *The Duchess of Malfi* is the sheer quantity and intensity of such images, and the way in which they become part of the play's structure. The first scene alone crowds blackbirds, crows, pies and caterpillars, leeches, hawks and dogs into its 81 lines – and they are all mentioned by Bosola. It is with him and with Ferdinand that animals are especially associated. The Cardinal is linked with toads at the outset (I,2,83) and dies, as he says himself, 'like a leveret' (V,5,45), but it is the Duke who takes the central animal role. In the conversation between Delio and Antonio (I,2,103) he is compared to a spider: by the play's end he has actually become a wolf. Strikingly, the doctor's description of Ferdinand's madness explicitly links him with Bosola and the Cardinal. People with lycanthropia, we are told, overflow with 'melancholy humour'. Both the Duke's brother (I,2,81) and his henchman (I,1,75) are described as melancholy. Up until now Ferdinand has appeared to be fiery and passionate, but at the end of the play his 'true' nature appears with his wolfishness: he, too, is a melancholic, one oppressed by dark, heavy feelings – the temperament associated with death and tombs and all the gloomy relish of mortality. This is a good example of the way in which imagery makes a dramatic point.

The play's animal images are closely bound up with questions of identity in a number of ways. There is the matter of how people see themselves and others. Webster often uses birds to express this. The Duchess sees herself as a pheasant, a quail, a robin and a nightingale: Bosola is a blackbird; Ferdinand an eagle. But the Cardinal contrasts his treatment of Julia as a hawk with her husband's approach, which put her under surveillance like a tame elephant. Ferdinand compares his sister to a crab, a hyena and a screech-owl, calls his sister's children cubs and thinks of Bosola as a politic dormouse. Antonio sees Bosola as a mole and a snake; various people call Ferdinand a salamander and a tiger, and his brother a porpoise and a fox; and Bosola dismisses the whole court as crows, pies, caterpillars and leeches. One might compare the play to a work such as Jonson's *Volpone* in which all the characters are given animal names and appropriate characteristics. The difference is that Webster varies his comparisons to suit the circumstances, and the shifting references add to the richness of verbal texture and to the kaleidoscopic presentation of character. His images also recur. In I,2 Ferdinand and Bosola are discussing the henchman's task. The Duke, telling Bosola to 'be himself,' says that:

> This will gain
> Access to private lodgings, where yourself
> May, like a politic dormouse . . . (I,2,206)

at which point Bosola interrupts with his own reflections on the image of the dormouse, which catches his fancy.

> As I have seen some,
> Feed in a lord's dish, half asleep, not seeming
> To listen to any talk: and yet these rogues
> Have cut his throat in a dream: what's my place?

At one level Bosola is merely completing Ferdinand's thought with added vividness. On another, he takes over the image and twists it to his own view: the harshness of 'these rogues/ Have cut his throat' goes to the point in a way Ferdinand himself avoids. Earlier he has rebuked Bosola:

Your inclination to shed blood rides post
Before my occasion to use you. (I,2,174–5)

The different uses of the image reveal something about their characters and situations: the Duke, urbane, careful – Bosola impatient of sophistry. And the added idea of the 'dream' adds another level of the passage's meaning: throughout the play Bosola seems to act, as he says at the end 'In a mist'. The metaphor of the sleepy dormouse, hardly aware of what he does, is therefore especially apposite. And the image's importance does not end there. In III,1 Antonio takes it up to describe Ferdinand's frightening calmness:

He is so quiet, that he seems to sleep
The tempest out, as dormice do in winter. (22–3)

And this reference recurs ironically when the doctor, confident of curing Ferdinand's madness, says 'I'll make him as tame as a dormouse' (V,2,74). The grotesque image of the dangerous mouse characterizes the Duke's indirectness and deceptive nature.

This use of recurring and subtly evolving images is common in the play. In I,1, for example, Bosola offers a striking description of the Aragonian brothers as 'like plum trees, that grow crooked over standing pools'. (49). Bosola later uses a comparable simile

... an honest statesman to a prince,
Is like a cedar, planted by a spring,
The spring bathes the tree's root, the grateful tree
Rewards it with his shadow. (III,2,262–5)

which recalls not only Bosola's earlier image but also Antonio's description of a good prince's court as:

... a common fountain, whence should flow
Pure silver drops in general. (I,1,12–13)

and Ferdinand's allusion to the prince's natural tendency to
suspicion:

You see, the oft shaking of the cedar tree
Fastens it more at root. (I,2,166–7)

This configuration of images is not determined by the characters who participate in it: it has a structure independent of the
drama, though each remark is appropriate in the dramatic
context. Other groups of images which undergo comparable
transformations are associated with disease and death – again
established in the play's first speech (I,1,15); hell and heaven;
and monuments, ruins, graves and sarcophagi. For detailed
commentary of these, readers should consult the textual notes
to each scene.

Finally, a word must be said about Webster's irony. Like
other dramatists in the period, he employs irony at different
levels, from the incidental to the structural. When the Cardinal says to Bosola: 'Would you could become honest' and
Bosola replies: 'With all your divinity, do but direct me the
way to it' (I,1,40–41) the Cardinal is being hypocritical and
Bosola ironic: he knows well enough how much 'divinity' the
Cardinal has, and his tone might suggest as much to the
audience. On the other hand, this is not confirmed until the
Cardinal has left the stage, and Bosola angrily identifies him
with the devil. But as the play develops, this exchange takes
on a deeper resonance, for Bosola does indeed become 'honest'
– in the sense that he faces up to the truth – and his honesty
brings him the reward of death. The Cardinal puts off his
'divinity' to become a general, and he too perishes as a result
of his own scheming, killed by Bosola. In retrospect their
exchange takes on a far deeper tinge of irony, which we can
assess when we reflect on the whole play. Other aspects of the
first scene can be interpreted in the same way. When Antonio
says:

Though some o'th'court hold it presumption
To instruct princes what they ought to do,
It is a noble duty to inform them
What they ought to foresee (I,1,19–22)

our immediate impression may be two-fold: that he is laying
down a general maxim, and that he has his own particular
court in mind. Antonio is the Duchess's steward, who marries
her with some misgivings – misgivings which only increase
with time. Yet never does he offer more than token resistance
to her will, though he suspects the dire consequences. His acts
contradict his own maxim. But we can also apply the notion
elsewhere in the play. Webster is preoccupied with flattery
and bad advice. Ferdinand tells Bosola that he is the only man
to speak out plainly to him (III,1,89–93) and makes just the
point Antonio does:

That friend a great man's ruin strongly checks,
Who rails into his belief all his defects. (III,1,92–3)

For men such as Ferdinand it is the height and refinement of
flattery to be told the apparent truth – but not, as in this case,
all of it. Bosola tells him enough to make himself appear a
plain-speaking man, but not enough to get himself dismissed
or dissuade Ferdinand from his wickedness: he criticizes his
master's personality not his moral values. And when he finally
does tell the Duke the truth, Ferdinand is on the brink of the
madness into which he then retreats, unable to face the 'fact'
of his sister's corpse. And there is yet another layer of irony
here. If we look back to Antonio's words, we find that he
recommends telling princes what they ought to *foresee* and not
telling them what they ought to *do*. In the face of Ferdinand's
perverse tortures, Bosola does tell his master what to do:
'. . . go no further in your cruelty . . .' (IV,1,116) but without
effect; and he does not, any more than the Duke, foresee what
the outcome will be: that they are both emotionally disturbed,
one despatched to madness, the other to repentance.

These are aspects of what we might call structural irony –
the long-range logical development of contradictions in the
play. Traditional dramatic irony is equally important. Irony –
the contradiction between what is said and what is meant –
depends for its effect on the fact that speaker and hearer both
understand what is not stated. Dramatic irony occurs when a
third party – the audience – is added, with its own kind of
knowledge. In III,1 the Duchess attempts to deflect Ferdinand's talk of marriage by complaining about the rumours

which affect her honour. A few moments earlier, in the previous scene, we have witnessed the Duke's almost insane fury at the thought of his sister's promiscuity; but the moment has not come for him to reveal his thoughts, and he assures his sister that he will not believe any scandalous reports.

When Julia tries to wheedle the Cardinal's secret out of him he poisons her in a moment which encapsulates the kind of macabre dramatic irony peculiar to Jacobean tragedy. Julia's death is as much a surprise to the audience as it is to her and to Bosola. The Cardinal, of course, knows all along that the book she swears on is poisoned; and Bosola's entry shows him that he has indeed caught Julia out in deception. Yet he, too, is caught out, for this action, witnessed by Bosola, seals his fate. And, as we later discover, it also seals Bosola's: by the end of the play, all three of them are dead – and death is the most ironic comment on all human aspiration. In this sense the play is pervaded by the final irony of mortality. All the main characters die. The muddle which remains at the end is hardly dispelled by conventional remarks about the Duchess's heir, as Webster makes clear in Delio's words:

> These wretched eminent things
> Leave no more fame behind'em than should one
> Fall in a frost and leave his print in snow ... (V,5,112–14)

And although Delio says that:

> Nature doth nothing so great for great men
> As when she's pleas'd to make them lords of truth. (V,5,118–19)

the ambiguity of his meaning is itself ironic. Does he refer to the Duchess? Webster, establishing the new order in a traditional manner in the person of the Duchess's son, does nothing to dispel the mist of error mentioned by Bosola. The truth of which we, the audience, are lords is neither optimistic nor simple. When Delio says, in conclusion:

> Integrity of life is fame's best friend,
> Which nobly, beyond death, shall crown the end.

echoing Bosola's commendation of worthy minds which 'ne'er stagger in distrust' (V,5,103) he also seems to echo Bosola's hint that there is, indeed, nothing else after the end: reputation is the only immortality. This is the final irony.

Literary terms

A few specialist usages are given below, but where there is a full explanation of a term in either the *textual notes* or *critical commentary* it is not defined here.

iambic pentameter This is the staple line of English narrative and dramatic poetry. 'Pentameter' indicates that there are five beats, feet or stresses in the line. Iambs are feet in which there is a short syllable followed by a long, or an unstressed followed by a stressed. 'Without' is an iamb, for example.

irony The conveyance of meaning by words whose literal sense is the opposite of that implied.

dramatic irony This occurs when a character is unaware of the true significance of his words or actions but other characters on stage, as well as the reader and the audience, know exactly what is happening.

metaphor This is a figure of speech in which two things are not merely compared (as in a simile) but identified. It is not introduced by 'like' or 'as'.

catharsis A word used by Aristotle to describe the effect of tragedy on the audience. According to the context it can mean either purging or purification

hubris Another of Aristotle's terms from the *Poetics*, hubris is the kind of blind pride characteristic of the tragic hero.

General questions and sample answer in note form

1 Examine Webster's presentation of Bosola
2 Webster calls his play a tragedy. Is this an accurate description?
3 How important is the development of individual characters within the play, and how subordinate to other elements?
4 Is there any significance in the fact that the Duchess and Ferdinand are twins?
5 Is the Duchess's drama a distinctively female one?
6 Comment on the character and role of Antonio.
7 Discuss the part played by visual spectacle in the play.
8 Give an account of the play's imagery, paying particular attention to recurring motifs.
9 To what extent and in what sense or senses would you call *The Duchess of Malfi* a religious play?
10 Ferdinand sees lust as his sister's main motive. Do you agree?
11 Support or refute the charge that *The Duchess of Malfi* is no more than a sensational melodrama.
12 Can Webster be said to present a coherent moral view in the play?
13 What different kinds of love are portrayed in the play?
14 In what ways does the play have any relevance for us today?
15 Discuss the proposal that Bosola is the real hero of the play.

Suggested notes for essay answer to question 1

A complex character undergoing change. Developed in more detail than other characters – set up for comparison with both Ferdinand and Antonio. Consider these comparisons in general terms.

Focus on presentation through the play. Act I – he both appears and is commented on by others – Antonio, the Cardinal, Ferdinand. Importance of the first scene – melancholy. Act II – his railing at Castruchio and the old Lady – his encounters with Antonio and the Duchess – realism: laughs at astrology. Act III – his frankness with Ferdinand – his deception of the Duchess and his cruelty to her. Act IV – his conversion to the Duchess's point of view – yet he still tortures and kills her – his remorse only after Ferdinand betrays him – his regret and tears – determination on revenge. Also consider his extraordinary assumption of different roles. Act V – his skilful intrigue against the Cardinal – his use of Julia – his last words to Antonio – his own last words.

Points to consider: Ambiguity of Bosola's last speech, especially in view of his habitual irony; his assumption of different roles, his conflict between 'duty' and honesty, the ways in which he sees himself and is seen by others; his change of heart over the Duchess; his melancholy.

Further reading

Gunnar Boklund: *The Duchess of Malfi: Sources, Themes, Characters* (Harvard, 1962)
Ralph Berry: *The Art of John Webster* (OUP, 1972)
M. C. Bradbrook: *Themes and Conventions of Elizabethan Tragedy* (Cambridge, 1935)
Clifford Leech: *Webster: The Duchess of Malfi* (London, 1978)
Una Ellis-Fermor: *The Jacobean Drama* (Methuen, 1965)

Brodie's Notes

TITLES IN THE SERIES

Jane Austen	**Pride and Prejudice**
Robert Bolt	**A Man for All Seasons**
Emily Brontë	**Wuthering Heights**
Charlotte Brontë	**Jane Eyre**
Geoffrey Chaucer	**Prologue to the Canterbury Tales**
Geoffrey Chaucer	**The Nun's Priest's Tale**
Geoffrey Chaucer	**The Wife of Bath's Tale**
Geoffrey Chaucer	**The Pardoner's Prologue and Tale**
Charles Dickens	**Great Expectations**
Gerald Durrell	**My Family and Other Animals**
T. S. Eliot	**Selected Poems**
George Eliot	**Silas Marner**
F. Scott Fitzgerald	**The Great Gatsby** and **Tender is the Night**
E. M. Forster	**A Passage to India**
John Fowles	**The French Lieutenant's Woman**
Anne Frank	**The Diary of Anne Frank**
William Golding	**Lord of the Flies**
Graham Handley (ed)	**The Metaphysical Poets: John Donne to Henry Vaughan**
Thomas Hardy	**Far From the Madding Crowd**
Thomas Hardy	**Tess of the D'Urbervilles**
Thomas Hardy	**The Mayor of Casterbridge**
Aldous Huxley	**Brave New World**
John Keats	**Selected Poems and Letters of John Keats**
Philip Larkin	**Selected Poems of Philip Larkin**
D. H. Lawrence	**Sons and Lovers**
Laurie Lee	**Cider with Rosie**
Harper Lee	**To Kill a Mockingbird**
Arthur Miller	**The Crucible**
Athur Miller	**Death of a Salesman**
George Orwell	**1984**
George Orwell	**Animal Farm**
J. B. Priestley	**An Inspector Calls**
J. D. Salinger	**The Catcher in the Rye**
William Shakespeare	**The Merchant of Venice**
William Shakespeare	**King Lear**
William Shakespeare	**A Midsummer Night's Dream**
William Shakespeare	**Twelfth Night**
William Shakespeare	**Hamlet**
William Shakespeare	**As You Like It**
William Shakespeare	**Romeo and Juliet**
William Shakespeare	**Julius Caesar**
William Shakespeare	**Macbeth**
William Shakespeare	**Antony and Cleopatra**
William Shakespeare	**Othello**
William Shakespeare	**The Tempest**

George Bernard Shaw	**Pygmalion**
Alan Sillitoe	**Selected Fiction**
John Steinbeck	**Of Mice and Men** and **The Pearl**
Alice Walker	**The Color Purple**

ENGLISH COURSEWORK BOOKS

Terri Apter	**Women and Society**
Kevin Dowling	**Drama and Poetry**
Philip Gooden	**Conflict**
Philip Gooden	**Science Fiction**
Margaret K. Gray	**Modern Drama**
Graham Handley	**Modern Poetry**
Graham Handley	**Prose**
Graham Handley	**Childhood and Adolescence**
R. J. Sims	**The Short Story**

 LVECHURCH

1200 YEARS OF HISTORY

Wilfrid Elliott English

OSBORNE
HERITAGE

Published by Osborne Books Limited,
Unit 1B Everoak Estate, Bromyard Road,
St Johns, Worcester, WR2 5HN
Tel 01905 748071

Printed by the Bath Press, Bath.

British Library Cataloguing in Publication Data
A catalogue record for this book is available from the British Library

ISBN 1 872962 61 0

CONTENTS

Acknowledgements	4
From Offa to Domesday 780 – 1087	5
From Domesday to the Bishop's Survey 1087 – 1299	7
Hard Times 1300 – 1485	15
Life under the Tudors 1485 – 1603	22
The Stuarts 1603 – 1714	33
The Hanoverian Kings 1714 – 1837	48
Victorian and Edwardian Alvechurch 1837 – 1914	68
The Twentieth Century	103
Appendix I – Alvechurch in the 1800s	108
Appendix II – The Seal of the Peculiar Jurisdiction of Alvechurch, 1742	114
Index	116

ACKNOWLEDGEMENTS

A lvechurch has had a long association with the Bishopric of Worcester – from Saxon to Victorian times – and the local historian has been fortunate in the retention of so many records amongst the Diocesan papers. The proceedings of the Manor Courts are extant from the early 1500s, the Bailiff's Book begins in 1603, and from the early Eighteenth Century there are Poor Law and associated papers, all of which throw light on how the people earned their living, where and how they lived, and what their interests were – all matters of greater interest to the local historian than political history or the doings of great families.

In the pursuit of this interest I must express my indebtedness to the Worcester Branch of the County Record Office and to the Alvechurch Historical Society whose records have proved invaluable, to Michael Fardon, who has guided me through the maze of publishing, to Rosemary Griffiths and Jon Moore, who have processed and set the text, and to Anita Sherwood who has designed the text layout and cover. Acknowledgments for permission to reproduce material are due to Alvechurch Historical Society, Birmingham Museum and Art Gallery, the Diocesan Registrar, Hereford and Worcester County Record Office, The Ordnance Survey and The Society of Antiquaries: and, on a more personal note, to Mr and Mrs John Davies, Mr Keith Garman and Mrs Rachel Hayes.

W. E. English, March 1997

FROM OFFA TO DOMESDAY
AD 780 – 1087

T he definitive history of Alvechurch begins in the reign of King Offa: although Icknield Street, the Roman Road running from Alcester to Metchley, runs through the easternmost part of the parish, the Romans left no mark, nor is there any real evidence of earlier settlement. By his charter of 780 Offa, 'King of the Mercians and of other neighbouring nations,', granted to the monastery of Bredon 20 measures of land in Waersetfelda (probably to be equated with the West Heath, Wast Hills area), Coftune (Cofton), and Wreodan Hale (Rednal). Soon afterwards the donation reverted to the Church of Worcester. When the Norse incursions began, in order to gain royal protection, the Bishop granted the land to the then King, Berhtwulf, but eventually peace was restored and in 934 King Athelstan re-granted the 20 measures of land to the Church: these were now described as being at Werst Felda, Coftune, Wam Ham Stealle, Wreodan Hale, Hoppwda, Waersethylle and Wihtlafesfeld - it will be noted that Hopwood is now identified. It is clear that up to this date there has been no mention of Alvechurch, and, indeed, it is unlikely that there was either a church or a settlement at what is now the village. There was a church by the time of Domesday Book, 1087, as the presence of a priest is recorded, but the fact is that one cannot say with any degree of certainty when the first church was built, or why it was named after a lady called Aelfgythe.

When was the church built? Certainly after Athelstan's Charter of 934, and, possibly, during the time of Bishop Oswald, 962 - 991, as he is known to have encouraged the building of churches and the establishment of the parochial system: later evidence shows that there were a few houses around the churchyard. Further, there is no reason to suspect that the Saxon church was sited other than where the church now stands. The name, Aelfgythe's church, suggests either that she founded it - which seems unlikely as the land belonged to the Bishopric - or that the church was dedicated to her. There is an Anglo-Saxon saint named Aelfgythe: she was sister-in-law to King Athelstan, and it is conceivable that the first church was dedicated to her, then being rededicated to St. Laurence when the Normans built the stone church some time in the 12th Century.

Domesday Book of 1087 provides the first opportunity to picture the village. Under the heading of the possessions of the Church of Worcester there comes the entry for 'Alvievecherche' consisting of 13 hides, or measures of land - smaller therefore than the donations of Offa and Athelstan - and comprising a priest, a reeve (farm manager), a riding man, 12 villeins (customary tenants), 7 bordars or cottagers, and 7 male and female slaves: much of the manor was forest: they have 8 saltpans in Droitwich: it is worth 100 shillings, as it was in the time of Edward the Confessor. The Bishop's manor does not comprise the whole parish, and later in Domesday, under the possession of Urse d'Abitot, Sheriff of the County, there is one hide of land at Osmerley, in the extreme south of the parish, with 2 villeins, 10 bordars and 2 women slaves, and now worth 13 shillings: this land later came to the Beauchamps and was granted by them to the Abbey of Bordesley.

In attempting to evaluate the information in Domesday Book one must bear in mind that it was essentially a fiscal document providing a basis for taxation. It seems that the only free man was the riding man - the radchemistre of the survey - as well as the priest. The rest were either customary tenants owing personal service to the Lord of the Manor, or smallholders with lighter duties, or slaves. Perhaps, with their families, they might have totalled between 200 and 250; they were scattered in four hamlets in the manor with a few houses around the church. That there was a church at this time is assumed from the mention of a priest, just as the lack of reference to a mill suggests that the mill on the Arrow was of later construction. It was a heavily wooded area, just outside the Royal Forest of Feckenham which covered most of the land west of the Arrow. The scattered population would be hard pressed to sustain themselves and grow sufficient cash crops to meet their obligations to the Lord of the Manor and to the Church.

FROM DOMESDAY TO THE BISHOP'S SURVEY 1087 – 1299

The 200 years that follow Domesday saw an expansion in production together with a steady growth of population: at the same time institutions became more formalised, and the duties and obligations of the different classes making up society were to be more closely defined. There are progressively more records, national and local, from which one can begin to build up a picture of life at the time, and in particular we have the Survey of the Manor of Alvechurch, 1299, preserved in the Red Book of Worcester, and, from the time of Bishop Godfrey Giffard, 1268, the Registers of successive bishops.

There is, in the event, a useful, if less comprehensive survey of the manor in 1182, from which it is evident that in the preceding century a large part of the manor had been granted to free tenants, of whom there were now 19: there were now 21 villein families holding in all 2 hides: there must have been a park as the park-keeper is named, and there was a smith who held his holding by the service of producing ironwork. The inhabitants are mostly scattered in the different berewicks or hamlets, and there are only a few houses around the church. At this time the great majority of the inhabitants have Saxon names but by the time of the 1299 Survey there is hardly a Saxon name to be found.

It is shortly after this 1182 Survey that there is evidence of more rapid growth. This took the form of the grant, in 1196, by Richard I, the Lion Heart, of the right to hold a weekly market, and this was followed, in 1239, by the grant of an Annual Fair to be held on the eve, the day, and the morrow of Saint Laurence's Day, 10th August

- the first evidence we have of the dedication of the church. In 1236 we learn that Bishop Blois died at his palace in Alvechurch so that we know that by that date the bishops were looking upon the manor as one of their regular residences and that the palace that stood within the double moat east of the Arrow was already in existence and in use. Then, finally, the Bishop's Survey of 1299 tells us that, as well as the freemen, villeins and cottars, there was a new element, 62 burgesses holding regular burgage plots within a borough. Alvechurch was a seignorial borough - there was no Royal Charter, but the status was granted by the Bishop as Lord of the Manor, and the date of the grant, if indeed there was a formal grant, is unknown. The effect, however, was clear, and has left an indelible mark on the shape of the village today. As happened in Stratford upon Avon, another of the Bishop's manors, a new town was laid out, in our case some 200/300 yards east of the old centre around the church, and nearer to the crossing over the River Arrow. It took the form of a carfax, or cross-roads, with a triangular shaped market place on what was then the main axis, the old highway between Worcester and Coventry, running down Bear Hill, over the Arrow, and along the Radford Road. Thus the new town lay along the present Red Lion Street, Swan Street, Bear Hill and Radford Road, while the market place was larger than the present square, as the in-filling of Nos. 1, 15, 16 and 17 The Square are much later developments. There is no direct evidence of the size of the burgage plots, but we know that at Stratford they were 19 yards wide and 66 yards deep: the depth of existing gardens in the old part of the village seems to agree with this figure, and, while it is difficult to correlate the frontage width with 19 yards, there does seem to be a relationship in some places, if one makes allowance for the division of the original plots into three or even four properties. What is noteworthy is that the basic rent of 10d per burgage remained unchanged until this century, although tenants had to pay quite heavy entry fines.

The grant of borough status did not bring self government. The only concession was that henceforth there were separate manor Courts Leet and Baron and View of Frankpledge for the Borough and for the Foreign, so that separate officers were elected and separate juries sworn, but one Constable, elected by the Foreign, served the whole manor. It is clear that the improved economic status depended heavily upon bishops continuing to make frequent use of the Palace. The

Bishops' Registers show that some, such as Godfrey Giffard, spent long periods here, and as medieval bishops moved with an entourage of up to 50 lay and clerical followers, the impact on the local economy was considerable. Once bishops ceased to make such frequent use of the Palace, possibly because of dilapidations, the village must have sunk back into torpor, and we know that by the time of Leland's Itinerary, around 1540, the weekly market had been discontinued.

During this period the Saxon church was replaced by the first Norman stone building, much of which survived until the rebuild of 1860, and fragments of which are still to be seen. Architectural evidence gives a date in the 12th Century to the nave and north aisle that was the original church. There is no historical evidence of the date of construction, but there is a record that Bishop Simon (1125-1151) dedicated the cemetery, and it is possible that this may relate to the completion of the new church. Of this church the only certain relic we have today is the South door, which was dismantled and re-sited in 1860 when the South aisle was built and a new porch erected. Compared with some local places such as Rock or Kilpeck it is a very simple affair. Later in this period, again date unknown, the chancel was lengthened: the priest's door that then gave the parson direct access to the chancel was re-sited between the North aisle and the vestry in 1860. The last relic is small but interesting. Victorian drawings show that the columns and capitals dividing the North aisle from the nave were faithfully copied in 1860, and one of the original scalloped capitals was reused in the westernmost pillar. It is not possible to tell whether there was a tower - the existing tower is 15th Century and there is nothing to suggest that it replaced a former building.

From the time of Bishop Godfrey Giffard, 1268, the Bishops' Registers are complete and throw authentic light on affairs temporal and spiritual. Although the first appointment of a rector to Alvechurch, and the first name on the board inside the church is that of Robert of Wych, of whom more later, we do know the names of some earlier rectors from casual mention in national records. The first is in 1221 in a case before the Justice in Eyre and concerns one Isabel who is described as the daughter of Hugh, parson of Alvechurch. This not only gives the name of the earliest priest, but also shows that married priests still continued despite the efforts of the Papacy to insist on celibacy. The next is in 1249 when there are two deeds in Ancient

Deeds of the Exchequer covering agreements between the Abbot of Bordesley and Matthew Cantilupo, Rector of Alvechurch, regarding fishing rights on the River Arrow and grazing rights in Sortewode (Shortwood). Matthew was the brother of the then Bishop of Worcester, and was already a canon of York, so that he was probably another absentee rector. In 1255 the Close Rolls contain an order from the King to the Custodian of the King's Forest at Kynefare (Kinver) to send six oaks for curved posts for making a grange to Henry de Wengham at his church at Alvethecherch, by gift of the King. Henry was a Royal clerk, was soon to be Chancellor of the realm, and held many benefices in addition to Alvechurch. Then, in 1260, in Pleas of the Forest, Thomas Molinton, Rector of Alvechurch, was fined the enormous sum of £20 - the annual value of the rectory - because his squire had offended against the Forest Laws. Lastly we know from the appointment of Robert of Wych that his predecessor had been Robert de Fangelos, Archdeacon of Gloucester. The rectory was by this time a 'peculiar' as it probably had been for many years: this meant that it was independent of the Archdeacon of Worcester, the Rector 'visited' himself two years out of three, and he dealt with the probate of wills within the parish and certain other matters normally reserved for the Archdeacon and the Consistory Court. This peculiar jurisdiction was to continue into the last Century.

We now turn to the remarkable career of Robert of Wych, a career that can be followed in great detail from the Bishop's Register and from national records. He first appears in 1272 when, as a clerk in minor orders, he is authorised to assist the Bishop's Official, and from then onwards is engaged in the business of the Bishopric - he is deeply involved in the litigation between the Bishop and the Prior of Malvern, he 'visits' the Deanery of Warwick as the Bishop's deputy, he is involved in the affairs of Parliament to which the Bishop was summoned, and in every way was concerned with the administration of the diocese. To remunerate him he had been granted the benefices of Tidrington and Twining as well as a prebend of Westbury, and in 1287 when he was collated to Alvechurch he retained Tidrington and Westbury. It was only then that he took priest's orders and he immediately asked for, and was granted, permission to be absent for three years for study. Although described as 'Magister', there is no record of his being at either Oxford or Cambridge. It is likely that he actually resided in Alvechurch as the 1299 Survey shows him holding several plots of land in addition to the substantial glebe. He was a frequent litigant and in 1306 was licensed by the Bishop to go to Rome to pursue a claim against the Prior of Gloucester. His downfall began in 1310 when a writ was issued to levy his ecclesiastical goods for a debt of £10, but it was in 1312 that articles were objected against him:

– of incontinence with Emma, keeping her publicly in concubinage, and having children by her,
– that he had bound himself to pay Emma 10 marks (£6.13s.4d.) two cows and other small things, and had broken his word,
– that in the parishes of Alvechurch and Tidrington he did no good, nor did he reside duly,
– that in Alvechurch, pretending that he had jurisdiction, he received money penalties for serious faults, contrary to the constitution of the Fathers.

Robert fought the allegations and used every legal delay that he could, but in the end he was condemned, but failed to appear for correction. In consequence, in June 1313 he was excommunicated: he appealed to Canterbury but this failed: the Bishop asked that Robert, being excommunicate for 40 days, should be arrested by the civil power: in August he is cited to appear to hear his sentence: the rectory is sequestrated and Robert deprived and removed, and a new rector is appointed: the story ends in August 1313 with a mandate to release him from prison, and no more is heard of him.

National records throw light on other aspects of current society. There appeared before the Justices in Eyre in 1221 one Osbert, of Alvechurch, accused of having killed Nicholas of Hagley, and Osbert offered the King one mark, or 13s.4d. to have an enquiry. The result of the enquiry is not given but Walter Beauchamp, Sheriff of Worcester, accounts for the chattels, 5s. of Osbert of Alvechurch, who has been hanged, so that it seems that Osbert would have been wiser to have kept his mark and become an outlaw. In 1224 Walter and Richard de Jerdele (Yardley) were taken as being of ill-repute and for many crimes, and the people of Bremmesgrave,

Norlfeld, Frankele and Auvinchirche said they knew them to be thieves with many robberies and to have stolen cattle and it was held they should be hanged: in the margin is 'Suspensi' so the sentence must have been carried out. In 1257, following a dispute, commissioners were appointed to make a perambulation by oath of the men of Worcestershire between the King's lands at Brimesgrove and the Bishop of Worcester's lands at Alvincherch, and this is done down to the least detail. In 1284 the Justice of the Forest this side of Trent is instructed to send six live bucks and six live does from the Forest of Kanok to stock the Bishop's park at Alvechurch. Eight years later a commission was authorised to determine who had broken into the park, hunted, and carried away deer. During the whole of this period poaching seems to have been rife, despite the heavy penalties that were incurred.

The peak of early medieval prosperity appears to have been reached around 1300, and it is apt that there should be the Bishop's Survey of the manor in the year 1299. The document is essentially fiscal, laying down the duties, with the cash equivalent of each, of every tenant, be he free or servile: it is also concerned with any way that the value of the manor could be augmented. It is unique in its detail - every tenant is named - and making adjustments for the large freeholders who must have had workers to till their holdings, one can make an estimate of the population of the parish. The Survey deals first with the demesne of 536 acres, the land which the Lord of the Manor cultivated direct using full time demesne servants such as carters and overseers, but relying basically on the day by day services of the customary tenants, the villeins, whose duties are laid down in the finest detail: where the villein commuted all or part of his service by a cash payment, then the cultivation of the demesne depended upon the work of paid labourers, of whom there was clearly a pool in the cottars whose holdings were too small to provide a living. After the Lord's demesne come the free tenants - 80 of them in all holding altogether $7\frac{1}{2}$ hides, say 900 acres, but they range from substantial landowners with a whole hide to small cottars with nothing more than a cottage and garden. Then come the customary tenants, the backbone of the manor, with 50 of them holding in all $3\frac{1}{4}$ hides, say 390 acres. Lastly there is a new feature, there are 62 burgesses, all freemen, holding a total of $74\frac{1}{4}$ burgage plots. All the tenants owe service, even if, in the case of the largest freeholders, it is only suit or attendance at the manor court.

Some hold by serjeantry or personal service, such as the keeper of the park, and the smith who had to provide the ironwork for two ploughs and the shoes for two horses. Two smallholdings were held on payment of ½lb of cumin, or 1d. each.

The standard holding of a villein tenant was approximately 15 acres, a half virgate, and for this the regular weekly and seasonal duties are precisely set out, and in addition to these there is a host of other tasks and restrictions - catching the horses in the woods, collecting nuts, helping with the hunt in the park, carrying goods to Worcester, paying toll on the sale of horses and oxen, paying pannage for pigs foraging in the woods for acorns and beech mast, paying toll on ale brewed, attending the Lord's ale feast, guarding prisoners to Worcester, not allowing a daughter to marry or leave the manor without permission - which had to be paid for, and as a final imposition paying a heriot, that is the best beast, to the Lord of the Manor on the death of the tenant. Every one of these labour services and special duties is priced, and to be free of them altogether comes to 12s. 2¾ d. for the year. The impression one receives is that by the time of the Survey most tenants had commuted all or most of their service and that there was a well developed money economy, for the peasant was also required to make quite substantial payments to the church. Some holdings have much lighter obligations, perhaps because they had to clear the forest first, but one cannot over-emphasise the infinite variations in the duties and the cash equivalent of different holdings, variations that are now enshrined in a formal document to which landlord or peasant will look in the future if there is any attempt to meddle with custom.

The arable land lay in open fields, whether on a two field or three field system one cannot tell, but a holding would be spread in a number of selions or single strips scattered over the field, so that each had his share of good and bad land, but this did not make for economic working and all must follow the same crop sequence. The meadow, similarly un-enclosed for most of the year, lay close to the village around the Arrow and its feeders, while the arable fields lay in a large arc from north-west to east. The Bishop's park was fenced and covered the present Alvechurch Lodge, Rowney Lodge and Mill farms: Bordesley Park belonged to the monks; the rector's glebe of over 100 acres lay in one holding around the Old Rectory in Old Rectory Lane, while it seems likely that the lands of the freeholders would be enclosed. There was still waste or common and access to this with the rights of pasturage and gathering fuel were of great use to the smallholders. The peasant on his half virgate was concerned with growing food to feed his family, and with growing sufficient in the way of crops that could be sold to meet his obligations to Lord and Church and pay for anything essential they could not grow themselves. This leaves unanswered the query how the burgesses, 62 of them, each presumably with a family to feed, earned a living. The Survey tells us there was a cook who had a shop, another held the Bishop's oven which all would have to use, and there were by then the two mills, the Bishop's and the Rector's, but for further clues we must look at the names - coupere, couherde, dysshere, faber (ironworker) ferrour (smith), mouner (miller), percaritor (carrier), skinner, tanner, turner, taylor, wodeward: in 1312 we are told that the demesne employed a woman making serfs' pottage. Undoubtedly the welfare of the borough depended very much upon the frequency and duration of the visits to the Palace by the Bishop and his entourage. Their consumption was conspicuously higher than that of the peasant and their needs must have raised the demand for produce for sale and given employment to local craftsmen. We know little about the Palace. It was of timber construction, apart from being moated it had no defences, excavations have shown that there was a building of stone outside the moat to the east, and casual references in Bishop Giffard's Register tell us that there was a chapel and a herb garden.

With so much detail about the inhabitants one is tempted to estimate the total population. The problem arises with the larger freeholders who must have had peasants, villein or free, to work the land, nor is there any mention of men directly employed by the Lord, but allowing for these uncertainties, and employing the generally accepted multiplicand of 4.5, we reach a figure of 1000. This figure was soon to fall drastically after the Black Death which came on top of crop failures: it was not until the second half of the 18th Century that the population would again reach the thousand mark.

HARD TIMES 1300 - 1485

These were troubled times. Four kings, Edward II, Richard II, Henry VI and Edward V were murdered and Richard III was killed in battle, the Hundred Years War and the Wars of the Roses bankrupted the country and decimated the old aristocracy, and the weakness of central government facilitated the rise of over-powerful lords as bastard feudalism flourished. As if this was not enough it is apparent that, either because of a worsening of the climate, or declining yields as newly cultivated land lost its fertility, productivity had already fallen and famine had occurred before the onset of the Black Death in 1348/9, after which things would never be quite the same again.

Alvechurch escaped most of the political troubles since it belonged to the Bishop who did not usually have to take sides in the disputes, whereas lay lords found it very difficult to be on the winning side all the time, and to be on the losing side usually meant the loss of one's head and the forfeiture of the family estates. There are a few occasions when outside events affected the manor and its people. The Bishop had refused to send support to the Scottish expedition of Edward II, and so escaped the disaster of Bannockburn. Much later, in 1486, one of the most important inhabitants, Thomas Porter was in receipt of a royal pardon, for which no doubt he paid dearly. The reason for the pardon is not mentioned, but there is little doubt that it was for appearing at Bosworth Field on the side of Richard III - not surprising, perhaps, as the Sheriff was Sir Humphrey Stafford, one of Richard's staunchest supporters, and it is likely that he took the shire forces to Bosworth. One family that was involved in the quarrels of the early part of the 14th Century was the Blaunfronts, or as they were more usually known, Blanchfronts, and their history is of interest as the effigy of a knight in armour, which lies in the North aisle of the

*Effigy of a Knight in armour, believed to be Sir John Blanchfront:
note the rare breast chain securing his dagger.*

church, comes from this family. Apparently their coat of arms once appeared in the adjoining window, while the experts say it represents Sir John, rather than his father, Sir Thomas. Their main interests lay in Staffordshire but they took over an estate in Alvechurch formerly held by the Norfolk and Warwick families and which was centred on a manor house in a moated site that is still recognisable to the north-east of the present Moor Green Hall. They evidently supported the baronial anti-court party opposed to Edward II and the Despensers as there is reference in 1322 to the lands of Thomas Blaunfront, a late rebel, being in the King's hands, and two years later he is presented as leading an armed band against the King's forces. By 1326 Edward II had been deposed and in 1328 a commission was set up to enquire into Blanchfront's complaint that his house in Alvechurch had been broken into and his goods carried away - presumably during the time when he was a rebel. He is evidently in favour in 1329 when there is a 'Grant by special grace' of the right of free warren over his lands - the right to keep coneys etc. Royal favour must have gone to his head because next year there is a complaint by the Bishop that Thomas and others carried away his corn and assaulted his servants. It is tantalising that they do not appear again in the national records. The effigy in the church has been dated probably to the 1340s and is exceptional as being one of only a handful that shows the knight wearing a breast chain from which a dagger would be hung. National records of this time contain many complaints of park-breaking and poaching and of commissions of oyer and terminer being appointed to trace the culprits: in 1359 the Prior of Worcester excommunicated the evil doers, unknown, who, with bows and arrows, entered the manors of the Bishop, including Alvechurch, and took rabbits and fish from the ponds - which seems a rather ineffectual action.

The Bishop was a major landholder, tenant-in-chief of the King, equivalent indeed to an earl, and in addition to his spiritual responsibilities he was a feudal lord with the customary duties to the King, such as providing knight service. Several entries in national and local records evidence this. In 1340 the Patent Rolls are rectifying a transfer of land by the Bishop where he had failed to obtain the King's prior approval. Feudal dues are paid according to custom, and two are worthy of mention - payments of £4, at the rate of £2 per Knight's Fee for the two Fees at which Alvechurch was rated for the Knighting of the King's eldest son, in 1347 for the

Black Prince, and in 1401 for Prince Harry, the future Henry V.

During the first half of the 14th Century it seems that there was above average rainfall and cooler weather - there was certainly a series of poor harvests - and for peasants on a subsistence economy and living from hand to mouth, and at a time when poor transport facilities made it difficult to transfer a surplus in one region to a shortage in another, such a pattern of events could be disastrous. The result was that when the Black Death struck it hit a people already weakened by famine and with poor resistance to disease. It was in 1349 that the peak of the infection was reached in Worcestershire, but the disease kept returning at intervals over the next 50 or 60 years, so that recovery was painfully slow. It has been said that over the whole country 35 to 40% of the population died in the first onslaught: in Alvechurch, from available records, Professor Dyer has estimated that the loss amounted to 43%. When the Bishopric was void on the death of a Bishop and before the appointment of a successor the income from the estate went to the King, and the Royal Accounts show that in the Michaelmas Quarter of 1349 the total receipts from the manor were 17s. 2$\frac{1}{2}$d. and this from an estate normally fetching £50 per annum.

The early years of the Hundred Years War had been very profitable to some of the aristocracy and their followers, but as it dragged on and became less successful new taxation had to be raised to finance it and the first Poll Tax was levied in 1377. This was at the rate of a groat - 4d - per head, a not inconsiderable sum when a labourer's daily wage was 2d. per day, and was paid by all over the age of 14 and not in a state of poverty. The returns for this tax for the Hundred of Oswaldslow to which Alvechurch belonged are in the Public Record Office, and, on a tiny slip of paper, held by string to the rest of the Hundred is the record 'VI 1. VII s. 11d. p'ochia de Alvechurch'. £6. 7s. 11d. does not exactly divide into fourpenny units but the amount remitted would be after collection expenses and there was always confusion when money could be estimated either by telling, that is counting, or by weight. The tax is important in that it offers an opportunity to make some estimate of the population of the parish. On the face of it there are therefore 384 payers, but if collection expenses were no more than 10% the total is raised to 422. If it is assumed that the paupers and those under 14 amount to one third of the total, then we reach a figure of 630, which should be compared with the estimate of 1000 in 1299. What is certain is that there were many empty holdings, duties owed by villeins could not be enforced and henceforth they are copyholders paying a cash rent for their holdings - their title is a copy of the manorial roll, their rent remains that fixed in the 1299 Survey, they hold for 'three lives', and fines, based on the level of current rents have to be paid when a 'new life' is inserted. Although the Poll Tax is said to have sparked the Peasants' Revolt of 1381 there is no suggestion of trouble in Alvechurch.

It is apparent that the well-being of the borough depended very much upon successive Bishops using the Palace. The evidence comes from the Bishops' Registers which normally recite where a document was signed or sealed, and it does seem that after the death of Bishop Giffard in 1302 there were long periods when the Palace was little used until we come to the time of Polton, 1426. From then to the death of Carpenter in 1477 the bishops were more frequent visitors and the parish church was used for ordinations and enquiries. After 1477 the house must have fallen into disuse and Leland writing in the 1540s says that the palace was lately in decay but that the Bishop Latimer repaired it.

More Diocesan records have survived from this period and the accounts of the Receiver General in the 1420s show that the manor was yielding between £72 and £75 per annum, the amount varying with the receipt of fines, sale of timber and the number of empty holdings. From this total there stood to be deducted the fee of the Bishop's bailiff £2. 13s. 4d. and a gown - a fee that was, like the rents themselves, to remain unchanged as long as the manor survived. With the Palace no longer used there was no need for a park and its deer, and the park was let for grazing, a tenancy that soon included the Palace itself, and the whole fetched £8 per annum, a figure that again would never be increased. In addition to the land comprising the old villein holdings now held by copy, other lands, some of which were probably the former demesne, were let on lease. One of these leases, to John Vele and his wife, of land in what was later to be Radford Farm, for 10s. per annum, is noteworthy in that the covenants might have come from a modern farm lease - to maintain hedges and ditches, to employ proper cultivation, not to sublet, and the landlord has the right to re-enter on non payment of rent or failure to observe the covenants.

Turning now to the church, the main event of the 14th Century was the rebuilding of the North aisle. The outside walls stand much as they did five hundred years ago although the windows have been altered and the aisle itself is now approximately four feet narrower than it was originally, as the Victorians when they rebuilt the church widened the nave at the expense of the aisle. They are also responsible for masking the lower part of the fine reticulated window at the east end of the aisle when they added the heating chamber. There is no documentary evidence to date the rebuild, but it may be significant that Bishop Orleton in 1330 ordered the Dean of Wych to report on dilapidation's of the chancel. What does help to date the aisle is the recess in which the Blanchfront knight lies: the double centred or ogee arch and its decoration date it to prior to the Black Death. Other features that belong to this period and were later re-incorporated in the church in 1860 are the fine sedilia or seats for the priests, in the south wall of the chancel, and the smaller recess that lies to the west of the sedilia. It appears to be an Easter Sepulchre, but that should traditionally be on the north wall, and so it is likely to have been a tomb that has disappeared or which was never used. Another mystery is presented by the tombstone of a priest that lies on the floor on the north side of the chancel: it depicts a chalice, so that it relates to a priest and it bears the coat of arms of Bishop Carpenter which would suggest that it was his tomb, were it not that there is ample evidence that he is buried at Westbury and there is a very full account of his funeral there. Until they were removed after the Reformation all churches had a rood screen dividing the chancel from the nave, on which were depicted the Saviour on the cross flanked by the Virgin and St. John. Writing in the 1820s the Worcester historian Prattinton tells us that the ancient rood screen at Alvechurch was re-used to form the front of the gallery that in his day ran across the west end of the nave: the present choir screen, with the over-painted panels that originally would have shown saints and fathers of the church, was clearly part of this rood and choir screen and is very fine work of this period. The most noticeable development of the 15th Century was undoubtedly the building of the tower. Its dating is on architectural evidence only, and despite having to be largely rebuilt after damage caused by the great gale of 1661, it looks much as it did when it was built, the only real difference being the balustrades that replace the earlier battlements.

The Bishops' registers now give a fairly complete list of rectors - there are one or two lacunae - but none of the names calls for special mention. One feature, especially of the 14th Century, is the extent that incumbents were involved in an exchange of livings - whether to move to a more convenient or salubrious spot or whether for pecuniary advantage it is hard to say. What is clear is that most of the rectors were absentees, and that the living, which was a valuable one, was used to pay diocesan officials, and in one case a Vice-chancellor of Oxford University, and that the cure of souls was covered by the employment of a curate at a fraction of the income from the rectory. Another development is the extension of papal provision. Although the right to present to the living lay with the Bishop there is increasing use of the Pope providing the next incumbent, i.e. making the appointment, and the Register of 1st July 1331 appointing John of Hereford to Alvechurch contains a full recital of the letters patent issued by Pope John XXII from Avignon where the popes were in exile. John of Hereford was one of the rectors who exchanged benefices freely. He had resigned Ripple on collation to Alvechurch, and in October 1332 exchanged Alvechurch for Hasleton and then exchanged Hasleton for Winterbourne in Gloucestershire, the object probably being to have a parish as close as possible to Oxford, where he was a lecturer, and which he probably never left. Priests with a living are at this time normally called either 'dominus' or 'magister'; the latter implies that he was a university graduate, and most of these can be traced and their careers followed in the printed Alumni of Oxford and Cambridge.

LIFE UNDER THE TUDORS
1485 - 1603

T he accession of Henry VII in 1485 is often taken as marking the end of the Middle Ages and the beginning of the Renaissance in England. Certainly, in the small cosmos of the village the importance of the medieval manor and its institutions now begins to diminish and the powers of the parish, as exercised through the vestry, increase, so that by the end of Elizabeth's reign the parish and its officers are paramount in local government, and especially in the administration of the Poor Law and the upkeep of the roads. The information available to us is greatly increased - the Manor Court Rolls are almost complete from 1523, the earliest wills are dated 1544, and from 1545 we have the Parish Registers which are complete until 1837, except for a gap of seven months in 1586/7 when 'this booke was negletted to be kept orderlye in the tyme of Rychard Carter, his clerkeshippe.' The manor still belonged to the Bishop of Worcester, but more than ever it was now only a source of income, no longer did bishops come to stay in the Palace - indeed the house and the park continued to be let on lease - and the borough continued in obscurity, starved of the trade that resident bishops had brought. Alvechurch's decline as a residence is mirrored in a note of 1577 which tells us that the bishops stayed in their Palace in Worcester from November to April, at Grimley from then to June, and finally, at Hartlebury all summer: it then goes on to say that 'in Allchurch there is wood sufficient to make charr coale for all his howses.' One lessee of the Palace and Park was Philip Chatwyn whose brass memorial is still to be seen in the church. Later, Bishop Heath in 1543 granted a lease to his brother

William. The Heaths remained true to the Roman doctrine and Dorothy, William's widow, suffered severe financial penalties as a recusant, that is refusing to attend the parish church, and was in 1595 at the centre of the martyrdom of a Catholic priest.

The Court Rolls are a mine of the most detailed information regarding the people and their lives. They are the proceedings of the 'Court Leet and Baron and View of Frankpledge' and they met twice a year. The View of Frankpledge is a relic of the arrangement whereby everyone had to be a member of a tithing and each tithing was responsible for the deeds of its members, but by now it related to minor criminal jurisdiction, normally reserved for the Hundred Court, but which had long ago been delegated by the King to the Bishop in the Hundred of Oswaldslow. There are in fact two Courts, one for the Borough and one for the Foreign, though they are held in the same day under the same Steward. All the homage - holders of free or customary land who owe suit at court - are required to attend, and those without essoins, legitimate excuses, are fined 2d. or 4d. The Jury is then named from the freeholders of the manor and its function is not to reach a verdict on the basis of the evidence placed before it, but to present to the Steward crimes, misdemeanours and any matters affecting the land, such as the death of a copyholder, the heriot payable on his death, who is the next heir and whether there is a widow with right of freebench. In this first Roll for the Borough the Ale tasters present a number who have brewed and broken the Assize and they are each fined 2d: one man did not send beer for tasting and is fined 2d: two who keep inns and brew excessively are each fined 2d: butchers who sell meat too dearly are fined 2d: as is the miller who takes excessive toll: there is only one misdemeanour, a hedgebreaker, who is fined 4d. Two ale tasters are elected for the ensuing year, the Bailiff is nominated and the Assize of Beer is fixed at 1d. per gallon and 1½d. per gallon for old beer. The Foreign, with its own homage and Jury, similarly present brewers and, in this case, the rector's miller for taking excessive toll: it orders the repair of a gate under penalty if it is not repaired by a certain date: it orders a tenant overstocking his land to rectify the matter: it orders that hedges enclosing the common pasture should be removed: it fixes the Assize of beer at 1½d. per gallon and it elects the Constable who is to serve the whole manor. The Tudor period is one where inflation is said to have been a serious problem and we see that by 1575 ordinary beer is fixed at 2d. and old beer at

3d. a gallon - a very modest increase in the light of inflation in recent years. Gradually the Courts build up a series of by-laws, which are repeated year after year - pigs are to be ringed, miskins (middens) removed from the streets, mounds between houses in the borough are to be kept up, marl must not be taken from the highway, and so on. Some items, taken at random, give the flavour of the sort of matter with which the Courts were concerned:

- the forfeiture of the chattels of a person convicted of felony;
- the heriot due from a holding - custom had established many 'silver' heriots in lieu of the best beast;
- a shop has been built obstructing the highway and is to be removed;
- there are many presentments of roads in need of repair;
- Edward Tursey, clerk, fought with Hugh Prine, chaplain (Prine had been the chantry priest and later became the curate);
- the tanneworks in the common road are to be removed under penalty of 5s.
- the borough is lacking archery butts, a pillary, and a cokynstole (ducking stool): although the rolls are in Latin, words such as these are in English;
- leather sealers, who stamped leather to show duty had been paid, are added to the elected officers in 1580;
- there is evidence of the exchange of selions or strips of land in the open field in both customary and free land - to create more manageable holdings.

The Subsidy Roll of 1523 lists the names of the 43 individuals who were sufficiently wealthy to have to pay the tax and the man at the head of the list is Philip Chatwyn who held the lease of the Park and the Palace. The 1576 Roll has also survived, but now there are five who pay on land and eleven who pay on chattels: this list is headed by the Lewkners who will later endow the Lewkner Hospital. The Muster Roll for the shire levies for 1539 shows that Alvechurch was responsible for finding 45 able-bodied men, archers and pikemen, while seven 'impotent' men provided harness, i.e. arms and armour, only.

This was a time of great religious changes - from Roman Catholicism, by fits and starts to the Elizabethan settlement, with an English liturgy and the Sovereign as Supreme Head on Earth of the Church of England. Furnishings that had been there for centuries were removed or destroyed - statues, wall paintings, stained glass windows, and, of course, the great rood screens, although in our case we know that the screen was retained and used. Bishop Bell - he had been an absentee Rector prior to his appointment as Bishop - held a Visitation of his Diocese, and we learn from this for the first time that there was in the church, and apparently in the North aisle, a chantry to the Blessed Virgin, that Hugh Prynne was the stipendiary chaplain, receiving his salary from Thomas Milward and William Hodges, who were guardians of the chantry lands. Although the Bishop's licence was needed to establish a chantry, and the King's licence to hold the land, there is no trace of either authority. The Survey of Chantry Lands of 1548 revealed that they were worth £5. 2s. 8d. per annum: the lands were sold and the chantry suppressed, but Hugh Prynne received an annual pension of £4 and continued to live in the village, being described as curate. This same Survey reports that there were 400 communicants in the parish, that the church had no silver plate or goods, that there was no preacher and no school. This was wrong in at least one respect. Four years later it was enacted that all church silver should be collected and sold, and the return for Worcestershire shows that one paten and one flagon came from Alvechurch. As far as the church was concerned this was a period of destruction rather than building, but there is one monument, the brass to Philip Chatwyn, that belongs to this time. The brass originally lay on the floor of the chancel but was moved to its present location in the blocked up north door in the North aisle. Chatwyn has already come to notice as holding the lease of the park etc., and of being the richest man: his memorial tells us that he had been a Gentleman Usher to Henry VIII, and national records show that he had been a petty captain in his brother's contingent in the Earl of Shrewsbury's forces at the Battle of the Spurs when the French were routed in 1513.

The oldest extant wills - all proved by the Rector within his peculiar jurisdiction - are dated 1544, and from this date on, and especially when there is an accompanying inventory, they are a mine of information. Thomas Schallowe made his will because he is 'intendyng to do my prince grace service towards France or els

[facsimile of manuscript text in medieval Latin script]

"Alvechurch. Sir Henry Furnivall curate there receives his stipend through Master Robert Cowper Rector there.
Sir Hugh Prynne Stipendiary there receives his stipend through Thomas Milward and William Hodges guardians of chantry of the Blessed Mary there."

Extract from Bishop Bell's Visitation Book: this is the first reference to the Chantry dedicated to the Virgin that was situated in the North Aisle.

where at hys graces pleasure and his most honorable councell': we have no indication of what the service was, but England was then at war with France. These wills date before the Reformation had been fully established and almost always start with gifts, usually of 4d. to the church for the high altar and for the 'light', that is the lamp over the pyx. They then usually dispose of household goods, personal clothing and farming stock down to the smallest detail. Thus we have a velvett nyght cappe, quylltyd doublett, peyrs of black hose, jerkyn, gowne, cote, the better of two wenynge calves, a bryndyd heyfer, the best cowe, and so on. Many wills are accompanied by an inventory. Thus Harry Handye who died in 1551 owned an old bras bane, a chafying dysshe, a table burde, a forme, 2 trestells, a coffer, a peyre of potthangles, a hatchett, and he had a cowe, a mare and 16 sheepe: the whole was valued at £7. 15s. 7d. It is apparent that living standards improved over this period. Writing in 1580 an observer quotes his grandfather as saying that the three great improvements he had seen during his lifetime had been the installation of a chimney to replace the smoke-hole in the roof, the introduction of bedsteads and mattresses in place of straw paillasses, and the general use of pewter to replace wood for domestic utensils. The elimination of the smoke hole made it possible for the lofty medieval hall to be divided into a ground and first floor, for greater comfort and privacy, and it also encouraged the siting of the kitchen in the house, rather than in a separate building outside. Many hall houses were thus divided, often extended, and sometimes entirely rebuilt during the high days of the Elizabethan age.

The extent of the improvement in the circumstances of the ordinary people is shown in the inventory accompanying the will of Humphrey Bryan, a labourer, in 1591. In the hall there were a table board and frame, a large board, bencher, 2 chair stools, cupboard, 2 brass pans, 3 cauldrons, 4 brass pots, 3 shelves, a spinning wheel, fire shovel, a pair of pot hangers, 12 pieces of pewter, 2 basins, 2 candlesticks, a skimmer, 4 saucers a brass posnet (small dish with feet), a weting pot, 2 strikes (bushell measures), a form, a stool, a board and two salt cellars. In the chamber were a feather bed, 2 twillies (woollen cloth), a flock bed, a covering, a bolster, 2 other twillies, 3 blankets, another cover, a great coffer, 6 pairs of hempen sheets, a table board cloth, a towel, 6 napkins, 2 other coffers and a painted cloth. The kitchen, which also contains farm tools, follows, and in the barn, in addition to oats and hay,

Will of Rycharde Levet 1544. Probate granted 13 March 1544/5

"In Nomine Dei Amen. In the yere of owre Lorde 1544 and in the yere of owre soverayne lorde kinge Henry the eight immediatelye under God supreme hedd of the churches of Englande and also of Irelande the 36th I Rycharde Levet of Alchurch within the countye of Worcester hole and perfect of mynde and syck and dyseasyd of my body make thys my last wyll and testament yn manner and forme as followythe Fyrst Y bequethe my soule unto Almyghtye God to owre Ladye Saynte Marye and to all the holye companye of hevin and my bodye to be buryed within the parryshe churche yerd of Alchurch   Item Y bequethe unto the hygh alter there 4d.   Item Y bequethe unto the torche light 12d.   Item Y bequethe to Sir Hugh Prinn 12d.   Item Y bequethe unto Margery Hodge 6/8d   Item Y bequethe to Elyzabeth Hodge the better of two wenynge calves Item..."

This is a typical will of the period in making provision for the high altar and for the light that perpetually shone over the pyx.

he has 4 cows, 2 heifers, a calf, a bacon hog, 2 pigs and 20 little cheeses, and the whole is valued at £18. 5s. 4d. and displays a relative affluence that will not be equalled by a man described as labourer for very many years. Edward Knightley in 1570 left his brother his 'cross bowe and backe' (armour), and to his son in law 'my sword and my dagger and my shirte of maile.' Margaret Butler, clearly a well-to-do spinster disposed of four silver spoons, two gold rings, and her 'best gown, white kirtle, second best gown, petticoat, French hood, blue gown and best caule.'

Thomas Cromwell, who was appointed Vicar General of the English church, ordered that every parish should be furnished with a parish chest, controlled by the incumbent and the two churchwardens, and should keep a Register of Baptisms, Marriages and Burials. There are two very old wooden chests in the ringing chamber of the church tower, and one presumes that one of these is the original. As for the Register, the entries for Alvechurch commence in 1545 and were in the first place on loose sheets, but in 1598 it was ordered that they be kept in parchment books and the first Register states 'This parchment booke was bought for the parish of Alvechurch at London anno 1600 by Mr. William Thornhill then parson there and the parish payed for it 26 shillings.' The following are a few of the more unusual entries:

1575   Baptised the daughter of James Valentyne and Elizabeth, vagaraunt Egyptians.

1580   Buried Nicholas Lewcknor, Gent. (Founder of the Almshouses).

1582   Buried Peeter Farmer, Raulfs his son, Joane his wife, dyed of plague.

1601   Buried John Ghest de Hopwood being of the age of one hundred and VI years.

1601   Buried Thomas Acton, quelled in a sand pytte in Rouwneywood.

Poverty and vagrancy are evidenced in the list of burials: a poore boye found dead this morning in a barowe of Thomas Porter's: a poore woman's child that went a beginge: a poore walking man which was not knowne: a poore wanring boye: son of Owen, a straglinge beggar. There are baptisms of children born out of wedlock - few as compared with today - but the description shows many variants '- patre incerto, born of his concubine, pellicis illis, illegitime nata, popule patre, si quidem lege anglicana patrem habuit populum, ex fornicatione genitus, illegitimus conceptus ac natus, filia populi,' as well as the straightforward 'born out of wedlock.'

We have a full list of Rectors, any gaps in the Bishop's Registers being made good from the Crown Receipt of First Fruits after the Reformation. They show the same pattern continuing, the rectory being held by a high church officer who is both an absentee and a pluralist. Thus John Lane was Principal of St. Alban's Hall, Oxford: Thomas Hannibal was Canon of York, Vicar General of Worcester, and Ambassador to the Holy See before resigning Alvechurch when he became Master of the Rolls: John Bell was Chancellor of Oxford before becoming Bishop of Worcester, when he resigned Alvechurch: Thomas Bagarde was Canon of Wolsey's new College of Christchurch, Oxford: William Thornhill was Canon of Worcester, and lived in the Cathedral Close. The parish church was served by a succession of curates, poorly paid, but responsible for the cure of souls.

The Elizabethan settlement of the Church was intended to be sufficiently broad to accommodate all consciences, from extreme Protestants to Catholics, and questions were not asked as long as there was outward conformity, but all was changed in 1570 when the Papal Bull was issued deposing Elizabeth and approving rebellion in favour of Mary Queen of Scots, who was said to be the rightful Queen, and thus compelling Catholics to choose between Queen and Pope. The adjoining parish of Beoley was a hotbed of Catholicism centred round the Sheldon family, but the only prominent recusant here was Dorothy, widow of William Heath, the brother of the former bishop, and she continued to hold the lease of the Palace and Park. She suffered severely financially for her adherence to the old faith, but worse, was involved in a great tragedy. She sheltered a priest, known as William Freeman, a Yorkshireman who had been trained at Reims, and who came to England in 1589. Ostensibly a serving man, he was tutor to her son, and, no doubt conducted services for local Catholics. He was betrayed by William Combes, whom the Heaths had befriended, and by Dr. Boardman, a former Rector of this parish, but by then Vicar of Warwick. The house was searched, but Freeman was away; unaware of what was happening, and not warned by any of the villagers, he returned to Alvechurch and was arrested on the road outside the Palace. He was taken to Warwick Gaol and tried:

the conclusion was inevitable and on the 13th of August 1595 he was hanged drawn and quartered at Warwick, in accordance with the barbarous laws of the day.

One institution that still exists dates from the Elizabethan age - the Lewkner Hospital, or Almshouses as they were more commonly known: now that there is no element of alms they are simply the Lewkner Houses. How and why the Lewkners came to Alvechurch is not clear as the family comes from Oxfordshire, but it is likely that they 'married into' the village through an heiress. Be that as it may, we know that Thomas Lewkner, the father, bought the former lands of the chantry and that he and Nicholas his son were well-connected locally. Nicholas died in 1580 having made his will some ten days earlier, and in it he charged his manor of Hadzor with a perpetual rent charge of 100 marks, that is £66. 13s. 4d., for the maintenance of almshouses in Alvechurch to accommodate twelve inmates, and he also gave a house and two acres of land on which the almshouses were to be built. There were problems in carrying out the will - it was claimed that Hadzor could not stand so heavy a rent charge, and in any case as it was held in chief of the crown the charge could not be valid as it stood, but the matter was resolved by the issue of Letters Patent by the Queen in 1588 and by these the Hospital was to consist of a Master six men and two women: the existing house was divided into two, and seven more erected, to give the total of nine dwellings. The date of completion is unknown, but the Parish Register records the burial of one 'Margaret Prettie, of the Almshouses' in 1598. The owners of the Hadzor estate attempted to divest themselves of the rent charge and especially of the responsibility for repairs, but they did not succeed and it was only in 1884 that it was commuted for a cash payment that was invested in Government funds. As for the houses themselves, it was evident that they must have been rebuilt or substantially altered some time in the late 18th or early 19th Century, but their state was such that they were demolished, and new houses built in 1980, on a site farther back from Station Road, and this was done under the aegis of a Housing Association: there is no longer any question of free accommodation or of a weekly dole since the tenants are required to pay a full rent. There is an interesting connection with the Lewkners in the inclusion in the stained glass window in the west window of the tower that was erected by public subscription to mark Queen Victoria's Jubilee of the family coat of arms.

The Lewkner Hospital was founded by the will of Nicholas Lewkner who died in 1580: this shows the almshouses before their demolition and rebuilding in 1980.

THE STUARTS 1603 - 1714

This period saw great constitutional change. It commenced with the personal rule of James I and Charles I, when years went by without a Parliament being called, through the Civil Wars and the Commonwealth to the Restoration of the 'Merry Monarch' Charles II and then his brother James II, the flight of James in the Glorious Revolution of 1688 which brought in Dutch William and Mary, and then the last of the Stuart line, Queen Anne, who died in 1714. By this time the constitutional monarchy was firmly established. Generally speaking it was a period of improving living standards, though this was mainly seen amongst the upper and middle classes, and the lot of the poor, and particularly of the agricultural labourer, worsened. The parish continued to be predominantly agricultural, with by far the greatest part of the population dependent upon farming; the average holding is modest, as far as possible self-sufficiency is the rule, and, even where an individual has a trade, such as carpenter or smith, he usually has a small holding to supply a proportion of the needs of himself and his family.

Our knowledge of life in the parish is much wider by reason of the so-called Bailiff's Book which runs from 1603 to the 19th Century and which contains the accounts of the Churchwardens and other parish officers, as well as additional casual but interesting information. There is also an Estate Map of 1701, which covers not only the Park, its main object, but the centre of the village as well. On the face of it there is little change in the manor: the arable land is still largely cultivated by the medieval open field system, with individuals holding one or more selions each a furlong long, and the strips are often spread across different fields. Indeed, this strip cultivation was to survive at least to 1791, though gradually there was some merging and exchange to achieve holdings that could be worked more economically, and

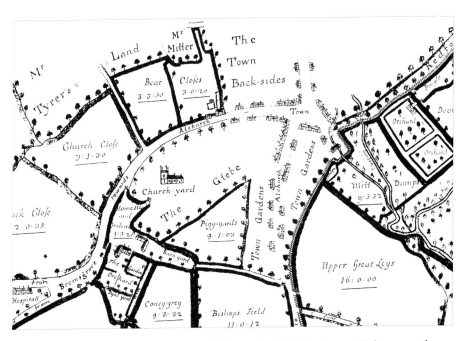

The map of the lands of James Booth drawn in 1701 by James Fish covers the former Park, and also the centre of the village. The church, the Lewkner Hospital, and the houses are depicted in elevations and appear to reflect their actual appearance.

though there is no formal enclosure Act of Parliament there was undoubtedly more enclosure of the common or waste. The rental of the manor improved from £58 to £78 between 1582 and 1603 'because the herbage of Rowney Wood is let and waste has been newly enclosed.' Illegal encroachment of the common or waste was always happening, as is clear from the manor court proceedings, and this was especially the case during the Commonwealth period. After the Restoration in 1663, and in subsequent years, there are many injunctions to individuals to pull down their cottages and fences on the waste: the orders are repeated year after year, notwithstanding the penalties, and one suspects that in the end the cottages remained and the Steward accepted a small rent in acknowledgement. There is also evidence of enclosure on a much wider scale. In 1704 it was reported that a considerable area of what had been common waste, lying between the Beoley boundary and Weatheroak and centred on Rowney Green, i.e. the present Seechems Farm, had been encroached upon and enclosed, originally by Thomas Milward during the Commonwealth as he had been a Justice and a 'great man in those times', and had erected gates and enclosed old common land, and the process had been continued by the next owner, James Booth, until almost all had been enclosed. It was by such enclosure, with the consequent loss of free grazing and firewood, that the farm labourer, and more so the day labourer, were slowly reduced to pauperism.

The episcopal system was abolished by Cromwell and the Bishop's lands were confiscated by Parliament. Prior to being offered for sale a Survey was undertaken in 1647, and in its detail it is second only to the Survey of 1299 in the way it provides a picture of the manor, and hence of the parish. There is a perambulation and the boundaries are hardly changed from medieval days. Then we have the tenants by indenture, by custom, by lease, or by burgage holding, with the payment due from them. The total receipts from the tenants are £76. 19s. 8d. and from this there now stands to be deducted £10. 13s. 4d., made up as to £2. 13s. 4d., the Bailiff's fee £1. 10s. to the Bailiff for 8 loads of firewood etc. due to him, £1. 10s. for the repair of the mill, £1 for the repair of Court Bridge and Radford Bridge, £2, the Steward's Fee for holding the Court, and £2. for the Leet Dinner, twice a year. Both the Park and the Mill were sold for £990 and £451 respectively, but the property was recovered by the Bishop after the Restoration. The Survey also recites the Customs of the Manor, the customs that the homage and the jury of the court had to interpret. The main elements of the Customs are:

1. It hath bin longe and antiently the custome for the coppie holders to take what tymber they have need of from off their coppie hold landes and tenements without assignment for houseboote heyboote carteboote ploweboote and fireboote and to sell cropps and lopps and underwoode from off the same without licence from the Lord.

2. According to the custome of this manor there is a herriott in kind viz the best beast or goodes of the deceased due upon the death of every coppie holder dying seized if it be not expressed or referred otherwise in their coppies. And every widowe of a coppie holder marrrying ought to pay a herriott but the freeholders doe pay only a reliefe upon death and nothing upon alienation. But there is neither herriott nor reliefe due to the Lorde for any land within the liberty of the borough.

5. The coppie holders and other tenants there have the benefitt of common of pasture in all the commons and wastes within the mannor and common of estover (taking wood) upon the same as belonging to their several messuages and tenements only the trees growing on the waste doe belonge to the Lorde And that the coppie holders only may digg marle upon their own coppie hold lands without licence.

6. The antient custome within the said mannor hath bene that the coppie holders have had their estates graunted unto them by coppy of Court Roll sibi and suis in the nature of inheritance and upon reasonable fines. As appears by severall antient coppies produced dated in the Raigne of Edward 6 and Philip and Mary and the antient Court Rolls remayning amongst the late Byshopps Evidence.

7. The Lords of the Mannor have there a Court Leet usually kept at twoe severall tymes in the yeare as the lawe directs, and a Court Baron which they may keep one every three weeks And the Lords have all the Perquisites of Court there and all Royalties belonging to a manor, and deodands (any animal or object that caused a death is seized by the Bishop) and other things granted by Charter to the precedent Bishopps within their severall mannors.

The Survey then goes on:

> There is a fair in the town once in the year upon the tenth day of
> August (Saint Laurence Day) where toll is paid for horses but the same
> toll is claimed and taken by the Baylife of the borough within the town
> for the time being to his own use and dynes the Jury of the Borough at
> every leet from the profit of the same. The site of the mannor is within
> the park, antiently the place of the Bishop's abode but now very ruinous
> by the violence and spoil of soldiers and partly by the negligence of the
> tenant - stabling and outhouses are fallen down and the rest of the
> building is not fit for habitation yet is very large - 70 feet in length and
> 30 feet in breadth, and the park has long been disparked and divided into
> several closes, and timber trees are very few not sufficient to repair the
> buildings.

As the Parliamentary Survey tells us, the Manor Court continues to meet at intervals,
but, gradually, its business becomes more and more restricted to copy-hold land
transactions and the issue of local bye-laws, a movement that receives added impulse
during the Commonwealth. The Justices of the Peace, individually and in Quarter
Sessions, deal with misdemeanours and minor criminal matters that had been in the
jurisdiction of the Court Leet, while the vestry became the authority for
administrative matters. However, there is still plenty of interest in their proceedings:

1603   John Morris, in contempt of the King, assaulted made an affray and fought
        with a pistol against William Underhill, Constable: fined 26s. 8d.

        John Morris and Tristram Lett made an affray against the peace and Morris
        gravely wounded Lett with a pistol and caused an effusion of blood: sent to
        the Assizes.

1608   William Mason, Hugh Blick, alias Wood, John Liddiatt and Roger
        Sommerfield are night walkers in disturbance of the peace: each fined 12d.

1609   Three individuals are ordered to clear their dunghills from the street.

1613   The inhabitants are deficient in bows and arrows.

1613   Thomas Taylor is presented for selling bad meat.

1616   John Milward took marl from the King's Highway.

1619   Thomas Veale is a night walker and of ill fame.

1640   No inhabitants of the manor shall cut 'anglice fearne' until St. Lawrence Day. (Court proceedings are still recorded in Latin, and will be for many years, but where the Latin word is unknown, resort is made to English).

1664   Five individuals are presented for building cottages on the waste.

        John Field is presented for failing to scour his drains so obstructing Eggle Street (Icknield Street) towards Beoley.

1673   A penalty is laid on those pasturing beasts other than their own on the waste.

1676   Hoebrook Bridge is in need of repair. (This is the bridge over the brook by the Baptist Church in Red Lion Street).

1691   There is a list of tenants of the manor, in Latin. There are now 122 tenancies yielding £69. 8s. 11d. Two tenancies raise an unsolved problem. Simon Degg held a house in Weatheroak Hill once belonging to William and Edward Moor, formerly, as they say, a parcel of the land of the Green Knight. The other holding is by Humphrey Moor of land formerly Richard Whiam, and again, as they say, once of the Green Knight. There does not seem to be any other reference to the Green Knight, or Knight of the Green other than a much later doggerel poem, but there is evidently some old tradition relating to the Blanchfronts.

1708   Eleanour Dunn bakes bread to sell within the borough it being 5lb 3oz in a sixpenny loaf and very coarse, it being 12oz lighter than our town's bakers' bread, and has been sufficiently warned: fined 10s.

1709   The bridge at Lea House is out of repair and by a majority of voices the repair falls on the parish.

1710   A penalty of 40s. on Jonathan Haynes one of the Overseers of the Highways sufficiently to repair Ecklestreete Way (Icknield Street) leading from Weatheroak Hill towards Beoley before Christmas next and to bring in the tenants of Bordesley Park to restore the same.

By this time the old Hundred Court is moribund and it is the Quarter Sessions that takes the leading role in administration as well as in the discharge of criminal justice. Cases where the death penalty could apply - and these include theft of goods worth more than a shilling - are sent to the Assizes, and many of the matters dealt with by Sessions are relatively trivial in our eyes. People from Alvechurch appear before Sessions for evading the muster, for fathering a bastard child, for assault, theft, non-attendance at church, and the parish is assessed to pay 5s. towards sufferers of the plague in Redditch. There are two cases which illustrate class distinctions of the day. In 1612 a number were indicted for shooting sparrows with a hand gun loaded with powder and hail shot, and in 1619 William Lett was indicted for using a fowling piece to shoot at pigeons on the church roof: by a statute of Edward VI it was illegal to shoot with a gun charged with hail shot, and it was also illegal for anyone other than a Lord in Parliament or one of similar rank, or their servant, to shoot at certain birds, including house doves. The Quarter Sessions item that is most frequently quoted is in 1642 when the Constable laid complaints of immorality against the Rector, William Hollington, and the gravamen of this will be dealt with later.

What is unique to Alvechurch and of great value historically is the so-called Bailiff's Book, in which, from 1603, there are recorded the Churchwardens' Accounts and those of the other parish officers, Overseers of the Poor, Constable and his deputy, the Thirdborough, and the Overseers or Surveyors of the Highways. In most cases the accounts are in summary form, but occasionally contain full details of receipts and outgoings: they are scrutinised, with or without comment and sometimes after expenditure is disallowed, at the Easter Vestry meeting when the Parish Officers are elected for the ensuing year. Expenditure was financed by levy on all householders, not paupers, and based upon a historic valuation that became unfair as land usage changed: each officer raised a separate levy, often in a number of instalments, and the officers changed each year, so that arrears and confusion often reigned. The Book was also used as a place for permanent record, and contains details of the Lewkner Hospital, the lands held for the Free Grammar School, charitable gifts to the poor etc. A flavour of the earlier years can be obtained from 1629 when the total expenditure of the Churchwardens came to £7. 3s. 4d. which included £2. 13s. for a Bible (almost certainly the 1616 Edition still in the Church), £1. 17s. for 71½ gallons of muscadin wine from The Lamb in Birmingham for Easter, and 1s. for liquor for the bells. The 1636 accounts reflect the changes introduced by Archbishop Laud - 'sawying the tymber and carrying the pillars from Lea End to the church 10s. 4d.: Thomas Newnham had for rayling of the Comunion table 15s.: John Moore for hynges 2s. 6d.: for carridge of tymber for the Comunion table 1s.: For certifying the Courte about the comunion table that it was done -.' Other expenditure for that year includes '6d. to destroyers of noysome foule and vermine: for a fox head - : for destroying of urchings 1s.: and for washing the surplis and for licker for the bells 3s.' That year the Churchwarden's expenditure totalled £8. 11s. 3d., that of the Overseers of the Poor £33. 14s. 2d. and that of the Constable £12. 6s., but the vestry meeting disallowed some of the Constable's expenditure, namely '1s. 4d. the drom Maiaers pencon, 2s. paid to John Glover for giving the watch and 2s. 5d. for hues and cries.'

Exceptionally, the Constable's accounts for 1655 are given in detail. With more than 50 items it is not practicable to give them in full, but one case by itself illustrates the burden placed upon the unpaid Constable and his Deputy, and the cost to the community:

Chardges with Richard Williams for foure meales meate before he went
to jayle and one to looke to him .... 1s. 9d.

His charges in Worcester for victualls and drinke .... 1s. 0d.

The hire of a horse to carry him to jayle .... 1s. 0d.

My owne chardges goinge with him .... 1s. 6d.

Chardges with Richard Williams before he went to jayle the second time
for three meals meate and twopennyworth of drink .... 11d.

And to Robert Veale for watchinge him one Sunday and Sunday night.......... 1s. 0d.

The Constable's assistant, the Thirdborough was also involved:

While Williams mittimus was rittinge spent on ale .... 6d.

Payde for their dinner .... 1s. 0d.

Puttinge him in prison and expenses .... 1s. 2d.

To the clarke for making his mittimus .... 1s. 0d.

My oene chardges goinge with him .... 1s. 6d.

Payde for Robert Veale's supper and lodgings and two days jorney .... 2s. 0d.

Unfortunately we do not know the nature of Williams' offence or the result of the trial.

The Restoration of Charles II is reflected in the Churchwardens' Accounts for 1661:

For two service books for a fast upon consideration of our old king's death .. 2s. 4d.

For one book for another fast and form of prayer for our Queen .... 1s. 6d.

For a new Common Prayer Book .... 6s. 0d.

Paid to Mr. Hollington for a new surplice .... 70s. 0d.

In that same year, 1661, we have detailed accounts from the Overseers of the Poor, and the way relief was granted is illustrated by two cases. The first relates to Widow Grinsell who receives 4s. in relief in April and then, later that month for washing Widow Grinsell, 2s.: in November, for a neck of mutton for Widow Grinsell, being sick, 1s.: in January, charges laid out at the burial of Widow Grinsell 3s.: and paid Widow Grinsell before she dies, 1s. In the other case, in April, 5s. is paid to Widow Veale and 4s. for keeping Veale's son: in July 1s. 5d. is spent on shirt cloth for Veale's son and 3d. for making the shirt, and in September a pair of stockings for him cost 6d. The sick and infirm received regular weekly payments such as 1s. per week paid to Widow Grinsell, and special payments were made to meet crises such as childbirth, funeral expenses, accident, sickness. The assistance was not always in cash but in kind - a cow, flour, coal, cloth etc. For paupers without accommodation or too feeble to look after themselves the Overseers in 1705 rented a house in Dog (now Meadow) Lane to house poor families at a rent of £2. 6s. p.a., and eight years later they rented houses belonging to the Grammar School Trust for the same purpose.

Children who were a charge on the parish - orphans, illegitimate, or just of pauper parents - were apprenticed at the age of 7 or 8, to 24 in the case of boys and to 21 or marriage in the case of girls. All ratepayers were required to take their turn at accepting an apprentice - an unwelcome burden as it meant another mouth to feed - so that where possible they were apprenticed to a master in another parish, a policy that became easier to carry out as the mining and metal industries developed in the Black Country. The master received a small cash sum - £1. 6s. 8d. in 1662 - while boys were usually to be taught husbandry and the girls housewifery. Parishioners sometimes paid to avoid having to take an apprentice. In 1711 Samuel Warren, for many years curate in the parish, took Mary Ryalls as an apprentice upon promise that the parish excuse his lands at Rowney Green, and as a further obligation Mr. Warren clothed Hannah Penter, a hired servant with John Horton.

Illegitimacy was punished in the church courts, the guilty parties usually having to appear in church and acknowledge their sins, but it left the parish with longer lasting problems in the maintenance of the offspring. Sometimes an outright cash payment might be made to the Overseers, as in the case of John Freeman who paid £13 in 1692; in other cases a bond might be required to cover the eventuality of the child becoming a charge, as in 1669, when John Colcut entered into a bond for £40; but in most cases when the child came into the care of the parish the man was required to pay lying-in expenses and a weekly sum, and the mother was often required to make a small weekly payment.

The cost of administering the Poor Law increased inexorably - a familiar story - and parishes took steps to ensure that they only relieved those who were legally entitled, that is those who had a legal settlement. Any one not having settlement and judged likely to be a burden on the parish became the subject of a Removal Order, signed by two magistrates, and instructing that the individual and any dependants be sent to his parish of settlement. The poor vagrant was subjected to harsher treatment, being examined, whipped, and sent on his way. Thus in 1678 Dolphin, a vagrant, was whipped and sent to Tanworth, the place of his birth: in 1688 Isaac Marriott, age 14, and his brother John, age about 9, were whipped according to law and sent to Feckenham, and Joseph Marriott, who must have had a different settlement, was whipped and sent to Studley. In 1700 James Simister, vagrant, aged about 40, was whipped according to law, and was sent to Hatfield, Hertfordshire, with Oma, his wife, and son Thomas. These were hard times, and the burden on ratepayers heavy, but these are harsh penalties on men and children whose only crime was that of suffering misfortune.

Turning now to the church, the most important event was the destruction of the tower in the great gale of 1662. The extent of the damage is not clear as there is no obvious break in the masonry, but it was not until 1676, as the inscription on the west face tells us, that it was rebuilt by two local stonemasons, Thomas and Samuel Richards. That it was rebuilt was the result of steady pressure from the church authorities: the cost, £150, was raised in three levies, and collection was often delayed and difficult. Apart from the parapet and crocketed finials that replaced the earlier battlements, it seems that the original design was faithfully copied. At some time during this period the accommodation was increased by the erection of a gallery at the west end of the nave. Apart from the statement that the old rood screen was used to form the front of the gallery we know nothing about it, but as the roof line was then much lower, it and the nave below it must have been very dark. The church plate had been confiscated during the reign of Edward VI and there is no mention of any replacement until 1686 when the then Rector, Dr. Hickes, Dean of Worcester, arranged for Lady Margaret Coventry to donate a silver flagon, chalice and paten: these items were stolen in 1820 and never recovered. There is no record when the original peal of bells was installed, but we do know that the original five were recast in 1711 to give a peal of six bells. Each bell has an inscription and those on numbers five and six leave no doubt as to the date, reading 'if you should know when we were runn it was March the 22 1711' and 'Joseph Smith in Edgbaston made mee 1711.'

There are indications of political and doctrinal differences. The curate in 1623, one Humphrey Vincent, must have had Puritan leanings as he is presented as not using the 'Forme of Praier' and of not wearing a surplice. In 1646 the Rector,

February the 17th 1674

A Leavy made for the rebuilding of the steeple of the parish Church of Alvechurch after the rate of Eight pence ye tile for Humfrey Moore and John Bate Churchwardens By us whose names are subscribed

The ffoley Esqr and his tenants	8	0	0
Mr Richard Boothe & his tenants	8	+	8
William Coombe Esqr & his tenants	2	12	8
The Extendors of Mr Milward land and tenants	2	10	8
Thomas Jolly Esqr	0	4	0
John Tyrer gent for his owne	0	15	0
William Tyrer gent & tenants	0	6	8
For Church leasowe	0	1	8
Mris Estopp and her tenants	0	5	4
Sam: White gent & his tenants	0	8	0
Clement Milward gent & tenants	0	4	8
Mr William Moore for land purchased from Bittell	0	7	4
Edward Newnam for Bittell land	0	7	0
John Savage gent & tenants	1	14	8

A copy of the third and last levy on ratepayers to cover the cost of rebuilding the Church Tower, which had been blown down in the great gale of 1662.

William Hollington, was ousted, and Richard Moore, of a prominent local family, intruded. During the Commonwealth, weddings were celebrated before the magistrates, though some were still recorded in the Parish Register, and a civil registrar took over the responsibility of maintaining the Register. Although baptism was no longer recognised as appropriate it is significant that in 1657, they were once more being recorded in the Register, some three years before the Restoration. With the Restoration, Hollington was reinstated and Moore, in his turn, ejected. The Glorious Revolution of 1688 had its repercussions when a number of clergy, the non-jurors, would not give the oath of allegiance to William and Mary, having already given their oath to James II. Among these was the Rector, Dr. Hickes, Dean of Worcester.

Of the incumbents during this period William Hollington is the most worthy of note, if not notorious. A staunch Royalist and Chaplain to Charles I and II, it was he whom the Constable of Alvechurch complained to Quarter Sessions in 1642 was a frequenter of alehouses, keeping riotous and idle company, causing drunkenness by forcing others to drink whole cups, of incontinence with neighbours' wives, of favouring Papists, of being a curser and a liar. It does not seem that Sessions took any action, and it is likely that the complaint was part of the campaign to have him ejected. Hollington held the Rectory until his death in 1686. He was the exception in that he resided in Alvechurch and the family connection continued until 1766. Richard Moore who was intruded was a Puritan divine, noted for writing a pamphlet 'The Pearl in the Oyster Shell', but while rector he lived in the Cathedral Close in Worcester. After the Restoration he was for a short time curate of Wythall Chapel until his views became too extreme for the Bishop and his licence to preach was withdrawn. He is then said to have preached from an upper window at his house, Moor Green Hall. Dr. Hickes, the non-juror Rector and Dean, was a friend of Samuel Pepys, also a non-juror, and attended him on his death bed. Dr. Jephcott, Hicke's successor, was another pluralist and non-resident: the account book of the agent he used to collect his tithes has survived, and, in addition to demonstrating the practicalities of tithe collection, it shows that Jephcott was not blind to the needs of his parishioners and made generous payments towards the education of the young.

Apart from some gaps during the Commonwealth, the Parish Registers are complete. Some of the unusual items are:

1605   was buried Nicholas Giles: this man travelling towards Worcester before day was robbed and murdered nere unto his house the revenge of whose death lyeth in the hande of God.

1607   was buryed Maister William Sheldon servant to Mr. William Combes Esquier. This man ridinge from Hewell towarde Alvechurch was found dead lening one a hedge his purse being taken from him.

1618   was buriede Thomas Crosse being a chylde starved in a hollow tree: bastard.

1626   was buriede Thomas the sonne of William Taylor that the corner satt on suspectinge him to be slayn.

1684   buried Elisabeth Johnson, widow, her age was thought to be 109 years old.

We know rather more about the village from national and local records. The introduction in 1662 of the Hearth Tax, based on the number of hearths in a house tells us that there were 104 that qualified, and the number in the categories, but with the exception of some of the larger properties such as the Old Rectory, it is almost impossible to identify the houses. In 1676 Bishop Compton's Census shows that there were 209 adult churchgoers, 2 Papists, and 4 non-conformists. Analysis of the Parish Registers suggests that life expectancy was around 32 years, and if that is approximately accurate, the population of the parish would seem to lie between 500 and 600. In the years 1703 and 1704 all entries in the Parish Register give the occupation of the man and whether he was a pauper. Of the 51 entries, 24 were described as labourers, almost all agricultural, and of these 16 were paupers: 11 were husbandmen, i.e. small farmers, and one was poor: 4 tailors, 2 poor: 2 yeomen, i.e. more substantial farmers: 2 shoemakers: 2 weavers, one poor: and one each of collar-maker, chair-maker, wheelwright, blacksmith and butcher. It is noticeable that one in three is ranked as pauper and this at a time when conditions were by no means at their worst. In fact the Government took active steps to protect industry and trade and one measure was that a shroud wholly of wool should be used at all burials. In accordance with this we have a certificate sworn before Thomas Hooman, curate, that the wife of Robert Haynds was wrapped in sheep wool only. In 1686 the accounts show the receipt of £2. 10s. from Richard Bellamy for his wife to be buried in linen.

In 1663 there is the first indirect reference to the Free Grammar School in the licence by the Bishop's Official for Thomas Whoman as 'a fit person to instruct children within the parish of Alvechurch.' In 1697 the Churchwardens present that Thomas Hooman and Samuel Biddle are schoolmasters, so that it appears that Hooman was both curate and schoolmaster. Biddle's will is in the County Record Office, and while spelling at this time was not fully standardised it does not suggest that he was well educated. There is no earlier reference to the Grammar School, nor how it received the lands from which the schoolmaster's salary was paid, but it seems to have occupied the same property in 1 to 3 Bear Hill, where the Post Office and other shops now stand.

THE HANOVERIAN KINGS
1714 - 1837

During the period covered by the reigns from George I to William IV England was changed from being a predominantly agricultural country into one which was becoming increasingly industrialised as the Industrial Revolution turned her into the workshop of the world. In 1715 transport facilities were little better than they had been in earlier centuries - there were a few turnpike roads and no canals - but by 1837 there was an efficient road network with coaches covering distances at un-thought of speed, there was a wide-reaching web of canals, and the railway boom was about to begin. In 1715, apart from wind and water mills the only source of power was animal or human: by 1837 the steam engine and the factory system that inevitably followed had profoundly changed the industrial out-put of the country. Against this background of progress Alvechurch was to show little change. The population grew considerably but there was little new housing; agriculture continued to be by far the most important employer and as late as 1792 the medieval open fields with their narrow strips or selions still formed the background to much of the farming, though over the next 20 years there was to be much merging of holdings and enclosure: the influence of the nearby towns of Bromsgrove and Redditch led to a significant number being employed in the manufacture of nails, needles and fish hooks.

That great medieval institution the manor, that had existed at least since the Conquest, was now in terminal decline. By 1837 it was only concerned with transactions to do with copyhold land and burgage plots in the borough, and when in

1860 the Ecclesiastical Commissioners took over the Bishop's estates no more Courts were held in the village. During this time the Steward continued to take the traditional rents on the properties and the Bishop continued to claim and take heriots in cash or in kind and to this extent the yield of the manor was no more than it had been centuries before. However, in addition to these payments, and amounting to much greater sums, were the fines that were payable when a new life was put into a copyhold, traditionally held for three lives, or a new lease was granted, because these fines were based upon the current market rents. During the French Revolutionary and Napoleonic Wars rents soared, and when two lives were put into the lease of the Park in 1795 the fine was £2,085, although the annual rent remained at £8.

In the earlier years the two Courts, the Borough and the Foreign, continued to exercise jurisdiction over the manor. Thus, in the Borough:

1719   The pound is still out of repair - it is the responsibility of the Bishop. The stocks are out of repair - they are a charge on the Constable. (The pound, for stray animals, was situated on the present Memorial Green by the Post Office. The stocks were behind the house that formerly lay next to 1 The Square, before it was demolished for road widening).

1730   A pain on all Ev's Droppers that go about to hearken under people's walls and peep in at people's windows or drop lybels to breed difference amongst neighbours at 20s. apiece.

1773   A pain of £5 to be paid by the Churchwardens and Overseers of the Poor if they do not amend and repair a certain well or pump lying in the Swan Street within 40 days, it being a very dangerous and unsufferable place.

1820   A nuisance of a drain or privy leading from the premises of Mr. John Gaunt and Mr. John Hitchcocks and lay a pain on £3. 3s. on Mr. John Baylies, the landlord, if it be not removed in 3 months. (Gaunt was the surgeon and then lived at Punch's Castle, now 42-46 Swan Street).

Turning to the Court for the Forcign:

1717   A pain of 10s on the Lord's Bailiff if he does not drive the Common at least twice per annum.

1728   A penalty on three individuals if they do not throw down and keep open enclosures on the Lord's waste. (This is repeated next year and is a further instance of the pressure on the common waste).

1738   Twentyone individuals are placed under a penalty of £5 each to throw down their common plecks. Next year they are recorded as having forfeited the penalties, but there is no evidence of the penalties being paid.

1762   A penalty on every cottager who shall keep more than one cow and six sheep or two cows on the Waste: a fine of £5 on any servant man or boy who shall keep any sheep on the waste. (As enclosure of the common waste took place albeit without any Enclosure Act, there must have been increased pressure on what was left).

1791   George Moore was killed by a fall from his horse within the manor, and the Lord is entitled to a deodand. (This is a late survival of the doctrine that, in causing Moore's death, the horse did a criminal act, and as in the case of a felon, it fell to the crown, but in this case the crown rights had long ago been granted to the Bishop).

For many years each of the Courts, Borough and Foreign, had repeated a series of injunctions, or bye-laws, and the latter years this was the sum of their activities. Those for the Borough in 1807 were repeated verbatim to 1860 and read:

First of All We lay a Pain of 10s. upon every Householder of this Borough who does not make good their mounds, between neighbour and neighbour, within Ten Days after Notice given for that purpose.

Also   We lay a Pain of One Pound Ten Shillings upon every Householder who does not pen up their Swine, from Lady Day to St. Bartholomew's Day, and we Likewise Order that they Pay all Damages done by such swine going about.

Also   We lay a Pain of Ten Shillings upon every person who doth break any hedge and steal any Wood thereof.

Also   We lay a Pain of Five Pounds upon any Person or Householder who doth entertain any Stranger, or Inmate, to Damnify the Borough. (This reflects the fear that anyone without legal settlement might become a burden on the parish).

Also   We lay a Pain of One Pound upon any Householder who shall breed any Disturbance between Neighbour and Neighbour.

Also   We lay a Pain on any Householder who doth not clean their Dunghills out of the streets within Ten Days after Notice given by the Bailiff.

Also   We lay a Pain of One Pound on any Householder who is known to Drop any Libel within this Borough.

Also   We lay a Pain upon every Householder who shall be guilty of Erecting any Nuisance, or Encroachment, which shall reduce the Width of the Street, Contrary to the General Act of Parliament.

Also   We lay a Pain of Ten Shillings upon every Person who doth not serve upon the Jury, after being duly summoned by the Bailiff.

Also   We amerce every Person in Two pence who owe Suit and Service to this Court, and who hath not make their Appearance this Day at Court.

Also   We lay a Pain of One Pound upon every Householder who doth not keep their Children and Servants in Good Order and due Subjection on the Lord's Day, and likewise, We lay a Pain of One Pound on the Headborough If he doth not take due Notice and punish all them that Offend or break the Sabbath.

Many of the regulations of the Borough relate to the problems of neighbourly relations and conduct; those of the Foreign are more concerned with the day to day routine of farming:

Imprimis   We lay a pain of 40s. on every person who shall make any marlpit upon any of the Commons within the manor and does not secure the same within ten days.

Item   We lay a Pain of £10 on any person who shall erect a cottage within the manor.

Item   We lay a Pain of 10s. on every person who after one month's notice shall neglect to scour his Ditches lying and being in the roadside.

Item   We amerce every cottager at 6d. each and every other person at 2d. each who owe sute and service to this Court and have not made their Appearance this Day.

Item   We lay a pain of 40s. on every Person that shall make any encroachment upon the Lord's Wast.

Item   We lay a pain of five pounds on every person who shall gett or cause to be got any sand upon Barntgreen to Damage the Road and does not secure the Breach Immediately after the getting thereof.

Item   We lay a pain of 10s. on every person who shall cary or cause to be caryd any of the soil off the Lord's wast for the manuring of his land.

Item   We lay a pain of 20 shill. on every person that shall cutt fern on any part of the Lord's wast before Midsumer day.

Item   We lay a pain of 5 shill. on every Person that shall suffer his swine to go about the Neighbourhood Onwrong to damage theire Neighbours.

Before leaving the subject of the Manor Court we have an eye witness of the formalities that followed the election of the 'Mayor' of the Borough. It comes from the little book entitled 'Martha', the story of the life of Martha Harber. She was born in 1820, the daughter of John Harber who that same year was transported for stealing the church silver: she spent most of her life in service, until she became too aged, when she maintained herself by keeping a small sweet shop. She said that in October each year the new 'Mayor', dressed in a red cloak, was carried round the borough on a chair. Two 'sidesmen' bore a mace, painted and lettered, and a tall pole topped with a crown. In front marched the twelve jurymen, each holding a lighted candle. The outgoing Mayor gave a feast at The Crown to all attending the Court, and by tradition this was paid for from tolls at the Fair.

The situation regarding the Fair is confusing. The original grant had been for it to be held on the eve, the day, and the morrow of St. Laurence's Day, the 10th August, and it must have been held on 10th August 1750 because it is mentioned in the Quarter Session papers in connection with a standstill order on the movement of stock following an outbreak of cattle disease. In 1794 there is a reference to the Alvechurch mop, or hiring fair, being held the week before Michaelmas. The Victoria County History says that by the end of the Eighteenth Century two Fairs were held, one on St. Laurence Day and the other on 22nd day of April. In his Rambler in Worcestershire, Noakes says that in 1851 there were Fairs on 3rd May and 22nd September, and ox-roast at the Statute Fair at Lady Day. In 1901 there were said to be two fairs, one on the first Wednesday in May and the other the first Wednesday in October. It seems to be the latter that has survived as the Mop, now only in the form of amusements brought by travelling showmen.

As the responsibilities and functions of the Manor Court declined, so local government within the parish became the responsibility of the Vestry, under the general supervision of the Justices of the Peace. The vestry consisted of all who paid rates, i.e. the whole body of householders other than paupers, and included Roman Catholics and Dissenters, who not unreasonably, felt aggrieved that they should pay the church rate, though it was normally very small compared with the Poor Law Rate. A greater problem was that the rates were based upon a very old assessment since when development and enclosure had taken place. It was agreed that there should be a fresh assessment, and to this end in 1792 a large scale map was surveyed and with it is a terrier which gives the name of owner and occupier of each parcel of land, together with the area, the field name, and whether it was arable or pasture or waste. It is of great interest to the historian, being approximately 50 years before the Tithe Map, which is also nearly 50 years before the first large scale Ordnance Survey map. It proved, however, easier to survey the parish than to reach agreement on the assessment, and it took three tries before this was achieved. The Vestry elected the church-wardens and other officers at the annual meeting at Easter: all the offices were onerous and the more substantial parishioners were expected and indeed compelled to take their turn. The Vestry had responsibilities for oversight of payments made by the Overseers of the Poor during the year, but although all were entitled to attend, few actually did so, with the result that there was not proper control. Taking advantage of recent legislation, in 1821 it was agreed that there should be a Committee of the Vestry, the Special Vestry, to carry out the oversight.

The churchwardens themselves did not in fact have further responsibilities thrust upon them. They continued to be responsible for the fabric and furnishings of the church, for meeting expenses by raising a church rate, and they had to make their presentments each year, to the Rector, as Peculiar, in two years, and to the Bishop the third year. Examples of their presentments etc. are:

1717   The churchyard, parsonage house, and parsonage mill are out of repair.

1719   The parsonage house and chancel are out of repair, but materials are got ready to repair each.

1720   Where As Complaints have been entered against those persons that offend by their talking in the Church yard in the time of divine service We the Curate churchwardens and other substantial inhabitants doe agree to allow twenty shillings a year concluded at our meeting on Easter Tuesday to be given to a person by us chosen to see good orders observed and that he shall take good care to minde such as shall offend and warne such as shall offend in the premises. We also appoint him to whip the dogs out of the church And to rouse such as shall sleepe And to take care to inform against such offenders to the churchwardens That such offenders might be punished According to due Course of Law as the ordinary shall think fit.

1750   The Gallery at the East End of Alvechurch Church, consisting of seven seats, made of deal, was built (the licence of the Rector, Dean Lyttleton, being first obtained) in the year of our Lord 1750 by the direction of Mr. John Moore, who then served the office of Churchwarden with Mr. William Fish. The Charge of building the said Gallery (including materials and workmanship) amounted to the sum of £39. 1s. 1d. which sum was paid by the following gentlemen being (for the most part) Inhabitants of the said parish of Alvechurch who first purchased the seats - the names follow. Memorandum that on the fifth day of May 1752 the above said John Moore did sell unto Mr. John Birch the seat which is between the seat of Mr. William Stable and the north side of the said arch which is next the pulpit at two Guineas.

1807   Resolved that the present pulpit and reading desk be taken down, that a new pulpit and reading desk out of the old materials be made . . . as well as necessary alterations to the pews . . . such pulpit and desk to be erected against the church wall between the South door and window.

1828   J. A. Sharman is appointed organist at a salary of £20 p.a.

1829   Ale for the ringers, 12s.: paid to R. Court for ringing the morning bell £1. 1s.

1830   At a Public Meeting to consider the propriety of defending an action brought against the Churchwardens by J. A. Sharman, it was ordered that the organist be paid the sum due to him and the parish have no further use for his services.

1830   Expenditure of £3 on forms for children in the Sunday School.

The parish officers with the most onerous task, and one where the burden increased all the time, were the two Overseers of the Poor. The increase in the total population, the growth of pauperism, and the practice of augmenting the low wages of the agricultural labourer from the Poor Rate are responsible for the increase in expenditure on the Poor from £146 in 1715 to over £1,200 in the early 1830s. As the number of paupers rose, so the number who had to meet the higher rates diminished.

Payments by the Overseers fell into two main categories, the Weekly Poor, and Extraordinary Payments. The Weekly Poor were those who from age or infancy or infirmity were in need of regular assistance either to provide the whole of their maintenance or to augment their meagre earnings, and they received a weekly allowance. In 1784, for example, there were 58 families in receipt of sums ranging from 6d. to 6s. per week - the basis seems to have been to make up the cash income to 1s. 6d. or 2s. per adult. Extraordinary payments were made to meet particular problems - temporary unemployment, long spells of bad weather, childbirth, funeral expenses etc - and assistance might be given in cash or in kind. Typical examples of these payments are:

1743   William Field to serve the Poor with what coals they shall have occasion for the ensuing winter at the price of 7d. per hundred.

          The Overseers shall pay Edward Malkin towards the charg of the cutting of his servant's leg .... £2. 15s.

1784   Midwife for delivery .... 3s. 0d.

          Anne Ward for child's funeral, shroud, coffin, fees .... 10s. 7d.

          A paer of shoes for Mr. Rabold's prentice .... 3s. 0d.

          A petticoat and shift for children .... 4s. 0d.

          Half a strike ($^1/_2$ bushell) of flower for Tong .... 3s. 4d.

          $47^3/_4$ yards hempcloth at 13d. per yard .... £2. 11s. $8^3/_4$d.

          Mr. Freeman for Dockterin .... £6. 19s. 4d.

For many years there had been a workhouse for those without accommodation or who could not look after themselves, and the control and supervision of the often unruly people presented problems. In 1792 a warrant was issued to the Constable to bring Mary Wilkes before the Justices at the Fox and Goose at Redditch on complaint of having misbehaved herself in the workhouse by refusing to work and using abusive language. That same year the management of the workhouse was put out to tender and agreement was reached with two men from Bromsgrove who, for £270, undertook to take all the poor and impotent persons, that is for the management, diet, clothing, washing, funerals, etc., excepting litigation regarding settlement. Peace with France in 1815 was followed by an increase in unemployment and a greater call for relief. In 1817 it was resolved that there should be a Committee to assist the Overseers in paying the weekly poor at 3 p.m. on Saturdays, with fines for non-attendance. Next year it was resolved to accept the tender of Eleanor Wainwright to maintain the poor at an annual charge of £1200, any expenditure over that sum to be met as to two thirds by the parish and one third by Mrs. Wainwright. In 1819 Richard Boulton, shopkeeper of Alvechurch, undertook the maintenance for £1050, excluding Quarter Session Rates, the Constable's bill, suits of bastardy, militia expenses, and with additional allowances for each lying-in, but he would pay for a doctor for the care of the poor.

For many years the accounts of the Overseers of the Poor had been passed every four or five weeks at a Vestry Meeting: these meetings were poorly attended and the work fell upon a few, and to remedy this the parish took advantage of an enabling Act and chose a Select Vestry who became responsible for the oversight of the Overseers. One of the first actions of the Select Vestry in 1821 was to review the 78 cases of recipients of regular relief, giving a brief note of the circumstances and the amount of relief granted. A cross section of these cases shows:

Betty Coley, 80, widow, lame, earns little .... 2s. 6d.

Widow Buckley, 70/80, earns 1s per week for turnpike gate .... 1s. 6d.

Widow Hollom, 30, has 3 children, earns 2s. per week .... 5s. 6d.

Widow Birch, 45, 3 children, earns 1s. sewing and 1s. keeping school .... 5s. 6d.

Joseph Hill, 40, wife and 4 children, earns 8s., wife idle .... 2s. 6d.

Widow Cotton, 67, earns 1s. 6d. wheeling sand .... 2s. 0d.

Mary Harber, 43, husband transported, 4 children, earns 1s. 6d. .... 6s. 6d.

Widow Hanson, has 6 children, girls 11 and 9 work in the brickworks, boy
7 picks manure, boy 5 turns a wheel .... 9s. 0d.

Examples of the treatment of extraordinary payments after the Special Vestry took over control are:

- Elizabeth Wiggett, 7, to be apprenticed to a needlemaker until 17 at a premium of £1. 10s. and a pair of shoes.

- Spain, wife and 5 children, aged 13-5, he earns 10s. and family 11s.: no pay but to have a pair of shoes, pair of sheets, 6 yds. linen, 5 yds. cotton.
- Thomas Morrall, given 12s. for sheets, calico and flannel, and 1s. against his wife's confinement.

Meanwhile the problem of the parish workhouse remained. In 1822 the Special Vestry accepted Thomas Pulley's offer to provide bread meat and drink for paupers in the workhouse, together with soap candles and firing, at 2s. 3d. a head and to have 10% of what they earned from their labour. Dr. Gaunt was to be retained at £30 p.a. to attend paupers, medicines, accidents and midwifery, and to be excused Poor Rate. A subscription of £2. 2s. was paid to Birmingham General Hospital in order to have the right of nomination to the hospital. Pulley's contract was renewed until 1826 when the following advertisement was placed in the Birmingham Gazette: - 'Wanted - a person to reside in the Workhouse in Alvechurch to provide for and take care of the Poor in the house at a certain sum weekly. The Contractor will be allowed a house and large garden exempt from all payments.' This must have been unsuccessful as Pulley was re-appointed at 3s. 6d. a head and 2 tons of coal.

In the subsequent years each year seems to have seen a fresh manager and new problems arose. Bad weather and unemployment are reflected in the long list of families who in 1829 were given shirts, blankets, petticoats, sheets etc., and in 1830 the manager was allowed an extra £5 because there had been several cases of heavy illness and a lunatic woman. Worse was to follow in 1832 when a parish meeting was held to consider what steps should be taken to prevent the present cholera epidemic from spreading. It was recommended that:

1. A stock of coffins, especially pitched, be maintained.
2. All bodies of cholera victims to be coffined at once.
3. Dr. Gaunt is authorised to spend on food and clothing for the victims and to buy 2 gallons of brandy for the use of patients.

4.   Cottages are to be whitewashed, the poor advised regarding diet, and attention drawn to the state of the privies in Dog Lane.

5.   A parish meeting to be called to consider establishing a Board of Health.

In the event no further cholera deaths were reported for several days and it was decided that a Board of Health was not necessary: Dr. Gaunt was voted a further £20 because of the epidemic. The Reform Parliament passed the Poor Law Amendment Act in 1834 which sounded the death knell of the arrangements that had run with only modest change since Queen Elizabeth's reign. In 1835 the Bromsgrove Union, which included Alvechurch, was established. The parish still paid a poor rate and the ratepayers elected the Board of Guardians of the Poor who administered the Workhouse and out-relief.

The ancient and onerous office of Constable continued to be the representative of law and order. Writs and warrants were addressed to him, he was the man responsible for the apprehension and safe keeping of accused persons and where appropriate delivering them to gaol or the House of Correction, and he was also responsible for militia matters, including collecting the County Rate. Although a parish officer, he continued to be elected by the Jury of the Foreign: every one had to take his turn: the appointment had to be confirmed by the Justices: on at least one occasion, in 1741, the elected Constable hired a deputy to act for him: he had an elected assistant, the Thirdborough. The establishment of the County Constabulary in 1842 was soon to usher in a more modern approach, but over the whole of this period the old system prevailed. His expenses were most often modest, and met by a separate rate. In 1716 in order to meet a deficit, the Constable sold 'one old musket for 10s.': in 1722 he raised a penny rate which yielded £6. 19s. 9d. but 'Balmy Bati Brodbery did not pay': in 1732 the old parish weights were sold for 1s. 6d. - presumably because new countrywide standards were in use.

With the Revolutionary and Napoleonic Wars came a rise in prices, especially of bread, and this led to civil disturbances and an increase in theft. Except for the most serious offences a complainant had to meet the cost of prosecution, so that an individual would be reluctant to take minor offenders for small theft or hedge-breaking or trespass to court. The answer lay in joint action by land owners and farmers and forming an Association for the Prosecution of Felons. In the event it was not until 1828 that a public meeting was called at the Crown Inn, now 6 The Square, following which the Alvechurch Association was formed. Every member paid 5s. entry fee, and the fund was maintained at this total by an annual levy: in addition, a dinner was to be held each year, after the Annual Meeting, costing 2s. for the meal and 1s. 'to be spent' - presumably on ale - and absentees were fined 5s. which went to the funds. A substantial part of the expenditure went on notices for members to display on their property, and on handbills to advertise a theft or loss, and on payments to the crier, while rewards were paid for the apprehension and conviction of offenders against the property of members:

For a Capital Offence .... £5. 5s. 0d.

For a Transportable Offence .... £3. 3s. 0d.

or an Imprisonable Offence .... £1. 1s. 0d.

For stealing turnips, potatoes, damaging gates etc. .... 10s. 6d.

The first year's accounts show:

The crier for giving notice of an offence .... 6d.

Mr. Green Expense of handbills when he lost his pony .... 6s. 6d.

Mr. Hunt Expense of prosecution when he was robbed of his hat .... 4s. 6d.

Other items in the early years were robberies at The Bear and at Stonehouse, the loss of horses, and the theft of sheep, bees, fowls, hops etc., but seldom does it seem that the property was recovered or the thief apprehended. After the County Constabulary was established in 1842 the main items of expenditure were rewards to the village constable and the local sergeant of police.

Parliament transferred the responsibility for the upkeep of the King's highway from the manor to the parish in 1555, but it is not until 1700 that we find the appointment of a Surveyor of Highways in Alvechurch. There was a duty on every householder to give six days' labour for repair of the roads, or four days if he had a cart. Alvechurch is a large parish, and one can understand that someone living in Barnt Green would be reluctant to work on a road at the other end of the parish, say at Dagnall End, and in any case would spend half the day getting there and back. In consequence there were a number of Surveyors for different parts and each raised his own rate to cover any expenditure. As might be expected, the labour was granted grudgingly and was largely ineffectual so that eventually the Surveyors relied upon paid labourers and the expense was recouped from the levying of a rate.

The most important road through the village had been the King's Highway from Coventry to Worcester and beyond, which entered the parish at Weatheroak and proceeded across Radford Bridge and Radford Road to enter the village by the Lord's Mill, then across the Square and up Bear Hill and Scarfield Hill on its way to Bromsgrove. This road appears on the 14th Century Gough Map, and is shown in greater detail, with Alvechurch appearing, on Ogilby's Road Maps of 1675 as part of the road from Leicester to Hereford. The 1792 map of the parish shows this road, and the road to Redditch, but no direct road through Hopwood and West Heath to Birmingham: it seems likely that Birmingham traffic went along the Radford Road to Icknield Street and thence to Birmingham. This was all to change when the Birmingham to Evesham Turnpike Trust was established by Act of Parliament in 1825. The road entered the parish at West Heath and continued on the existing line through Hopwood to Jay's Crescent and the Old Birmingham Road past The Leys to Roberts Corner and the village: it then continued along the present line to leave the parish at Bordesley. There were toll cottages at West Heath, in the centre of the village in Swan Street, and at Bordesley, and the Bordesley Toll House was only demolished some 30 or so years ago. The toll was charged at each stage and varied from 6d. per beast pulling a coach to $\frac{1}{2}$d. for a calf or a sheep. From this time there were regular coach services - The Hope - between Birmingham and Redditch, and regular carriers serving Birmingham and Bromsgrove.

Even before the turnpike the situation had been changed by the construction of the Alvechurch section of the Birmingham to Worcester Canal. It had been authorised as long ago as 1791 but had always been under-funded, and had to meet an early problem in tunnelling under Wast Hills, so that it was 1802 before it reached Hopwood. For a short while this was the terminus, but in 1807 it had reached Tardebigge: with the Tardebigge tunnels and the drop to the Severn to overcome it was 1815 before it was fully open to Worcester. It was not long before it had to contend with competition from the Birmingham to Gloucester Railway, but meanwhile it facilitated the movement of bulk goods, such as coal and agricultural supplies and produce, and it was a factor in the establishment of Alvechurch Brickworks. For a while there was even a passenger boat service to Birmingham. The main effect on Alvechurch was undoubtedly the loss of agricultural land, not so much from the line of the canal - though it divided fields and holdings - as from the construction of the Bittell and Upper Bittell Reservoirs in 1813 and 1832 respectively. These, in turn, were held to interfere with the flow of the River Arrow, and so with the mills dependent upon its water.

The Parish Registers continue to be a mine of information until 1837, when the Registrar General took over the function that had for so long been performed by the church. In some ways there is more information available, but there are fewer of the interesting asides that appeared in earlier years. From 1813 the entries for burials include the age of the deceased, and this suggests a life expectancy of 36, as against earlier estimates of 32. However, from 1801, and every decade thereafter, there was a National Census, and while the early information is limited in its detail, at least we know the population total. In 1801 it was 1228 and by 1831 it had risen to 1548, that is 26%. Notwithstanding the expansion in population there seems to have been little new housing, increased accommodation being gained from the division of some of the larger properties and what we should regard as overcrowding in existing cottages. Another new feature in the Registers was the requirement in 1813 that the principals and the witnesses of marriages should sign the Register. If literacy is measured by the ability to sign one's name, then the figures for the ten years 1813 to 1822 are:

Male literates	81
Female literates	60
Total literates	141
Male illiterates	46
Female illiterates	62
Total illiterates	108

Also, from this date, the occupation of the father is given at each baptism. Extracting the figures over the next 25 years, 65%, nearly all described as labourers, are directly involved in agriculture; 10% are engaged in manufacture, nail, needle and fish hook making; 19% are artisans supplying local needs - shoemakers, tailors, carpenters, blacksmiths, bricklayers etc.; the remaining 4% are in retail trade and sundry occupations. Nail making and some aspects of needle and fish hook making were cottage industries, but the sharpening and burnishing depended upon water power at both the Town and the Rector's Mill. There are fewer 'asides' in the Registers, but two entries are of interest:

1743   On Sunday May ye 8th abt 11 at night died at HARTLEBURY CASTLE ye Rt. Revd. Dr. John Hough Bp of WORCESTER & LORD & PATRON OF ALVECHURCH full of years and good works in ye 53d year of his Episcopacy & ye 93d year of his age.

1752   September ye 2. N.B. According to an Act of Parliament passed in ye year of our Lord 1751 the Old Style ceases here, & ye New takes place; & consequently ye next day wch in ye old account wd have been ye 3d, is now to be called ye 14th; so yt all ye intermediate Nominal Days from ye 2nd to ye 14th are annihilated ys year. (This is the change from the Julian to the Gregorian Calendar, to bring us into line with Continental practice).

There are now many more wills and accompanying inventories and these show that the general standard of living of the better-off element of the community had continued to rise: one must bear in mind that the poorer people as well as those officially classed as paupers had so little to leave that a will was not necessary. Most of the wills are proved in the Peculiar Jurisdiction of the Rector of Alvechurch, and the following Notice of Visitation for 1794 sets out the scope of the Peculiar:

'Richard Kilvert clerk Master of Arts Rector of the Rectory and parish church of Alvechurch . . . Judge and Ordinary of the Peculiar and exempt Jurisdiction to the said Rectory belonging lawfully constituted To all and singular literate persons in and throughout the Jurisdiction Greeting Whereas We charge and command . . . to appear on Friday the 25 instant between the hours of 9 and 12 in the forenoon of the same day the said curate and schoolmaster to show their letters of orders and licence the old churchwardens to make their presentments and the new churchwardens to take their oath of office the said Executors to prove their wills or to renounce the execution of them and the possessors of personal estate of persons dying intestate to take Letters of Administration and further to do and receive as the law shall require. Given under seal 21 July 1794 John Clifton, Proctor.'

From the time of Charles Lyttleton's incumbency there dates a silver seal of the Peculiar Jurisdiction: this is now held in the Worcester County Record Office, and shows a view of the church with the arms of the Bishopric and the Lyttletons on either side.

The churchwarden's presentments report irregular liaisons. While the civil authorities were concerned that any irregular offspring was not a charge on the parish and made orders for the father and often the mother to make weekly payment the Church authorities attended to the moral aspect. The guilty parties were cited to appear at Worcester and were ordered to perform penance, as in the following example:

Friday the fourth day of August 1769 between the hours of nine and twelve in the forenoon before the Reverend Edward Taylor Clerk, Surrogate in the Registrars Office within the precinct of the Cathedral Church of Worcester appeared personally Sarah Search of the parish of Alvechurch, spinster, and acknowledged that she hath been guilty of committing the crime of fornication with John Hall and hath been delivered of a bastard child begotten by her body by him and submitted herself and Whereupon the Surrogate accepted her confession and enjoined her a Public Penance to be performed in the Parish Church of Alvechurch on Sunday next in the afternoon and admonished her to certify the performance thereof within one month And the said Sarah Search making oath of poverty was admitted in forma pauperis. Before me Edward Taylor, Surrogate.

Cases of slander also fell within the jurisdiction of the Church Courts. The number of cases and the evidence suggests that relations within the borough were not always neighbourly - one must bear in mind that there must have been overcrowding and that there were many observers. Some of the less extreme cases are:

1766   Elizabeth Baylies v. Sarah Webb wife of John Webb (the schoolmaster): 'Thou art a whore, has whored with her servant Harry Knight and the mother of Elizabeth Baylies caught her in bed with him.'

1744   Sarah Mills v John Mills: 'You thou or she is are or art a whore, stinking whore and a brimstone whore.'

1783   Edward Moore v William Howard or Howarth: 'committed the crime of adultery fornication or incontinency with Nancy Wiggett. You took her into the old Drink House and stitched her.'

1812   Proceedings begin with a Summons to John Wainwright or Wainright to answer the Rector, J. F. Tonyn, in a cause of defamation. One witness, John Strain, needlemaker, said that, being in The Crown Inn on the night in question at between 9 and 10 he heard John Hughes address John Harber, husband of Mary Harber, 'Are you not the man that married the parson's whore?' meaning, the witness believed, that Mary Harber had been guilty of the crime of fornication or adultery with the parson with whom she had lived as a servant. On examination he said that he does not recollect any quarrel between the parties, that he was not drinking with the defendant but was in the same room, and that the defendant was not very sober. The second witness was more politic. He was in The Crown on the night in question with John Harber, John Hughes, John Moore and John Wainwright and others 'but there was such a great noise that he could not take himself to say whether the words were spoken as he did not hear them.' As in so many of these cases the outcome is unknown, but once more we meet John Harber.

There were a few charitable bequests during this period, notably £100 by Dr. Worth, in 1742, and £70 by the curate, John Welch, in 1800. The principal charities, the Lewkner Hospital and the Grammar School continued. From their appearance prior to demolition in the 1970s the almshouses may well have been rebuilt at this time, but there is no documentary evidence and repairs were in any case the responsibility of the foundation. There are several notes of men and women being appointed to fill a vacancy: in 1831 James Nicholls was appointed 'as long as he maintains the good character which has this day gained him the appointment.' The Lewkner Hospital faced a crisis in 1821 when the annual payment was disputed, but after costly litigation the charity won its case and the money was received.

The Free Grammar School continued to provide tuition to the elected scholars and their number appears to have increased from 12 to 20. In 1744 we have the names of all the scholars, and for most of the time we know the names of the masters. As the years went by the annual stipend of £20 must have become more and more unattractive, and it seems that from the beginning of the 19th Century, if not earlier, the schoolmaster was taking boarders as additional private pupils in order to augment his income. The 1821 Census records 37 males on the premises although a report of 1833 talks of 12 foundationers and 2 boarders. In this latter year, consequent upon an Act of Parliament, there was an 'Inquiry concerning Charities, Hundred of Oswaldslow, parish of Alvechurch' and then the Trustees, or Feoffees as they were known, held the Parish House in Church Street with two gardens, three houses in Church Street or Bear Street, four houses near the Parish House in Swan Street, and a small amount of land.

Turning now to the Rectors, mention has already been made of Dr Worth and Charles Lyttleton. They were succeeded by Corfield Clare, Martin Smith and

Richard Kilvert. They were all absentees but Kilvert is of interest because of the connection with the diarist, Francis Kilvert. Richard Kilvert was a Canon of Worcester and Vicar of Kempsey and lived in the Cathedral Close in Worcester: he left one daughter, Maria, who continued to live in the Close, and to whose funeral Francis Kilvert and his father went as principal family mourners, and which is so graphically and comically described in the Kilvert Diaries. Kilvert was succeeded by Francis Tonyn in 1801 and he continued as Rector until his death in 1854. He was resident, the first since Hollington's death in 1686, and lived in the Old Rectory in Old Rectory Lane in the middle of the glebe.

By the latter years of the period places of worship other than the Established Church had been instituted. Although Protestant Dissenters had been tolerated since 1688 it was only in 1811 that a Methodist Chapel/Meeting Place commenced in Rowney Green. It was in Gravel Pit Lane - now a cottage - and was in use until the existing Chapel was built in 1869. Other Dissenters were registered in 1813 as meeting in John Culter's house in Weathercock Hill, and in 1817 at John Humphries house in Alvechurch. The Baptist archives record that a Sunday School was started by Edward King of Bordesley Park Lodge Farm and was the forerunner of the Baptist congregation and Church in Alvechurch. In 1826 Thomas Parsonage's house was licensed for worship, and in 1834 a building in Red Lion Street was licensed for use as a chapel by the Particular Baptists. This was a small cottage and smithy on the site of the present Baptist Church in Red Lion Street.

VICTORIAN AND EDWARDIAN ALVECHURCH 1837 - 1914

T he age from the accession of Queen Victoria to the outbreak of the First World War in 1914 saw the United Kingdom develop into a predominantly industrial nation and a major world power. Although situated so close to Birmingham and the Black Country - one of the main power houses of the Industrial Revolution - Alvechurch was little affected by what was happening only a dozen miles away. One area where it differed from many nearby communities was in the static nature of the population. Between 1841 and 1911 the numbers rose from 1633 to 1731, or 7%, whereas in the country as a whole the increase was over 95%. For centuries there had been an excess of births over deaths in the parish and there had been emigration elsewhere, but now this movement was accelerated by lack of opportunity in the village and more work to be found elsewhere.

Agriculture continued to be the main employment. The small mixed farms continued to be typical and the level of profitability fell after the inflow of cheap wheat and other farm products from North America and Australasia. Horse power was now widely used not only for ploughing, but also for seeding, reaping, binding etc., and the steam-driven threshing machine had replaced the laborious hand threshing and winnowing, but farming was still labour intensive and was the lot of most young men, either hired by the year or as day workers. Industry found its way here, mostly as overspill from Bromsgrove and Redditch. From Bromsgrove came nail making, a cottage industry employing the whole family down to the youngest child, and in the 1851 Census there were 54 following this trade. However, the hand nailers were already facing the competition from machine made nails, and after several bruising strikes the manufacture was concentrated in factories. Old nailers shops were recently still to be found at the rear of 22 Swan Street and 28 Bear Hill. From the other neighbour, Redditch, came the making of needles and fish hooks. Some found employment in the factories in Redditch, some were engaged in processes that could be performed at home, while some worked at the two mills, each of which was engaged in sharpening and scouring: in 1851, 23 men, women and boys were employed. The Rector's mill had something of a chequered career, suffering more than once from fire, and in 1912 was briefly used by Dunckleys for the manufacture of perambulators. What did become the largest employer in the village was the Brickworks, started in 1860 by a Mr. Wynn, a Birmingham ironmaster. It made use of deposits of clay near Scarfield Farm, and the canal side site made for cheap transport of coal and of the finished bricks. The tannery which had given its name to Tanyard Lane seems to have gone out of business by the time of the 1851 Census. The Bishop's, or Town Mill, in Radford Road was active, using water power from the Arrow to grind corn and cattle feed, and for a time to scour needles. Flax spinning took place at what is now the Butchers, 4 The Square, and Boultons, at 7 The Square, had a thriving candle making business as well as dealing with cattle feed etc. At Hopwood, on the site of the present Westmead Hotel, there stood Southam's Brewery and for those who preferred non-alcoholic drinks mineral waters were made at the factory on the site of the Village Hall in Bear Hill. The village had its own craftsmen and tradesmen - smiths, wheelwrights, saddlers, carpenters, bricklayers and so forth while the larger houses provided work for gardeners, grooms and footmen for the young men and domestic service for the girls. Writing about Alvechurch as it was shortly before 1914 Mrs Burman wrote: 'Alvechurch was a small prosperous village with very little real poverty. There was no unemployment. Domestic Service was the chief source of employment for girls, and also for boys as gardeners, grooms, coachmen, footmen etc. The Brickyard, the Canal, the Mills both the flour and the Needle Mill and Boultons were all employers of local labour. Redditch also provided employment in the Pin and Needle industry and Herbert Austin was just starting his works in Longbridge.' This may be rather an idyllic view, looking back from afar, but it depicts a community more at ease with itself and more self sufficient in every sense of the phrase.

As one goes round the village it is evident that there was a measure of rebuilding on existing sites, and of extending and refacing existing buildings, but that there was relatively little real expansion of the housing stock. There were new houses in School Lane - the School House, the Clergy Lodge, the Rectory itself, and along the Birmingham Road - the Police Station at No. 6 is an example - and a number of larger properties were built away from the village centre on Scarfield Hill, the Radford Road, Coopers Hill and elsewhere, but, by and large, there was remarkably little difference between the centre of the village in 1914 and that described in the 1299 Survey. Having said this, the services and the degree of comfort in the dwellings had been improved immeasurably if we compare 1914 with 1837. A great step forward in public health came with the sewerage system, with works at Lye Bridge, in 1903, to replace the earth closets and the services of the night soil man. Around this same time piped water came to replace reliance upon wells. While the larger houses had their own wells, many poorer people had to rely upon the parish well off Swan Street, and the state of this well had been adversely mentioned more than once. Town gas came in 1909 and though used almost exclusively for lighting, the better level of illumination and the convenience improved the lot of the ordinary people. What probably improved general living standards most was the introduction into even the small cottage of the kitchen range to replace the open hearth. Cheaper iron and steel made production possible: the range gave a more manageable and economic fire for cooking and usually included an oven and a side boiler: by the end of the period the larger houses had ranges with back boilers to provide hot water on tap, and made possible the indoor bathroom in modest dwellings.

The turnpike continued to be the main artery through the village, and, until the advent of the railway there were regular coach and omnibus services to Birmingham and Redditch, and carrier services continued to serve Birmingham, Bromsgrove and Redditch right up to 1914. Initially the roads continued to be a parish responsibility but personal service was no longer required and a paid Surveyor covered his expenditure by raising a rate. With the establishment of Worcestershire County

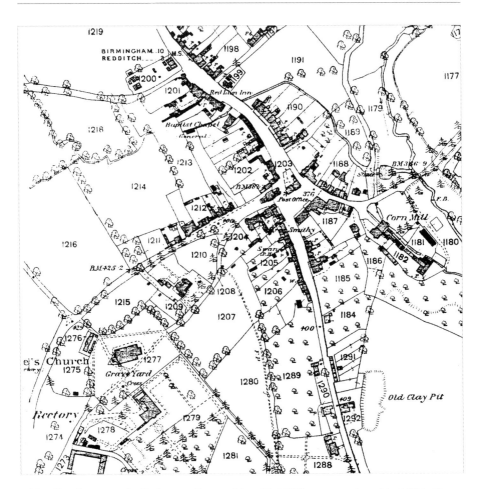

The first large-scale Ordnance Survey Map (1:2500) was produced in 1884. Note how little has changed since 1701. By permission of the Ordnance Survey.

Council in 1888 the major roads were taken over, and the minor roads were taken over by the newly formed Rural District Council in 1894.

The Canal had reached Worcester in 1815 and had 25 years before it had to meet the competition of the railway, but once the Birmingham to Gloucester line was opened it had to struggle to maintain its share of the traffic, and the struggle became more desperate when the Barnt Green to Redditch line was opened in 1859. Nevertheless, the canal was important to the Brickworks and for the movement of agricultural produce, and the canal folk were a regular phenomenon in the village. In hard winters, when the canal froze over and traffic ceased, soup kitchens were set up to help the marooned families. Every effort was made to keep the canal open, including the use of a specially strengthened boat which was manned by a large crew whose function it was to rock the craft from side to side and break the ice.

The construction of the Barnt Green to Redditch line in 1859 linked the village to the whole rail network, and this was extended when the line reached Ashchurch, near Tewkesbury in 1866. Alvechurch Station was opened in 1859. This coincided with the first issues of the Redditch Indicator, and the event was marked by the comment 'What is that? Alvechurch Station? What a funny looking thing. Like a great cow crib.' There was a coal and goods yard in addition to passenger facilities. Despite a regular and frequent service between Redditch and Birmingham the advent of rail services seems to have had only a marginal effect on the community, in contrast to Barnt Green where the coming of the train led to widespread and expensive housing development.

The Manor Courts continued to promulgate bye-laws for the Borough and the Foreign, but they lacked the authority to enforce them, and their only practical function lay in regard to Copyhold tenure, where title to the land rested upon a copy of the Court Roll. Even this function disappeared when the Ecclesiastical Commissioners took over the Bishopric estates in 1858, so breaking a link that had existed for over a thousand years. The Vestry and Special Vestry had become responsible for most of the aspects of local government that had formerly lain with the Manor Courts, but now, in its turn, it was being superseded by the broader based County Council and the Rural District Council. The Poor Law Guardians had already taken over the care of paupers, and the Highways were lost to the Councils by the end of the Century, and the responsibility for law and order fell to the County Constabulary. The year 1846 saw a resident constable from the new Force replace the elected Constable and Thirdborough, and after one or two false starts a custom-built Police Station, with a small cell, was erected at 6 Birmingham Road. The Alvechurch Society for the Prosecution of Felons had really lost its purpose when the Constabulary was formed, but now its funds, apart from paying for notices and for thefts to be 'cried' through the village, were largely expended on rewards to the constable and sergeant. The principal interest then became their Annual Dinner at the Red Lion, an event that was held right up to 1914. An amusing offshoot from the 'Felons' was the Sparrow Club, formed in 1892. One can only imagine that it was established because the small boys who in earlier generations had been available for bird scaring were now in school, and the Club was evidently concerned with the depredations of birds on their crops. Each member without land had to produce 12 sparrow heads and those with land one head per acre held, while failure to produce the required number of heads involved a fine of 1s. per dozen heads, and excess heads were paid 3d. per dozen heads and 2d. per dozen for eggs. One hopes the RSPB never heard of them. Most of the crime reported in the Felons' Reports are of a petty nature - the theft of potatoes from a field, trespassing for game, and so forth, but there was one serious crime that shocked the neighbourhood. This was the murder in 1885 of PC James Davies, Constable of Beoley, by one Moses Shrimpton, a poacher from Redditch, the attack taking place on Icknield Street, just within Alvechurch parish. A memorial stone now marks the place of the crime.

Having lost all its additional responsibilities the vestry was left with its first duty, the church itself. Costs were covered by raising a church rate, and this had always raised two problems, namely the fairness of the basis of assessment and the resentment of ratepayers who were not members of the Church of England. The assessment had been revised when the 1792 Map was prepared and was again revised on the basis of the 1844 Tithe Map. The problem of who should pay was resolved in 1866 when the Church Rate was abolished and thereafter the cost had to be met by collections and donations given voluntarily. Other relics also disappeared. There had been no mention of the ducking stool for very many years, or for that matter of the pillory, and the stocks appear to have been in use up to the 1830s when

Billy Brown is said to have been the last person to occupy them. The parish pound, where stray animals were placed pending their being reclaimed, was moved in the 1850s from the old site where the Memorial Green now stands at the foot of Bear Hill to the corner of Old Rectory Lane and the Radford Road.

A major problem facing the vestry was the fabric of the church itself. Over many years the Churchwardens' Presentments had drawn attention to the need for repairs, and sooner, or more often later, necessary repairs had been carried out. However, no major work had been undertaken and the medieval structure was evidently reflecting the decay of centuries: also, it was claimed that it was now too small to meet the increased population of the village. In keeping with the old arrangements, the nave was divided into box pews which were the property of a family or went with a particular property, and the only free seats were the 'paupers' seats.' Feeling was now strong that all seats should be free, and this was another factor in the decision that radical steps were needed. In his early years John Tonyn had been responsible for improving the internal layout of the church, but illness and age had dampened his enthusiasm in his later years, and it was to be his successor, John Sandford, who was also Archdeacon of Warwick, whose enthusiasm gave momentum for change. A man of great ability and drive, he had objected to the Old Rectory as being too far from the church, inconvenient in its facilities and noisy from the nearby needle mill. One of his first acts therefore, in 1855, was to employ the leading church architect, William Butterfield, to build a new Rectory - now The Lawns - on land close to the church and donated by the Windsor family of Hewell Grange. Next, in 1858, he was the prime mover in building the larger new National School in School Lane - also employing Butterfield. Meanwhile in 1857 the first move had been taken when it had been resolved to ask Butterfield to report on the condition of the church. Butterfield was a builder rather than a restorer, and we are probably fortunate that so much of the old structure was retained. The tower and the wall of the North aisle were kept, and a new chancel, nave, South aisle and porch were built, and the nave widened and made much higher, with a clerestory to give more light. Items from the old church - notably the Norman South door, the priest's door, the tomb recess and sedilia from the chancel, and many monuments - were re-sited in the new building, while it is clear from an old drawing that the pillars and

William Bourne, Belfry Bill, Workhouse Bill, Bill o' the Work'us, was sexton and bell-ringer, and here is holding the crier's bell.

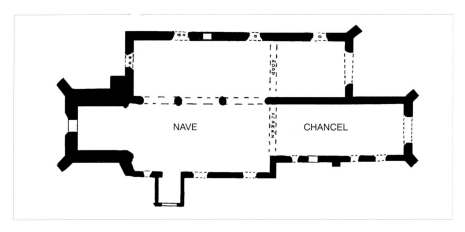

Plan of St Laurence Church before restoration of 1861.

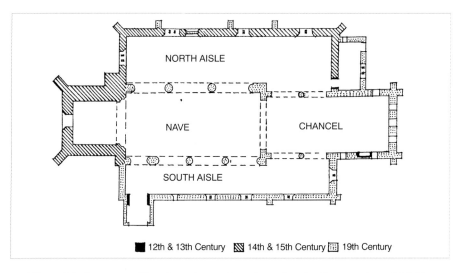

Plan of St Laurence Church as it stands today after the Restoration of 1861.

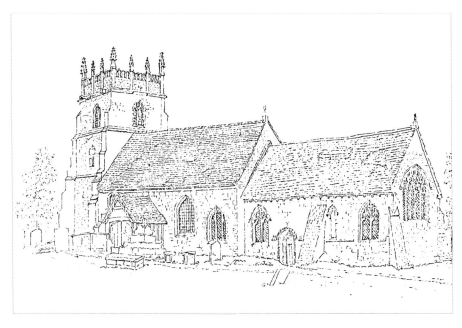

St Laurence Church c.1820. By courtesy of The Society of Antiquaries.

*South door of St Laurence Church, c.1855. The door casement has been
re-erected in the restored church, while it will be seen that the pillar and
capital have been faithfully copied from the original pattern.
By courtesy of Birmingham Museums and Art Gallery.*

St Laurence Church c.1855. Note the fine east window of the chancel, and the east window of the North Aisle - now partly obscured. The medieval cross is in its original position, and returned in the 1920s after having been banished to the Rectory garden. By courtesy of Birmingham Museums and Art Gallery.

capitals that divide the North aisle from the nave are an exact copy of the original, and close examination shows that some of the old stones were re-used. The total cost of £3,230 was met as to £485 from Church Building Societies, on condition that seats were free, £500 was borrowed from the Public Works Loan Board, and the balance was raised by public subscription, led by Baroness Windsor and the Rector himself. The result was highly admired at the time, although it was acknowledged that the roof line was too high in relation to the tower, and there were not enough funds to raise the tower. At the consecration in 1861 there were over a hundred clergy present together with the Bishops of London and Worcester. During the demolition the removal of the old pews revealed fragments of medieval wall paintings, and a coin of Edward IV's reign was found under the porch. The medieval cross that had stood outside the South porch was removed - fortunately only to the Rectory garden - and a new cross, in memory of Baroness Windsor's two sons, was erected on the old base, which was re-sited a short distance away. The medieval cross was rescued in the 1920's and replaced in the same relative position by the South porch. Various of the Rector's friends gave stained glass windows, ornaments etc. and the East window in the chancel is in memory of the Archdeacon: his tomb, also designed by Butterfield, lies near the South porch. The other window that deserves special mention is the West window in the tower. It was erected by public subscription to mark the Queen's Jubilee, and is rare in depicting Victoria as a young girl. Not satisfied with increasing the size of St. Laurence, mission churches were built in Rowney Green to hold 125 in 1862 and in Hopwood to hold 150 in 1864: both were to be closed almost exactly one hundred years later.

The rebuilt church was up-to-date in having hot water radiators but it was to be two years later that oil lamps were installed, thus permitting Evensong to be moved from 3 p.m. to 6.30 p.m. The organ appears to have been a casualty of the changes, as for a time an organ was hired, but in 1875 a new organ was installed and dedicated - this time in the presence of only 36 clergy - and this organ, which cost £450, a sum raised by public subscription, gave service until 1969. It will be recalled that the bells were recast in 1711 as a peal of six. In 1892 Thomas W. Jex Blake who had been appointed Rector in 1887 after having been Headmaster at Rugby School for 12 years, was made Dean of Wells, and to mark the occasion two bells were added to complete the peal, at a cost of £266. The curfew bell was no longer rung - the old custom had been stopped by Sandford - but the bells were almost invariably tolled for funerals, the passing bell. National events were also marked by the bells: thus in 1882 12s. was paid to the ringers for a muffled peal on the death of Prince Leopold, in 1892 £1 was paid to mark the passing of Prince Victor Albert, and £2 was paid for ringing in the coronation of Edward VII. There was also an ox roast in The Square to celebrate that occasion.

From 1801 onwards all the rectors were resident, and, certainly from the time of Archdeacon Sandford they were a power in the village and parish, in some part taking on the role of the squire in other villages. For most of the time they were assisted by a curate - and often by two - and without exception they were men with academic degrees. Curates were necessary to give general assistance to the rector, particularly if like the Archdeacon he had other heavy duties, and they were also needed to take the services at the mission churches. After the new schools were built in School Lane and the earlier buildings near the church had been freed, the premises which included a school house were used to accommodate a curate, until the Clergy Lodge in School Lane was built for that specific purpose.

No description of the church would be complete without a reference to one of the village's most odd characters, Will Bourne, Workhouse Bill, Belfry Bill, he had several nicknames. Tiny - he was only 4ft. 6in. in height - the Poor Law papers describe him as 'imbecile' but he was the grave digger and responsible for ringing the morning bell at 5 a.m. and the evening bell at 8 p.m. until both were discontinued. The 1851 Census has him living in Swan Street, but tradition has it that he lived in the church tower, and, armed with sword and pistol, he guarded the graveyard from the attentions of the 'resurrection men' who stole recently buried corpses for anatomy lessons for medical students. When the old church was being demolished, the Redditch Indicator printed that 'Poor Will, the demented bell ringer prowls around the ruins like an old raven and says 'The French be coming'.' Notwithstanding this, he had a wide reputation as a clock repairer, perhaps a result of his years living in the tower. There is a good portrait of him in the choir robing room in the tower, and a daguerrotype of him looking not quite so respectable in the Historical Society's Museum.

Alvechurch had always been a well endowed benefice. The emoluments came from the glebe lands of over 100 acres, the tithe of produce throughout the parish and fees from weddings etc. Apart from minor exceptions the tithe had not been compounded for a money payment, but had physically been tithed in the field by the rector's agent, or by the person to whom he had farmed it. This ancient arrangement ceased when the Tithe Commutation Act was passed in 1836, as this translated the tithe into a rent charge on each individual field or holding, the amount of the charge varying with the price of corn. It was 1844 before it was implemented in Alvechurch and the Map and the accompanying Terrier are of great interest. The map comes just 50 years after the 1792 map and 40 years before the first large scale Ordnance Survey map, and as in the earlier case the terrier gives very full information on ownership, usage etc. The field names present a strange mixture: some continue the names that were seen in the 1299 Survey, but others reflect the black humour of the farmer – Botany Bay, France, Follies, Ireland, Long Legs, Pudding, Picardy, Purgatory, Shoulder of Mutton. As time went by many of the rent charges were redeemed voluntarily, and they were finally extinguished under the provisions of the Tithe Redemption Act of 1936.

St. Laurence Church and its Mission Chapels were not the only places of worship. A small part of the ecclesiastical parish was lost to Wythall when that parish was formed, but few were affected by the move. What were more important were the Baptists in Alvechurch and the Methodists in Rowney Green. The Baptists built their church on the site they had used since 1834 in 1862 and the style, using red brick, is not dissimilar to that used by Butterfield on the parish church. It had its first pastor, shared with Kings Norton, in 1898. As mentioned earlier, the Methodist chapel in Chapel Lane Rowney Green was built in 1869 to accommodate 27 seat holders.

Like so many parishes Alvechurch had been the beneficiary of a number of charitable bequests over the centuries. The larger ones, such as the Lewkner Hospital and the Free Grammar School, were reasonably safe, but the smaller ones such as the 20s. p.a. left by Mrs. Christian Smith in 1634 and secured by a rent charge on her land, were likely to be overlooked or forgotten, and in any case their relative value had fallen with the passage of time. There were several enquiries to establish what charities existed and their funding, and by this time the principal distribution was on

St. Thomas's Day, and to those not in receipt of parish relief. Finally, in 1912, all the charities except the Grammar School were merged as the United Charities of Alvechurch to provide for the Lewkner Hospital. The Hospital still gave rent-free accommodation and a small weekly allowance to its inmates and some effort was made to provide further care. The original settlement had provided for a Master, but in the event it does not appear that there was anyone resident and responsible for the welfare of the aged inhabitants until 1863 when one Eliza Truman was appointed to be a nurse at a nominal rent of 1s. per quarter and a weekly wage of 2s. 6d. It is not clear whether she ever took up the post, nor is there evidence of the appointment of a successor.

The Grammar School had a brief flowering, and for a time it seemed that it might grow into a fully fledged Public School, as happened in a number of places at this time. It had taken boarders for some time in order to augment the Master's salary, but the real expansion came with the appointment of William Partridge as Master in 1836. Advertising itself as a Gentlemen's Academy, the curriculum offered Classics, French and German, also Reading, Writing, Arithmetic, English, Grammar, Elocution, History, Geography, Mapping, Globes, Practical Geometry, Mensuration, Surveying, Book keeping, Singing: French, German, Dancing, Drawing, Fencing and Music are £1. 1s. per quarter extra, and the fees for boys over ten were £23. 2s. per quarter. There were 34 boarders when the 1851 Census was taken and in addition to the statutory scholars there were day boarders and day boys, so that the numbers were quite considerable. The School continued to occupy the same premises, now 1 and 3 Bear Hill, and Partridge built the external staircase to the top floor which was used as the dormitory. He also made use of, and from his own statement spent £1600 on improvements to, other houses belonging to the Trust, and these he used for his staff etc. The playground was across the road where the Village Hall stands. In 1876 after a Public Enquiry it was decided that the free scholars could be more economically educated at the National School and it was then that Partridge said that he wished to retire and, on the basis that he had spent much of his own money on improving the Trust's property, asked that he be granted a pension. In place of a pension he was offered the premises for life, and he did not retire until 1882. The school seems to have been in decline in 1876 with 25 boarders and 4 day boarders,

This view of the northwest of the Square is c.1910: on the right is the Post Office, later demolished for road widening, and the large pale house towards the left is The Red House, a private school.

The Red Lion in the 1930s.

View looking east down Bear Hill towards The Square. By the 1930s the Post Office had moved to the former Grammar School premises.

This view of Swan Street is c.1910. On the left are the cottages commonly known as Bug Row, and since demolished and replaced by 31-43 Swan Street. On the right is Punch's Castle, formerly Billet's Place, a large half-timbered building then divided into three tenements, and demolished in 1931 for road widening.

The Grammar School, a relic of the Free School, finally closed in 1903, shortly after this photograph. The outside staircase led to the dormitory.

Looking up Bear Hill and the Old House, c.1900.

Looking up Bear Hill c.1900 with the Grammar School on the left.

The Square, looking east: the Post Office is on the left, and the butcher's shop and the former Crown Inn in the centre.

The Mill and Mill pond. This was the former Lord's Mill: there has been a mill on this site for at least 700 years.

and after Partridge's retirement there was a series of Masters – Rev. J. D. Knipps MA (Oxon): W. F. Matthews MA: and then Rev. George H. Ridley Fletcher BA, LID, who held the post from 1888 to the school's final closure in 1903. The property was then sold to Fletcher's wife for £500 and she later sold it to J. W. Partridge who used it in connection with his antique business. Once the foundation scholars were no longer at the Grammar School its income from the Trust property and investments was used to provide scholarships for Alvechurch children who proceeded to higher education at one of the nearby Grammar Schools, and the Exhibition Board, giving the names of the Exhibitioners is held in the Historical Society's Museum.

Following the lead of the nonconformist Joseph Lancaster with his British Schools, the Church of England replied with the National Schools in 1811, but it was not until 1839 that Alvechurch had its National School. The building, which included the schoolmaster's house, was erected on land adjoining the churchyard on the north side of the path leading from the church to Snake Lane, and the total cost of £417 was met by public subscription. Running costs were met from Government grant, based on attendance and efficiency, from fees which ranged from 1d. to 3d. a week, and from local fund raising. A feature of social life from now on is the number of concerts, plays, readings etc. that were held to raise funds for the school. The building by the Church soon proved to be too small, and William Butterfield, who had already built the Rectory and was to rebuild the church, designed the new building on a site in School Lane, at a cost of £852, again largely financed from local sources. It too was extended at least twice to meet the rising number of children, particularly after Forster's Act in 1870 which effectively introduced compulsory elementary education. The syllabus in the early days was restricted to the Three Rs and Religious Instruction, but gradually this was expanded. The school garden was an early introduction and Alvechurch was something of a pioneer in this development. The girls were given cookery classes at the Clergy Lodge in 1910, and in 1914 the boys began to take woodwork lessons for which they went to Redditch. In 1907 there was the first medical inspection – a direct response to the discovery at the time of the Boer War of the poor physique of the general run of recruits. The School benefited from the long incumbency of Mr. Thomas 'Tommy' Thompson who was Headmaster from 1878 to 1923, a total of 45 years. He was choirmaster at the church for 58 years and organist there for 34 years, as well as being Conductor of the Alvechurch Brass Band.

For part of this period the School Log has survived and is a mine of information. By 1910 there were 257 in the main school and 75 in the Infants. There are constant references to communicable diseases and time and again the school was completely closed because of epidemics of measles, German measles, chicken pox, scarlet fever, whooping cough, diphtheria, almost all now diseases of the past, but then of real concern for their morbidity and side effects. On a happier note, although the holidays were much shorter than they are today, there were days off when the school closed for the Annual March of the Women's Friendly Society, for the Beating of the Bounds, an event that had recently been revived, for the Relief of Mafeking and Ladysmith, and nearer at home, for the wedding of the Rector's daughter and for the Sale of Work at The Shrubbery. There were unofficial holidays for the boys when the Circus came to Redditch and when the Hunt met at Weatheroak. Finally, before leaving this aspect of elementary education, which by now had become the responsibility of the School Boards and the County Councils, because it was felt that the distances from Rowney Green and Barnt Green to Alvechurch were too great for infants to walk, Infants Schools were built in each, the children going to Alvechurch when they were seven or eight.

There had long been 'dame schools' – child minders rather than schools – but these disappeared with the advent of the National School. There had also been Ladies Academies, some of which offered boarding facilities, for those who sought a more genteel education for their daughters. Evidence from the Census Returns, Newspaper advertisements and Directories show that in 1842 there was a Ladies Boarding School in Meadow Lane kept by Mrs. Wainwright: in 1851 Mrs. and Miss Horton kept a Boarding School for Ladies at 14 The Square with 5 girls in residence: in 1855 Mrs. Frances Broomhill ran a Boarding and Day School, in succession to Mrs. Wainwright, at 8 and 9 The Square: in 1863 Mrs. Chambers, who lived at The Old Rectory and whose husband ran the Rector's Mill, advertised in the Redditch Indicator that her School was reopening after the Christmas holidays, and that there were vacancies for two young ladies there: in 1873 the Misses Chambers kept the school there: in 1882 Mrs. Cottrell advertised that she was moving her school to The

Red House, now 15 and 16 The Square, where there was more accommodation, and this school was still running in 1910: in the 1891 Census Miss Alice Whitehouse is recorded as running a school at her home, No. 1 Arrow Terrace, now 14 Red Lion Street, and the Directory shows her still there in 1912. It should also be mentioned that Alvechurch had the right to nominate needy children to the Bluecoat School at Oldswinford, under the Foley foundation. Lastly, on the topic of schools, one should not forget the Sunday School, which was certainly in existence in 1800, as the then curate, John Welch, left £20 towards its needs. Before the advent of the National School it provided a rudimentary education in addition to religious instruction.

From the incumbency of Archdeacon Sandford in 1854 the church played an increasingly important role in what we should now call social work amongst the labouring classes. The clergy and their families often provided the framework and the organisers, and they also acted as catalysts between the gentry and the middle classes on the one hand and the needy, particularly the deserving poor. The better-off became Vice Presidents, or subscribed as member without any of the benefits, and so effectively subsidised the clubs and societies. There were close relations with the National School – after all it was a Church School – so that the Rector was a frequent visitor, his daughter helped with needlework and took dictation, the curate's wife gave cookery lessons to the girls in her own home, and they were the prime movers, as well frequently the artistes, in the concerts and readings that took place in the school buildings to raise money for the school and other good causes. One of the most useful actions was when a few acres of the glebe were set aside for allotments, because many of the cottages did not have any facility for growing vegetables: further allotments were made available in Rowney Green. The major Friendly Societies – the Buffaloes and the Oddfellows – had lodges in the village and each year had their Annual Meetings and Feast when they marched through the village behind the Alvechurch Brass Band. The church entered this field in 1855 with the Men's Friendly Society and, next year, with the Female Friendly Society. The general principle behind this type of society was that, in exchange for a weekly subscription the member would be entitled to sick pay, a small pension in old age, and funeral expenses – and in the case of women, a sum on confinement. The benefits were modest, but they were meaningful when the alternative was most likely

The practice of beating bounds of the parish was revived in 1896, and this shows them starting from Lye Bridge - note the earlier bridge.

The Ox Roast to mark Queen Victoria's Diamond Jubilee in 1897 in The Square.
Behind the ox is The Hollies, a Nursing and Maternity Home, and, to its left is
Boulton's shop, suitably decorated for the occasion.

The circus comes to town, passing 36 Red Lion Street and the end of Meadow Lane.

Children's Party to celebrate the Coronation of Edward VII in 1901, at High House Farm: note Brittania with her trident in the centre (see inset).

The Shakespearean Society's production of The Merry Wives of Windsor in 1908.
The Rector, Bishop Milne, is in the back row on the right, and in the centre of the
front row is Thomas Cooper, whose gravestone, erected by the Shakespearean
Society, recited that 'he was an honest man and a good bricklayer.'

the Workhouse. As well as these mutual help societies the church organised a number of Clubs – Medical, Clothing, Shoe, Coal – and these were based on the principle of weekly savings set aside to meet heavy and seasonal expenditure. Because of the subscriptions of the Vice Presidents and the Honorary Members the participants got back rather more than they put in, which encouraged thrift.

What entertainment there was tended to be home grown. The old School near the Church was used as an Institute, usually with lending library facilities, and later, when the Crown Inn in the Square was closed, the Institute moved to that more convenient site. There were frequent concerts and penny readings and around the turn of the Century the Shakespearean Society was very active and produced plays in the Rectory garden and in the barn of High House Farm. The Brass Band held regular practices and led the different Societies on their annual marches through the village. Church Fetes became an annual event in the later 1800s, and the Fete in 1899 included a Lemonade and Ginger Beer Stall, Sweet Stall, Bicycle Gymkhana, Comediette, Conjuror, Coconut Shy, Sale of Rats, Hat Trimming, Dancing and a Darning Competition. One of the more bizarre events was the Pigeon Shoot at the Red Lion, and in 1870 the prize was a 38 score pig. The usual annual events continued. The Statute Fair and Mop brought a selection of sideshows – in 1871 these were an organ grinder, a 12lb rat, confectionery, toys, photographs, Shooting Gallery, Peep Show, Swing Boats and a Cheap John. There were sales of animals in May and September in the field behind the Red Lion, but the most prestigious event was the Alvechurch Horse Show which was held on Crown Meadow, off Tanyard Lane, where the Schools and Library now stand. Towards the latter part of the 19th Century Alvechurch had become something of a pleasure resort for Birmingham. At Easter 1888 it was reported in the Redditch Indicator that 600 had visited Hopwood Wharf where there were pleasure grounds, and to watch six a side football: on Easter Monday many came to Alvechurch itself: in April it was said to be a popular resort for cyclists: at Whitsuntide there were again many visitors to The Wharf, where there was boating, fishing and cricket, and at Alvechurch there were many visitors and there had been dancing to the music of the Alvechurch Brass Band.

The more traditional entertainment offered by the inns and beer houses had been freely obtainable in the earlier years, but the temperance zeal of Archdeacon

Sandford resulted in a drastic reduction in the number of licensed houses in the village itself. In 1851 there had been six inns or beer houses. The Bear Inn, now called The Old House at 32 Bear Hill, was the most prestigious and boasted of a ballroom in which in latter years the Manor Courts had been held. It was closed and became the home and surgery for the local medical practice for almost a hundred years. The Red Lion, on the site of the present Red Lion, was little more than a group of small cottages, but it was the favoured location for the 'Felons' Dinners, and for the Annual Meetings and Feasts of the Friendly Societies. The other inn with some pretensions was The Crown, at 6 The Square, but it too, was closed and was used for the Institute and Reading Room. The White Horse, a beer house opposite the Red Lion, was the stopping place for one of the coaches, but it was soon to be demolished and Trentham House was built on the site. The Swan, at 5 Swan Street, was also a beer house, and was soon to be closed. The Old Swan, now The Swan, on the other side of the road, had recently been rebuilt, and as a beer and cider house was popular with its bowling green near the churchyard as an added attraction. In later years we are told that it was strictly ruled by the Newboulds, the more substantial farmers being served in the snug out of pink and blue jugs, and men only allowed to cross the threshold.

The old days always seem to have been the happier time, as the benefits of more recent improvements are forgotten, but if one makes allowance for this the reminiscences of Miss 'Auntie Hatt' Cooper of life in the 1880s suggest that the village was one of the pleasanter places in which to live. She wrote these in 1952/3 towards the end of her life, and are given in full just as she wrote them as Appendix I.

THE TWENTIETH CENTURY

The eighty years that have elapsed since the First World War have seen greater changes than at any period in the history of the village. Briefly, the population and the built-up area have expanded enormously but the opportunity for local employment has diminished so that Alvechurch has become largely a dormitory suburb. The change may fairly be laid at the door of the internal combustion engine since the manufacture of motor vehicles, with Longbridge on our doorstep, has boosted local employment prospects, and the phenomenal spread of personal transport has enabled people to work far from their homes, and so facilitated the movement from the towns into the countryside.

Looking first at the population, it will be recalled that growth had been very modest during the reign of Queen Victoria, growing from 1,633 in 1841 only to 1,731 by 1911, but by the last Census in 1991 the total had reached 6,237, an increase of 260% in 80 years. At this last date there were 2,414 in full or in part-time employment, 1,090 were retired, and 159 were unemployed – a figure well below the national average. Housing development between the Wars took the form partly of the redevelopment of old sites, but, in the absence of planning constraints, mostly of ribbon development along the main roads. Thus, Punch's Castle, in Swan Street, was demolished and the Newbould Houses, 28–50 Swan Street, were built on the site, and there are other similar examples, but the main thrust of building development was by way of ribbon building – Tanyard Lane, Snake Lane, Birmingham Road and Redditch Road near the village centre, The Rise and The Drive at Hopwood, the Redditch Road at Bordesley and in the Alvechurch part of Barnt Green. The advent of the Town and Country Planning Act in 1944 saw Alvechurch placed in the Green Belt, as a buffer between Birmingham and what later was to be the New Town of Redditch, and later, the centre of the village was designated a Conservation Area. It might have been expected that this status would have inhibited housing development, but this has not proved to be the case as the demand for additional homes has come from Government to County Council to District Council and to the villages themselves. There has been a great deal of new housing, both local authority and private, and it has been concentrated in the quadrant north of Station Road and between Birmingham Road and the railway. This development has been some distance from the historic centre of the village but more recently the infilling of land in the area of Tanyard Lane and at the rear of Bear Hill has been more central. Conservation status has not really succeeded in retaining the character of the central part of the village, and the situation has been made worse by the closure of many of the smaller specialist shops that have found it impossible to compete with the super-markets. Another development outside the centre of the village has been the gentrifi-cation of old farmhouses and cottages and the conversion of barns into houses.

Despite the great growth in population and in housing, the opportunities for employment, far from keeping pace, have almost disappeared. Before 1914 farming continued to be the largest employer, and the small mixed farms, still dependent on horse and man power, were the norm. The trades allied to agriculture, the corn mill, the old Lord's Mill in Radford Road, the blacksmiths, wheelwrights, harness makers and so forth still served local needs up to 1939. The need to maximise the production of foodstuffs led to the general introduction of the farm tractor and the death of the small farm. The steady increase in mechanisation and use of artificial fertilisers, chemical sprays and improved strains of seeds has meant that one man is employed where a dozen worked prior to the War, yet the output is greater. After agriculture the main employer between the Wars was the Brickworks, on the canal-side site between Scarfield and Withybed. It changed hands in 1924 and expanded production into roofing tiles, hips, valleys, etc as well as bricks, and by the early thirties was employing 50 men and boys. It was a hard life – no shelter, no wet pay, no Union, and a 50 hour week – and as the depression took hold it was closed on several occasions while stocks were run down. Many of the workers lived in the cottages at Greenfield and at Withybed Green, and as some had been in-comers to deal with the new products they were regarded as a race apart by many villagers. The end came in 1939 when production was concentrated on the larger more economic sites, and the works were not restarted after the War, although the premises have been used for a number of purposes, but principally for storage.

A new undertaking, Flexible Manufacturing, was established in Tanyard Lane in 1926, but the main impetus in new employment came as a result of the 1939 – 1945 War. German bombs drove Delsons, manufacturers of fasteners, out of Birmingham, and they took over a site near the railway off Latimer Road. At one time the firm employed 175, and branched out into the manufacture of a small car, but changes in the industry and the take-over by a national company was followed by decline and eventual closure, the site being cleared and used for housing. The other large incomer was BICRA, now the British Investment Casting Trade Association, which was bombed out of its premises in 1942 when it moved to Bordesley Hall. It still operates from the Hall, but is on the edge of the parish and many employees come from outside. Another concern, Vernier Springs, was started on the site of the old slaughterhouse, but the accommodation proved insufficient and the firm moved to Redditch, leaving the property to be occupied by a Chinese takeaway. The Mill ceased to be used for milling some time after the end of the War, then the premises were used for a variety of purposes until now it is a restaurant. The old trades – smiths, wheelwrights, carpenters etc. – are no longer to be found, and within more recent years competition from supermarts and out of town shopping centres has led to the closure of many local shops, so that we have lost the haberdashery, boot and shoe shop, ironmonger etc. as well as two grocers, and are probably fortunate in retaining the chemist, baker and butchers.

The 19th Century saw great improvement in transport facilities – canal, turnpike and railway, but their effect has been nothing like so fundamental as the advent of the internal combustion engine, which has effectively meant that the bulk of the population has the benefit – and luxury – of personal transport. Nowadays, the canal has been reduced to an amenity for pleasure craft, the railway, now closed beyond Redditch, has been electrified and provides a half hourly service between Redditch and Lichfield, but it is the road that is supreme, not so much for public transport as for goods and the private car. The old road through the village, formerly the turnpike, was improved on a new line between Alvechurch and Hopwood in the Twenties, and has been widened and improved, but the long promised by-pass was not completed until the 1990s. More important, the completion of the M42 and later, the M40, have resulted in the area finding itself at a strategic centre in the country, with pressure for development.

For many centuries the parish was self governing and financing itself, initially through the manorial courts, then through the parish vestry, until the complications of modern society led to the need for larger units of administration in the form of the County Council and then the District Council. These are now far from independent, funded largely from Whitehall and their expenditure closely monitored, while the Parish Council finds that its responsibilities are little more than street lighting, playing fields, and so forth. Of the functions that were under local control, the policing comes under West Mercia, and there is no longer a resident constable; the relief of poverty has been subsumed within the Welfare State, and is administered by the County Council; the Highways, for whose repair every householder was required to give six days labour, are the province of the County Council; the schools, once built and in part maintained from local funds, are also controlled from Worcester. While the village has retained its First and Middle Schools, in new premises in Tanyard Lane since 1968, older children are bussed to Bromsgrove or Redditch for their further education.

The churches have remained a constant feature, although their influence is in no way as great as the peak that was reached in the 19th Century. In addition to St. Laurence's, the Baptists and the Methodists, the Roman Catholic Church, which had been using a room in the Village Hall, bought the former school premises in School Lane and altered them to St. Mary's. As for the parish church, new pews and wall panelling were installed in 1933, a new organ was installed in 1969, and since then there have been repairs to the floor, the east wall of the chancel, and the chancel arch. The Victorian Rectory – a country gentleman's house – proved to be a liability, and the building and grounds sold, and a new and more manageable Rectory built, in 1954. The Baptist Church continues to serve its congregation, and has expanded to meet changed circumstances with a Schoolroom in 1928, and more recently, a Hall at the rear. The Mission Churches at Hopwood and Rowney Green have been closed, but in Rowney Green, in a most interesting development, the Church of England holds regular services in the Methodist Chapel, which is now officially known as 'Rowney Green Shared Church.' Apart from the churches, there are many organisations and societies with their special interests ranging from the Cricket and Football Clubs, the Village Society and Women's Institute to the Dramatic and Historic Societies, and these activities have been made possible by the provision of village halls. In Alvechurch the Village Hall dates from the 1920s and owes much to a legacy from Mr. J. W. Partridge. Hopwood boasts of both a Village Hill and a Community Centre, while Rowney Green is served by the Peace Hall.

APPENDIX I

ALVECHURCH IN THE 1880s
by Miss H. Cooper

I remember it well, and as long as sight and memory last, I could never forget it. A gem of a village, in the emerald setting of green hills and woods as far as eye can reach. My father worked here for some time before he could get a house and came home to Birmingham at weekends. One day he brought us violets. We kept them in small glass jars and egg cups until they were quite dead. But although the violets were over the lanes were full of other flowers, Speedwell's darling blue, vetch, Ragged Robin, Batchelor and Billy Buttons, and high in the hedges wild roses, honeysuckle, foxgloves and every sort of lovely grasses and berries. The grass and growth was so long and thick we could play hide and seek in them.

Our first home was at the 'Tan Yard' and the brook was an endless source of delight and amusement, sailing bits of paper for boats. Often one of us fell in and got a wetting, once I let the baby in the pram fall in, and one of the boys who lived next door dropped some tallow candles that he had fetched from Boulton's shop into the brook. He got them out all right and when he got home put them into the oven to dry, and the fat from them ran out all over the hearth – we teased and ragged him about it for months.

We must have had a lot of rain one year, because I remember round the corner up Snake Lane the road was under water up to father's knees and he carried my brother and I under his arms till we reached the hill leading to the 'White Palings', then of course we went up by the Clergy Lodge and along the 'black path' to school. There were no houses then in Snake Lane: but there were two small culverts where brooks ran under the road, and we spent hours with a glass jar of water, some string and a bent pin, fishing.

We did not live at the Tanyard for more than a couple of years. We soon got a bigger house in Swan Street, but we often went for a walk that way, as our baker's house and shop were on the canal side at Callow Hill, and we had to fetch a loaf to last us till he came round with the bread. When I got bigger our favourite walk was up Cobley Hill and down Cooper's or vice versa. On Sunday evenings our father would take us for a walk, if mother was not too poorly to be left alone with the babies. My brothers all sang in the Church Choir as soon as they were old enough, so those treats were only in the midsummer days, there being no Summertime or Daylight Savings Bill then, but on Jubilee Day, June 1887, he took two or three of us up through Barnt Green up to the Lickey Monument ground to see the pile for the Beacon Fire. It was a lovely evening and though tired we did enjoy it. We returned by way of Bilberry Hill and alongside Cofton Woods (which were not then open to the public) under the railway at Barnt Green then home by Bittell Reservoir and Roberts Corner. On Jubilee Day there was an ox roasted in The Square and a large tent for all to come and feed at. The schoolchildren had a wonderful tea – I had just left school and started work but Mr. Thompson insisted I should come to the party and I was given a Jubilee Mug in commemoration of the event.

Coming into the village from Birmingham Road there were no houses between Roberts Corner and Tan Yard Lane. There were three cottages on the bank adjoining the Old Red Lion: on the corner was a nailers workshop, where you could see the worker, and the swarf fell through the open window into a heap and the children liked to play in it and feel for any small nails they could find. There were several of these nailers at work about the village; one was at the bottom of Swan Street, up the entry by the blacksmith's shop, and another next door to 'The Old House' on Bear Hill. When asked at school 'What is Alvechurch noted for?' some said 'Candles' others 'Bricks' but the correct answer was 'Nails', although bricks and candles were also made here. With the exception of the New Red Lion on one side, and the Garage and Petrol Station on the other, the main street has scarcely changed at all. Dog Lane, or Rectory Row, is much the same on the one side, but is now built up most of the way on the other side.

The Old Rectory Mill was very busy as a scouring mill for needles, brought from the factories in Redditch and taken back daily in a horse-drawn trap.

The meadows were always a favourite playing ground for the children, although not authorised and trespassers were supposed to be prosecuted, but of course there was a public path through to the Allotments as well as to the Old Rectory, and the path through the field on the left, with the stream where bullrushes and big golden marsh marigolds grew, was always popular. Turning right when you got out of the meadows brought you to the Radford Road, on the corner, turning right again, was the Pound, where any straying animals, cattle or horses, were safely kept till their owners fetched them.

I remember Radford Road was then very plentifully planted with hawthorn, or May, trees, red and white alternately. Only one dwelling before you got to the Mill, the Policeman's home. The Moat was on the other side, but we couldn't see it from the road, but sometimes during a spell of hard frost we came for skating and sliding. Just before we got to the Mill pond we crossed the old bridge over the Mill stream and could see a nice view of the waterfall, then we came to the Mill pond and the Mill. It was at work full time in those days and was very interesting. We used to come for 'Sharps' and corn for the fowls and were always willing to do that errand. It was fun to listen to the 'Chug Chug' of the hoppers as they tipped the corn and divided the chaff and bran, running down from the floor above, then on again to the floor below. Tucked away in the corner was the Mill House, such a cosy looking retreat, then another house, Mill Bank, and on the other side of the road a rather large white house where Mr. Corbett, the miller, lived.

Now we have got back to the village, on the left hand side it's all Boultons stores, warehouse and stabling, till we reach the Shop, facing the Square. On the right hand side was the Reading Room, and then, as now the Butcher's Shop, (I have omitted to mention the Candle Factory was among the buildings I have called the Boultons Warehouses etc.) and on the other side of The Square, facing the Redditch Road was the Post Office. On the corner piece of ground at the back of the Post Office stood the Stocks, where drunkards were secured if they were noisy or troublesome. On the corner of Red Lion Street and facing Redditch Road was an old established grocery shop, now the fish and chip shop. The other block of buildings used to comprise a private school for girls and a market gardener's house and shop, and the Village Hall is built on what used to be the playground for the school. There was always a large bakehouse and baker's shop on the other side of Bear Street, and the blacksmith's shop was always busy too, horses waiting patiently to be shod and ploughs and other agricultural implements wanting attention.

The houses on Swan Street are much the same, but the widening of the road has done away with the sloping grassy side paths and the last block of three cottages and some stabling and a yard for the carrier's carts were all demolished. So also was the old-fashioned half-timbered house (then comprising three small homes) called Punch's Castle. But they have been replaced by modern semi-detached dwellings and the old cottages on the other side of the road are still in use. The old Lodge at the entrance to the field path to Rowney Green used to be the last house in the village. The school has been several times enlarged, but the School House is about the same, so apparently is what is now called the Clergy House, but at that time the Rector kept cows and poultry and had a bailiff and his wife in residence there. Some of the sick poor were provided with milk and eggs in times of trouble. The farmyard and the big barn were at the top corner of the lane and the barn was often used for harvest suppers and other festivities. Once I remember the Shakespearean Society staged The Merchant of Venice there (there were no ladies in the casts in those days) but every year a play, or scenes from one, were produced in the School, and the room was packed for three nights at least: and also at Garden Parties, in the Rectory Gardens, at the Old Rectory, or Bordesley Hall, usually in aid of the Nursing Association. From the top of School Lane and from the Churchyard is the loveliest view of Barnt Green and the Lickeys and the Monument, and from the path that leads from Church to Schools we could see all up to Rowney Green and the Forehill. The Clergy Lodge was used for Bible Classes, Mothers' Meetings, and sometimes for reading and rehearsals for concerts and plays, and this was the curate's residence, too.

The Brickyard was busy in those days and Alvechurch bricks were considered very good and found employment for most of the younger men of the village, and most of them were sent by barges on the canal, to the wharfs at Scarfield and Callow Hill. There were scouring mills at the Old Rectory, worked by the water wheel, and fetched from the Redditch factories and taken back in a horse and trap.

Quite a few men, women and boys worked in the factories at Redditch and walked there and back. We could see or hear them go by at 7 o'clock in the morning. The farms found regular work for their own men, and in the summer for the women, too, and a few Irishmen came to help with the harvest. The milk from the farms was brought to the Railway Station in floats.

There were two 'Carriers' services every week to Birmingham with eggs, butter and any surplus vegetables and fruit, which found a ready sale, and the carriers would do shopping for housewives: boots and shoes, clothing and bed linen, and take one or two shoppers (or sellers). There were no trains between Redditch and Barnt Green on Sundays, but a brake and wagonette from Redditch took passengers who had to visit the hospital.

Aelfgythe 5,6

APPENDIX II

THE SEAL OF THE PECULIAR JURISDICTION OF ALVECHURCH 1742

The Rector of Alvechurch exercised Peculiar Jurisdiction. It meant that he was independent of the Archdeacon, so that, instead of being subject to the Archdeacon's Visitation, when the Churchwardens made their presentments of any errors or shortcomings of the incumbent, of the church, or of the congregation, he 'visited himself' in two years out of three, and in the third year was visited by the Bishop, or, more generally, his deputy. In addition, he granted probate of wills and grants of administration in the case of intestacy, where all the assets lay within the parish, and he corrected – and received the appropriate fees – for minor ecclesiastical offences committed by the laity. The Peculiar Jurisdiction was abolished in the 1850s.

This seal was introduced by Charles Lyttleton, second son of Sir Thomas Lyttleton, and brother of George, a leading politician of his day. He was Rector of Alvechurch from 1742 to 1762, retaining the rectory although appointed Dean of Exeter: he only resigned when he became Bishop of Carlisle. A keen historian, he wrote a manuscript history of Alvechurch which is the basis of the Alvechurch section of Nash's History of Worcestershire, and was a founder member of the Society of Antiquaries.

The seal is of particular interest as it shows, in great detail, the church as it was before the alterations and additions of 1860: on either side of the church are the arms of the Bishopric and of the Lyttletons.

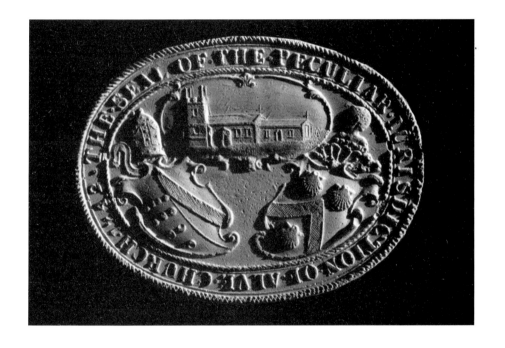

INDEX

Agriculture 68

Ale tasters 23

Allotments 95

Alvechurch Lodge 13

Annual Fair 7

Apprentice 42

Archbishop Laud 40

Archery Butts 24

Assize of Beer 23

Association for the Prosecution of
    Felons 60,73

Athelstan, King 5,6

Austin, Herbert 69

Bagarde, Thomas 30

Bailiff 19

Bailiff's Book 33,39

Baptist Church 67,82,106

Barnt Green 52

Battle of the Spurs 25

Bear Hill 69,86,89,90

Bear Inn, The 102

Beating of the Bounds 94,96

Bible 40

BICRA 105

Billet's Place 87

Birmingham General Hospital 58

Bishop Bell 25,30

Bishop Bell's Visitation Book 26

Bishop Carpenter 20

Bishop Godfrey Giffard 7,9

Bishop Heath 22

Bishop Latimer 19

Bishop Simon 9

Bishop's Register 9

Bishop's Survey 8,12

Black Death 14,15,18

Blake, Thomas W Jex 80

Blanchfront, Sir John 15,16,17,20

Blaunfront, Thomas 15,17

Bluecoat School 95

Board of Health 59

Boardman, Doctor 30

Booth, James 34

Bordesley 6

Bordesley Hall 105

Borough 8

Bosworth Field 15

Boulton, Richard 57

Boultons 69

Bourne, William 75,81

Brass Band 94,95,101

Brickworks 69,72,104

Brickyard, The 69

Bromsgrove Union 59

Broomhill, Frances 94

Burgage plot 8,12,48

Burgesses 8,12

Butterfield, William 74,80,93

By-laws 24

By-pass 105

Canal 48,62,72,105

Candle making 69

Cantilupo, Matthew 10

Carrier service 61,70

Catholicism 30,106

Cattle feed 69

Census 62,81

Chambers, Mrs 94

Chantry 24

Charles II, Restoration of 41

Chatwyn, Philip 22,24,25

Cholera 58,59

Church (St Laurence) 5,6,9,19,20,76-79,106

    bells 43,80

    chancel dilapidation 20

    chantry 25

    curfew bell 81

Easter Sepulchre 20

evensong 80

fete 101

gallery 43,54

medieval cross 80

morning bell 55,81

nave 56

organ 80

organist 55

plate 43

pulpit 55

rate 53,73

reading desk 55

rood screen 20,25,43

tower 20,29,43,44

vestry 53

wall paintings 80

Churchwardens 54

Churchwarden's Presentments 74

Clergy 81

Clergy Lodge 81,93

Clubs 101

Coach service 61,70

Cofton 5

Combes, William 30

Common, the 50

Commonwealth 45

Conservation Area 103

Constable 23,40,59,73

Cooper, Miss 'Auntie Hatt' 12

Cottrell, Mrs 94

County Constabulary 59,60,73

Court, Baron 36

     Borough 23

     Foreign 8,23

     Hundred 23

     Jury 51

     Leet 36

     Leet and Baron and View of Frankpledge 8,23

     Manor 12,72

     Service 51,52

     Steward 23

Coventry, Lady Margaret 43

Crown Inn 60,65,66,91,102

Curate 21,43,81

Customs of the Manor 35

Davies, PC James 73

Delsons 105

Demesne 12

Deodand 50

Domesday Book 5,6

Domestic Service 69

Ducking Stool 24

Dunckleys 69

Dunghills 51

Ecclesiastical Commissioners 49,72

Election of the Mayor 52

Enclosure 35,50

Estate Map of 1701 33

Fair 37,53

     mop or hiring 53,101

     statute 53,101

Fangelos, Robert de 10

Farming 104

Female Friendly Society 95

Field names 82

Fields, open 13,24,33,48

Fines 49

Fish hooks 48,69

Flax spinning 69

Flexible Manufacturing 105

Forest Laws 10

Forest of Feckenham 6

Free warren 17

Freeman, William 30

Friendly Societies 95

Gaunt, Doctor 58,59

Glebe lands 82

Grammar School 39,47,66,82,83,88

Green Belt 103

Greenfield 104

Hannibal, Thomas 30

Harber, John 52,65,66

    Martha 52

    Mary 65

Hearth Tax 46

Heath, Bishop 22

    Dorothy 23

    William 23,30

Heriot 13,24,36,49

Hickes, Doctor, Dean of Worcester 45

Highway 61

Hodges, William 25

Hollington, William 45

Hopwood 5,62,80,106

Hopwood Wharf 101

Horse Show 101

Horton, Mrs and Miss 94

House of Correction 59

Housing 70

Housing development 103

Hugh, parson of Alvechurch 9

Hundred Years War 18

Icknield Street 5,38,73

Illegitimacy 42

Industry 68

Institute 101

Inventories 63

Jephcott, Doctor 45

Jerdele, Richard de 11

    Walter de 11

John of Hereford 21

Kilvert, Francis 67

    Richard 64,67

King Edward VII coronation 99

Kinver 10

Knight of the Green 38

Knight service 17

Ladies' Academies 94

Land, common or waste 14,35,38,50,52

    copyhold 48,49

    Survey of Chantry Lands 25

Lawns, The 74

Lease 49

Leather sealers 24

Legal settlement 51

Leland 19

Lewkner Hospital 24,31,32,39,66,82,83

Lewkner, Nicholas 31

    Thomas 31

Literacy 62

Longbridge 69

Lord's Mill 92

Lye Bridge 70

Lyttleton, Charles 64,66

M40 106
M42 105
Manor Court Rolls 22
Manor of Alvechurch, 1299 survey 7
Map of 1792 53,61,73
      of 1884 71
Market, weekly 7,9
Marlpit 52
Meadow 13
Men's Friendly Society 95
Methodist Chapel 67
Methodists 82,106
Militia 59
Mill 14,35,48,92,105
      Bishop's or Town 69
      Farm 13
      Rector's 69
Milward, Thomas 25,35
Mineral waters 69
Mission Churches 80,106
Molinton, Thomas 10
Moor Green Hall 17,45
Moore, Richard 45
Murder 73
Muster Roll 24

Nail making 48,68
National School 74,83,93
Needles 48,69

Newbould Houses 103
Night Walkers 37,38

Occupations 46,63
Offa, King 5,6
Old House, The 89,102
Old Swan, The 102
Omnibus service 70
Osbert of Alvechurch 11
Osmerley 6
Overseer of the Poor 41,54,55
Overseers of the Highways 38,61

Palace 8,9,14,19,22
Pannage 13
Papal Provision 21
Parish Chest 29
      Council 106
      Register 22,29,46,62
      well 70
Park 7,12,13,19,22,35,49
      Bordesley 13
      keeper 13
Parliament Survey 35
Particular Baptists 67
Partridge, J W 93
      William 83
Pauper 46
Peasant's Revolt 19

Peculiar Jurisdiction 10,64,114

Penance 64

Perambulators 69

Pigeon Shoot 101

Pillory 24,73

Piped water 70

Poaching 17

Police Station 70,73

Poll Tax 18,19

Poor Law 42,53

Poor Law Guardians 59,72

Poor Rate 55

Population 14,18,46,48,62,68,103

Porter, Thomas 15

Post Office 84,86,91

Pound 49,74

Prattinton 20

Presentments 54

Protestant Dissenters 67

Prynne, Hugh 25

Pumps 49

Punch's Castle 49,87,103

Quarter Sessions 39

Queen Victoria 80

    Jubilee 80,97

Radford Farm 19

Railway 48,62,105

Receiver General 19

Rector 21

Rector's mill 69

Rectory 106

Rectory, Old 13,74

Red House 95

Red Lion, The 85,102

Redditch Indicator 72

Rednal 5

Removal Order 42

Rent 19,35

Reservoirs, Bittell and Upper Bittell 62

Restoration 45

Robert of Wych 9,10

Rowney Green 35,67,80,106

    Shared Church 106

Rowney Lodge 13

Rowney Wood 35

Rural District Council 72

Saltpans 6

Sandford, John 74,81,95

Scarfield Farm 69

Schools 106

School house 81

    Lane 93

    masters 47

Seechems Farm 35

Select Vestry 57

Selions 13,24,33,48
Sergeantry 13
Sewerage 70
Shakespearean Society 100,101
Sheldon family 30
Shortwood 10
Shroud, wholly of wool 47
Slander 65
Southam's Brewery 69
Sparrow Club 73
Square, The 84,91
St Laurence 6
St Thomas's Day 83
Station 72
Steward 49
Stocks 49,73
Subsidy Roll 24
Sunday School 55,95
Surveyor of Highways 38,61
Swan Street 49,87
Swan, The 102
Swine 50,52

Tannery 69
Tanneworks 24
Tanyard Lane 69
Tenants customary 12,13
       free 12
Thirdborough 41,59,73

Thompson, Thomas 'Tommy' 93
Thornhill, William 29,30
Tithe Commutation Act 82
Tithe Map 53,73
Toll cottages 61
Tonyn, J F 65,67,74
Town gas 70
Turnpike 48,61,70

United Charities of Alvechurch 83
Urse d'Abitot 6

Vagrancy 29
Vagrant 42
Vernier Springs 105
Vestry meeting 39,57
Vincent, Humphrey 43

Wainwright, Eleanor 57,94
       John 65
Wast Hills 62
Weatheroak 94
Welch, John 66,95
Wells 49
Wengham, Henry de 10
West Heath 5
White Horse, The 102
Whitehouse, Miss Alice 95
Will 25,28,63

Windsor, Baroness 80

Withybed Green 104

Women's Friendly Society 94

Worcestershire County Council 70

Workhouse 56,58

Worth, Doctor 66

Wythall 82

Wythall Chapel 45